The Death of a Christian:
The Rite of Funerals

*Studies in the Reformed Rites
of the Catholic Church,
Volume VII*

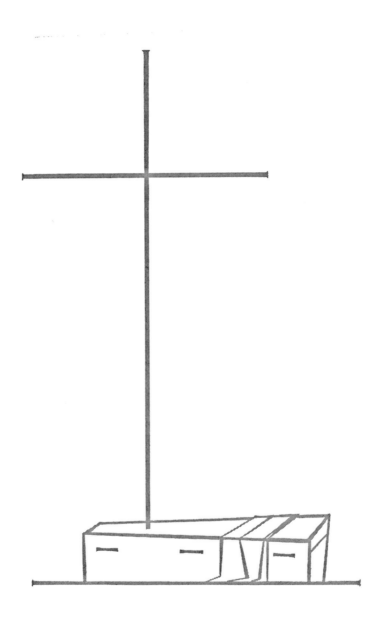

Richard Rutherford, csc

The Death of a Christian:
The Rite of Funerals

Pueblo Publishing Company

New York

Nihil Obstat:
✠ Paul E. Waldschmidt, D.D., S.T.D.
Censor Deputatus

Imprimatur:
✠ Cornelius M. Power, D.D., J.C.D.
Archbishop of Portland in Oregon

Design: Frank Kacmarcik

To
my sister Gail
who
loves life
and
knows the meaning
of death

Contents

Introduction

"Death is swallowed up; victory is won!" (1 Corinthians 15.54). This belief that life in the risen Christ undoes even the sting of death has typified the liturgy of the Christian funeral from the beginning. Yet the fathers of the Second Vatican Council were pastorally aware that Roman Catholic funeral liturgy today is frequently more a cherished, archaic gesture than a truly contemporary expression of this living Christian faith. Thus they urged in the *Constitution on the Liturgy* that funeral services be revised to express more clearly this paschal character of Christian death.

The death of a Christian involves the mystery of human death in the Christian mystery of resurrection as inseparably as Calvary was touched by Easter. Thus paschal faith cannot tolerate the denial of death or cosmetic life purchased at the price of a funeral. It is with sensitive respect for the full impact of death, its sadness and grief that the Christian dares to celebrate the funeral liturgy. Without attempting to hide the reality of death under superficial ceremony the *Rite of Funerals* invites all concerned—family, friends, the president and homilist, musicians and fellow Christians—to accept courageously the death of this person and to surround it with the Church's liturgy where the paschal death and resurrection of Jesus give it Christian meaning. Such is the paschal character of Christian death, and the *Rite of Funerals* its liturgy.

That liturgy is the focus of this book, and its celebration today motivates this review of its origins (Chapter One), its development in history (Chapter Two), and its present form and expression (Chapters Three, Four, and Five). By sharing the fruit of liturgical research and hundreds of pastoral conversations this book hopes to render ever more accessible the *Rite of Funerals* and its renewed expression of the paschal character of Christian death.

Many people have contributed to the birth of this book. Although most remain silent partners, two deserve very special thanks. The first is Professor Dr. Cornelius A. Bouman, Nijmegen (Netherlands), whose wisdom, erudition, and heroic kindness inspired and nurtured my original research into the funeral liturgy. More proximate in time, Miss Christine McCartney, M.Ed., is the heroine whose editorial and technical assistance transformed this work into a book. These two persons have taught me never again to read lightly over citations of gratitude. Truly, without them this book would never have seen the light of day.

The most personally enriching part of writing this book had been the privilege of so many conversations with Catholic laity and clergy about their pastoral experience with the new *Rite of Funerals*. Because it would be impossible to cite and thank every person, clergy and laity in the parishes and students in the classroom, who gave of their time and experience for those gleanings that help our appreciation of the *Rite* in pastoral practice, the principle of naming only those persons whose explicit ideas appear as unique and whose words are quoted *verbatim* has been followed. It is to the many others whose lives and deaths have given us the source of these gleanings that the book itself is dedicated in gratitude.

Finally, the dedication of the book embraces my mother and father. I alone, however, accept full responsiblity for what has become of their gift in these pages.

Evolution of the Rite

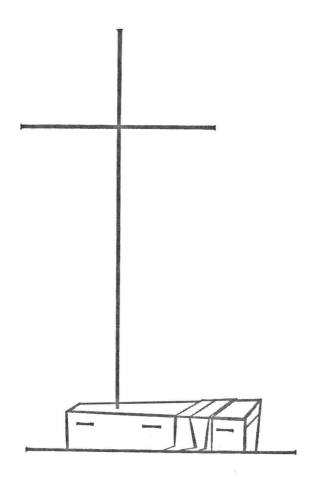

Chapter One

Origins

Long before medieval theologians began to write their tracts on the four last things, Christians had been expressing what they believed about death and about life after death in the care which they showed their dead. That the followers of Jesus took reverent care of the bodies of their dead and held their memory in honor was, of course, nothing out of the ordinary. They were simply continuing the customs of the culture into which the Church of Christ was born. Funeral ritual belongs to the very heritage of the human community. Speaking with the authority of scholarly consensus Margaret Mead has said, "I know of no people for whom the fact of death is not critical, and who have no ritual by which to deal with it."[1]

CULTURAL AND RELIGIOUS ROOTS

In the Mediterranean world of the first century A.D. the peoples absorbed into Greco-Roman culture observed funeral rites that represented both their own ancient heritages and the syncretism of the contemporary empire. Although customs differed widely from people to people, the funeral rites carried out for the ordinary Roman citizen were sufficiently widespread to give us an example of the kind of funeral first-century Christians would have known.

Jocelyn Toynbee, classicist and archeologist, provides a thorough description of this *funus translaticum*. Its ritual moments offer a good point of comparison with the early Christian funeral.

"When death was imminent relations and close friends gathered round the dying person's bed, to comfort and support him or her and to give vent to their own grief. The nearest relative present gave the last kiss, to catch the soul, which, so it was believed, left the body with the final breath. The same relative then closed the departed's eyes, after which all the near relatives called upon the dead by name and lamented him or her, a process that continued at intervals until the body was disposed of by cremation or inhumation. The next act was to take the body from the bed, to set it on the ground, and to wash it and anoint it. Then followed the dressing of the corpse . . . and the placing of a coin in the mouth to pay the deceased's fare in Charon's barque. All was now ready for the body's exposition or lying-in-state on a grand bed, if the family was well-to-do, with the feet towards the house-door. . . .

"From the following of the corpse to the place of its disposal by relatives, friends, and other invited persons (all wearing black *lugubria*) come the funerary terms *exsequiae* and *prosequi*. Traditionally, it was the ancient Roman custom for funerals to be conducted at night by the light of torches, which were still carried before the body when, in historical times, the funerals of all but children and the poor took place by day. In well-to-do families the deceased, still lying on the funerary couch, was carried from his or her home on an elaborate bier. The bearers, on whose shoulders it rested, might be the departed's nearest male relatives or closest male friends or his or her newly liberated slaves. . . .

"As soon as the funeral procession arrived at the place of inhumation or cremation, there was performed the essential rite of throwing a little earth on the corpse and, in the case of cremation, of the cutting off of a fraction of it to be subsequently buried. As regards inhumations, the poor were laid directly in the earth, generally fully extended, less often in a crouched position in simple trench-graves; or in the case of the Jews, other Semitics and early Christians, on shelves cut in the rock walls of hypogea and catacombs. The wealthy were placed in richly carved sarcophagi, the moderately well-to-do in less elaborate sarcophagi of marble, stone, terracotta, lead, or wood. Lead sarcophagi were usually placed in outer ones of stone or wood. . . .

"The burning of the corpse, and of the couch on which it lay, took place either at the place in which the ashes were to be buried or at a place specially reserved for cremations. The pyre was a rectangular pile of wood, sometimes mixed with papyrus to facilitate the burning. The eyes of the corpse were opened when it was placed on the pyre. . . . The relatives and friends then called upon the dead by name for the last time: the pyre was kindled with torches; and after the corpse had been consumed the ashes were drenched with wine. The burnt bones and ashes of the body were collected by the relatives and placed in receptacles of various kinds. . . .

"On returning from the funeral the relatives had to undergo the *suffitio*, a rite of purification by fire and water. On the same day there began a period of cleansing ceremonies held at the deceased's house; and again on the same day a funerary feast, the *silicernium*, was eaten at the grave in honor of the dead. There was also the *cena novendialis* eaten at the grave on the ninth day after the funeral, at the end of the period of full mourning."[2]

During the first century A.D. it seems that apprehension was the primary inspiration for funerary ritual. Personal emotions of loss and grief certainly played their part but it was fear far more than hope, aversion more than affection, that motivated the rituals of pagans at death. It was generally believed that the dead were inclined to be resentful and quick to take revenge. Funerary rites served to appease them. Burial, it was held, guaranteed a certain peace; otherwise one's shade might be doomed to

5

everlasting restless wandering and be a source of dread in the world of the living. That is the reason why burial of the dead was regarded as the minimum of ritual concern in the Roman world. Even the dead stranger was to be given a ritual burial. Both Greek and Roman literature attest how deeply rooted in popular religious sensibility was this last honor paid to the dead.[3]

The other primary influence on the early Christian funeral was, of course, its Judaic roots. In the history of Israel burial of deceased members of the community was an obligation as well as a work of mercy. The Book of Tobit, although never accepted into the Hebrew canon of sacred books, illustrates the importance of this practice in the life of a devout Jew who was tested and rewarded by God. In post-exilic times rabbis taught that the obligation to care for the dead included not only relatives and friends, but any deceased Jew. They repeatedly insisted that this duty of fraternal love likewise extended to the dead outside Judaism.[4]

Jewish funerary rites seem always to have reflected the realism and simplicity that characterize the present-day liturgy, "Justification of Judgment" (Tzidduk HaDin).[5] This liturgy dates from the ninth century, and it cannot of course serve to document first-century practice; nevertheless, as Geoffrey Rowell has concluded, "its stark simplicity and directness, and its consciousness of the righteous justice and faithfulness of God, who is to be praised in death as well as in life, exemplify the Jewish response to suffering and death, which is the context out of which the Christian understanding developed. Its very simplicity points us to a basic pattern of strongly biblical prayer, accompanying the few necessary actions of burial, which may be assumed, with the necessary Christological additions, to reflect what is most likely to have been the earliest Christian practice."[6]

Besides these two predominant influences the religious syncretism of the times brought still other active cultural forces to bear. Imperial Rome was strongly attracted to the mystery cults from the East and the religious beliefs and practices of Egypt.[7] One consequence of all this diversity contributes much to our understanding of the first-century milieu. In summary it can be said that "during the late Republic and throughout the Empire . . . belief in the survival after death of personal individuality prevailed and views on the nature of the life that awaited the soul beyond the grave were, in the main, optimistic. Both literature (to some extent) and funerary art (to a high degree) do, in fact, reveal that there was in this age a deepening conviction that the terror and power of death could be overcome and that richer, happier, and more godlike life than that experienced here was attainable hereafter, under certain conditions, by the souls of the departed."[8]

Interest, perhaps even optimistic interest, in life hereafter and ritual care for the dead were thus something Christians shared with the world around them as part of their human cultural heritage. Nevertheless, early Christian eschatology and the early Christian funeral were peculiarly Christian. While it would be a mistake to deny that the cultures in which the Church took root influenced the experiential faith of Christians, one cannot fail, on the other hand, to acknowledge the reciprocal influence which the faith had on the way those Christians lived their lives. "The world of Early Christendom," it has been documented, "is one which must be understood from within. It is not the prevailing form—which is usually that of late Classical times—but the Christian content which plays the determining role."[9] Just as important as uncovering the cultural and religious roots of Christian funerary rites, therefore, is interpreting them as the rituals of believing Christians.

CHURCH OF THE MARTYRS (A.D. 30–313)

During the first three centuries of the life of the Church, aptly called "The Church of the Martyrs," the earliest witnesses to Christian care of the dead are the cemeteries of the dead themselves. These were public cemeteries and not, as popular piety once believed, secret burial places of the persecuted Christians. Very few date from before the fourth century, and they reveal that Christians and pagans were buried in a similar manner, sometimes even side-by-side in the same cemetery. Only the decorative representations and inscriptions indicate any distinction between these early graves, and certain apparently neutral pagan motifs continued to appear with Jewish and Christian ones on the same grave.[10] Even these early decorations proclaimed in their pristine manner that for the Christians their dead "were no mere shades whom they remembered with sadness and resignation. These were the ones who had gone before to the Paradise of the Shepherd, to the 'place of refreshment, light and peace.' During the funeral meal [which Christians initially continued to celebrate as something quite ordinary], they linked the 'refreshment' with another meal, that of the Eucharist, the Food of Life. That is why, in the chamber of the funeral meal [in the catacomb of St. Priscilla, Rome] we see, on the arch above the center couch, the picture of the meal with loaves and fishes and on the walls that of the deliverance and the rebirth from the water."[11]

Their funerary decorations thus preserved for us the symbolic motifs by means of which those early Christians gave expression to their faith in face of death, a faith that speaks not of death but of life. This is not a denial of physical death but a proclamation of the belief that the life entered at baptism and nourished at the eucharist is of a different order. It is in no way affected by the fact of physical death. Its only paradigm is the life of the Lord Jesus, dead and risen, as the symbolism of Christian initiation connotes. Its food is the Body of the

Lord Jesus, broken and given as the bread of life. For those reborn to this life in the waters of baptism and fed at the Lord's eucharistic banquet in union with his Church, the idea that physical death might terminate such life simply has no place in the categories of the faith. This is not to say that physical death itself as well as its harsh consequences for bereaved survivors were experienced as any less real. The difference is this. In the face of grief, painful human loss, and separation, the Christian community found consolation in the promise of life. They had every hope that the life they once shared together in eucharist would be theirs again in the eschatological kingdom. Ignatius of Antioch, writing to the Ephesians, reminded erring Christians what it meant "to share in the one common breaking of bread—the medicine of immortality, and the sovereign remedy by which we escape death and live in Jesus Christ for evermore."[12]

This faith was stronger than the physical consequences of death for the body, whether natural decomposition or destruction by beasts or ill fortune. At the promised resurrection the all-powerful God, Lord of all nature, would restore all, for belief in an everlasting Christ-life pertained, of course, not to the soul only. The climax of redemption belongs both to spirit and to flesh; hence Christians paid care and respect to the mortal remains of the faithful dead while they remembered their souls in prayer.

The epitome of participation in Christ's redemptive death and resurrection was martyrdom, for such a death was believed to bear perfect witness to Christ and thus to enjoy the immediate reward of paradise with him. The tombs of the martyrs very early became places of special devotion. Simple shrines or memorials were erected at their tombs, some as adjacent crypts in the catacombs and others above ground nearby or in the homes of the martyred saints. Many of these precious places were to be the sites of future churches. Gradually lists of local martyrs with the dates of their death were compiled to guide the annual commemorations by the faithful. Thus the cult of the martyrs preserved an indication of the kind of commemorative rites that were held for the dead. Moreover, such annual commemoration mirrored the rituals of burial itself.

These few examples from church life, together with the earliest Christian iconography, demonstrate the spirit of prayer that characterized Christian burial and commemorations. The redeemed soul is shown with hands upraised in prayer to its Redeemer. Similarly, as we have seen, the conception of "refreshment" is frequently depicted as a banquet including the gospel motif of the loaves and fishes. This is an allusion to both the celestial banquet and the eucharist which was already becoming the Christian funeral meal *par excellence*. Funerary inscriptions have also preserved this attitude of prayer. The words "life" or "in peace," for example, express the *confidence* in faith that the deceased Christian is in peace and enjoys everlasting life as well as the *petition* for these blessings.

Thus besides references to the celebration of the eucharist and the singing of psalms, there are explicit allusions to other funerary prayers on the part of individuals and the community. The belief that prayer was appropriate to Christian care for the dead was taken for granted. Those early Christians needed no explanation to make them understand what their homilies, funerary inscriptions, and iconography meant.

The same can be said for Christian ritual at the time of burial. What can be gathered from scattered impressions showed Christians following the basic funerary customs of their neighbors, as we saw above. Only those practices which they believed to be contradictory to their faith were rejected.[13] The guiding spirit of their funeral

10

was the same perduring motif of "life" that permeated their early funerary iconography. Sources which pertain to the funeral of heroic martyrs and famous personages have been preserved in detail, and one sees there what was specifically Christian about their manner of burial: that is, above all, an attitude of prayerful joy. That joy is at once realistic in the face of human grief and at the same time expressive of the Christian faith that redemption unto life in Christ is not affected by physical death. An apologist of the mid-second century, Aristides of Athens, for example, defended the way Christians behaved at the death of a "just" Christian, explaining that they "rejoice and give thanks and accompany the corpse, for he has emigrated from one place to another."[14] A century later in North Africa, Cyprian urged with pastoral concern that his people not fall back into pagan ways of mournful despair at the death of dear ones.[15]

It was Cyprian who also declared that the martyrdom of constant Christian commitment should be a source of deepest consolation to the living when so many fellow Christians were dying in the plague. Eusebius cited a pastoral letter describing Alexandrian Christians in similar straits a century later:

"With willing hands they raised the bodies of the saints to their bosoms; they closed their eyes and mouths, carried them on their shoulders and laid them out; they clung to them, embraced them, washed them, and wrapped them in grave-clothes. Very soon the same services were done for them, since those left behind were constantly following those gone before."

The author of that letter, according to Eusebius, did not hesitate to assert that "death in this form, the result of great piety and strong faith, seems in every way equal to martyrdom."[16]

Evidence such as this assures us that when the Peace of Constantine opened the way for the established "Church of the Empire,"[17] the fundamental spirit and structure of future Christian funeral liturgy were already tradition. From the beginning Christians had buried their dead as an act of faith in the redemption that their baptism into the death and resurrection of Jesus promised. They imbued everything surrounding burial with this faith; thus even the most human activities, such as washing and anointing of the dead, and the tomb itself became symbols of liturgy. To the spiritual inheritance of Old Testament psalms they added Christian hymns; the eucharistic banquet came to supersede the memorial funeral meal; Jewish and pagan funerary art inspired new Christian representations expressing the mystery of redemption. Thus the Christian experience that burial was an occasion of praise and thanksgiving acquired its own proper ritual expression. Little by little favorite psalms and hymns came to be sung more frequently; certain prayer formulas were found to be especially fitting; repeated ritual practices became characteristic. It was this attitude of faith and the increasingly familiar ways Christians translated that faith into worship that constituted the origin of a Christian liturgy of burial.

THE CHURCH OF THE EMPIRE (A.D. 313–600)
During the four centuries following the Edict of Milan church life became increasingly more complicated. The pristine faith which once voiced itself in worship at the burial of a Christian could no longer always be taken for granted. Following upon Christian emancipation by Constantine, new masses of converted peoples began entering the ever-expanding Church. Their budding experience of the faith had not known the fervor passed on to the primitive community from the Lord's own companions or of that new sense of mission as a "third race" in a world of pagans and Jews. Accounts of living

12

faith sealed by the martyrs' blood were past history to these new Christians. Furthermore, many of them were often conquerors themselves. They brought with them cherished funerary customs that were bound to have an effect on the developing Christian liturgy of burial. During these centuries the Church was becoming a church of the masses and its liturgy, even something so personally-laden as the funeral, tended more and more to become highly formalized rites performed by a specialized clergy.

The impressions one gets of church life during this era point nevertheless to a funeral liturgy that had developed from the seeds of primitive Christian tradition.

Once again Christian cemeteries preserved art and epitaphs that provide valuable evidence from across the Constantinian Empire. From the fourth century alone some one thousand sarcophagi, entire or in fragments, are the best preserved monuments of the period. Of them it can be said,

"The old symbols: shepherd, fisherman, banquet, have disappeared. The unveiled figure of Christ makes its appearance, mostly in the representations of the miracles of Christ, with Old Testament prefigurations alongside. Small historical and symbolical cycles develop: the passion of Moses-Peter and the childhood of Christ. As a series, the 'deliverance' motifs hold their own the longest."[18]

Among the miracles of Jesus, the healing of the blind man and the raising of Lazarus from the dead, both symbols of baptism, continue the theme of "life" that death cannot destroy. Peter's denial "at the crowing of the cock" came to represent the dawn of new life after the forgiveness of sins. Nearly all known Christian cemeteries that date from after A.D. 313 continued to decorate the resting places of the dead with Old Testament scenes of "deliverance" by God: the sacrifice of

Isaac, Daniel among the lions, Jonah freed from the sea monster, the three young men in the furnace, and Job delivered from misery.

Fifth-century sarcophagi preserved a new, purely symbolic decoration. There one sees, for example, the late classical cliché of vine branches, now inseparably entwined with the XP of the Christ monogram. Such a composition could not fail to remind Christians of their life in Christ the vine, and of the fruit of that life untouched by physical death (John 15). Examples of funerary representations from all over the late Roman Empire, although in varying styles and motifs, thus continued to preach symbolically the kerygma pure and simple: redemption through Christ Jesus the Lord.[19]

With its freedom the Church of the Empire also became more vocal. Sermons and writings that were intended explicitly to teach the Christian faith also bear witness to Christian liturgical practice. These literary witnesses confirm without a doubt that the central motif of Christian teaching concerning death is indeed the belief, proclaimed from the beginning in word, liturgy, and art, that life in Christ is not undone by physical death. Nor is there any groping or hesitation here, as if something new were emerging with the emancipation of the Church. Rather, the freedom to speak out reveals simultaneous agreement among the Fathers from all corners of the Empire as to the centrality of this belief. Ambrose (+397), for example, grounding his teaching on the very promise of Jesus, summarized the tradition:

"'Do not fear,' that is, do not fear because of this world, do not fear because of the iniquities of the world, do not fear because of the waves of bodily passions: I am the remission of sins. Do not fear because of darkness: I am the light. Do not fear because of death: I am the life. 'Whoever comes to me will not see death forever,' because he is the fullness of divinity, and honor, and

14

glory, perpetuity is to him forever from the beginning of time both now and always and forever and ever."[20]

Ambrose's expression of belief in deliverance through God's mercy echoed the familiar theme of contemporary iconography.

Similarly prayer for the faithful dead revealed faith in Jesus' promise of life without end for those who believe in him and live the Christian life. Those who died outside communion with the Church were believed beyond the help of prayer. For Ambrose, "church" embraced the faithful, both living and dead. Augustine too elaborated on this notion of a communion of saints living and dead.[21]

The corollary to this belief also enjoyed universal adherence in patristic writings: final resurrection and restoration of the body was imperative, for the perfect life in Christ was unthinkable without the reunion of the complete person, understood as union of soul and body.

In Christian funeral orations one is struck by the way in which faith in life and resurrection renders *mourning* unchristian whereas it respects the genuine *grief* of the bereaved. In fact this faith becomes the greatest source of consolation for that grief.[22] Mourning the deceased in pagan culture flowed from *despair*. One mourned emotionally, on the other hand, because death for the ordinary person was believed to be the absolute and definitive end of any really true life; religiously, on the other, because fear led to appeasing the dead in their miserable lot of half-life. For the Christian, mourning of this kind (especially with its drastic expressions of personal physical mutilation and dramatic wailing) had no meaning. Grief, on the other hand, had its place and was a respected emotion, a natural movement of the heart and soul of the bereaved at such loss.[23] Grief was not to flow from despair nor was it to take expression in the mourning practices of nonbelievers. Although, as we shall see, some of these mourning customs would survive to plague and eventually become reconciled with Christian practice, devout Christians had developed their own appropriate expression of grief in their rites of burial. Instead of wailing in despair they sang psalms and hymns, thus expressing from the depth of their grief both their confidence in God and their solemn joy in the belief that Christ's promise of life would indeed be fulfilled for their deceased. Thus Christian grief found consolation in the same hope that iconography depicted.

Prayer too expressed itself at this time in the same symbols as funerary art. "Light," "rest," and "deliverance" characterized the hereafter according to Ambrose in his funeral address in memory of the Christian Emperor Theodosius. Ambrose prayed on that occasion:

"Give perfect rest to Thy servant Theodosius, that rest which Thou hast prepared for Thy saints. Let his soul return there, whence it descended, where he cannot feel the sting of death, where he knows that this death is not the end of nature but of error. For in that he died, he died to sin; so that now there can be no place for sin; but he will rise again in order that his life may be restored perfectly by renewed gifts."[24]

The popular image of the "bosom of Abraham" remained a manner of concretizing the meaning of "rest." Far from localizing a place of rest, Ambrose interpreted its meaning: "The just are said to rest in the bosom of Abraham, for they rest in his grace, in his rest, in his calm peace, who had put on faith like unto his and who transformed one and the same will into good works."[25] Elsewhere too the Bishop of Milan referred to Abraham's bosom in the context of lived faith as the holy patriarch's cloak of good deeds. This "cloak" embracing the saints was to become the distinguishing mark of Abraham in medieval art.[26] It is above all Augustine who impresses upon us the way symbolic images of the faith defy definition. Using this scriptural image, he writes of a dead friend, "Now he lives in the bosom of Abraham. Whatever is signified by that bosom, there my Nebridius lives, that sweet friend of mine."[27]

Another contemporary prayer, this one taken from the so-called *Euchologion* of Bishop Serapion, exemplifies well how faith in the fourth century took expression in symbolic language, the only language capable of rendering the inexpressible things of God. Note also the realism of the faith that prays not only for the deceased but also for the consolation of the bereaved and for the community present:

"... we beseech thee for the repose and rest of this thy servant or this thine handmaiden: give rest to his soul, his spirit, in green places (Ps. 22, 2), in chambers of rest with Abraham and Isaac and Jacob and all thy Saints: and raise up his body in the day which thou hast ordained, according to thy promises which cannot lie (Titus 1, 2), that thou mayest render to it also the heritage of which it is worthy in thy holy pastures. Remember not his transgressions and sins: and cause his going forth to be peaceable and blessed. Heal the griefs of those who pertain to him with the spirit of consolation, and grant unto us all a good end through thy only-begotten Jesus Christ, through whom to thee (is) the glory and the strength in holy Spirit to the ages of the ages. Amen."[28]

Many other patristic writings also illustrated aspects of faith and practice at Christian burial. Among them Augustine recounted the Christian death and funeral of Monica, his mother; Chrysostom explained the Christian name 'cemetery"; Jerome described a joyful funeral procession in Jerusalem where the chanting of psalms and alleluia reverberated off the gilded roofs.[29] Augustine's many references confirming "the practice of the universal Church" constitute a special source of impressions. For example, his short treatise entitled *The Care to Be Taken for the Dead* explained the value of the customary Christian care for the dead, especially of prayer on their behalf. It was not the place of burial, or even the fact of burial itself, but prayer that was advantageous for the deceased.[30] Augustine argued also that the value of such prayer depended on the good or evil of one's life before death, according to Scripture, and this is consistent with his own prayer for Monica.[31] It is not for us to distinguish who is helped or not, and thus none of the faithful dead are to be excluded, according to Augustine.[32] Furthermore, however good one's life had been, Augustine believed that no one except the martyrs died without sin. Thus the precise nature of the help accorded the faithful dead through the prayer of the Church was, for Augustine, the forgiveness of certain sins remaining after death. Through the intercession of the saints and the prayer of the Church, Augustine taught, God in his mercy and justice could forgive such remaining sins or at least grant a more tolerable damnation.[33] It was to be considered a duty in Christian charity to plead with God on behalf of the dead. This included the hope that one would receive the same care when death came. Augustine was insistent therefore that prayer, almsgiving, and especially offering the eucharist were efficacious for the dead. Furthermore, he asserted, burial and commemorative practices demonstrate respect for the body that once housed and served the soul, not in the manner of some decoration but pertaining to the very nature of man. They reflect God's own care for humanity and point to a strong belief in the resurrection. But above all they serve to assure continued prayerful remembrance by the living of those who have gone before.

We have devoted more space than usual to these impressions, and it was Augustine more than any other single influence who set the course and interpretation that "the practice of the universal Church to pray for the dead" would take in the medieval West.[34]

Aurelius Prudentius Clemens

The poet Prudentius (+ca. 405) has left a rare and exceptional mirror of this Christian faith in the resurrection of the body and the consequences of this belief in the life of the Church in the hymn *God, the Blazing Fountain of Souls*.[35] This hymn on funerals, considered a masterpiece of its kind in literature, was composed with a literary audience in mind and presumably reflected the faith of lettered Roman Christians of the fourth and fifth centuries.[36] Prudentius, a layman, proclaims in verse the same faith in the resurrection found in the writings of contemporary Fathers.

The natural, mortal condition of creatures flows from creation, the poem commences, and yet resurrection of the body is the God-given remedy for death. It is for this reason that Christians care for their dead (verses 1-16). Next, Prudentius reflects on the mystery of death and resurrection (verses 57-112). Death is the suffering one must go through—the giving up of life—to truly live and appreciate life. The hymn closes with an exhortation and a commendationlike prayer at burial (verses 113-172).

For Prudentius, the care Christians showed their dead and their burial customs themselves were signs that took their meaning from Christian faith in the resurrection of the body. They are one more confirmation that the faith found expression in the life of the Church. Ritual practices noted in the poem did not differ much from those of the Empire generally in the fourth and fifth centuries. Yet, one senses a Christian spirit which gives special meaning to them. For example, there was a wake of some kind where the Christian homilist placed greater emphasis on the imminent restoration of life than on life's end or on the accomplishments of the deceased. Other customs such as the attention given tombs, the funeral procession, the manner of wrapping in white linen and preserving the body with myrrh, the final and even the regular decoration of graves with flowers and perfume, and the honor of burial itself all make sense, according to the poet, because the body thus cared for is believed to be "asleep" until called forth to life beyond death. Thus one understands why the characteristic wailing and disruptive mourning practices of the pagans were so out of place among Christians. For death, already so natural and familiar, had become the path to unending life, the path that had been symbolized in the experience of the elder Tobias and laid open by the crucified Lord for all to follow. At a time when more fearful concerns began to preoccupy extant funerary references in literature, it is important to recognize that there was always a continuity of belief with the earlier tradition.

The occasion for the composition of this hymn is unknown, and commentators agree that it was not immediately intended for public worship. Nevertheless, Prudentius left us a glimpse of how lettered Christians at the turn of the fifth century saw in their funeral practices a liturgy expressing the faith that death does not destroy life. It is fitting to close this brief review of Prudentius' masterpiece of resurrection faith with a selection of verses from the poem:

God, the blazing fountain of our souls
who joined two elements, one living
and the other dying, to create
man out of your divine fatherhood, (1)

remember that both are yours. For you
they were combined, it is you they serve
while together they cling, flesh and soul
stirred and moved by the life you give them . . . . (2)

We see the body without its soul,
resting before us; but before long
it will seek to be joined to its soul
so that they together live on high . . . . (9)

For this reason do we take such care
of graves; for this reason do we give
these honours to a lifeless body
which we carried here in procession. (12)

For this same reason do we spread white
linen cloths over it and sprinkle
it with a precious preservative,
myrrh, which has been carried from Saba. (13)

What do the carved tombs and monuments
mean if they do not say that something
precious, something sleeping, has been placed
in them for safety as in a vault? (14)

This far-seeing care is expended
by the followers of Christ because
they believe that all who are asleep
and cold will one day return to life . . . . (15)

Why should you who are living lament
with these loud and silly noises and
rail against the eternal laws in
such a senseless display of mourning? (29)

Let your doubting sadness be silent;
let your flowing tears be dried, mothers.
Let this mourning come to a quick end
because death is not the end of life. (30)

When a dried seed is dead and buried
it comes to life and produces shoots.
When the seed is returned to the earth
it repeats the harvest of the past. (31)

Receive now, Earth, our brother's body.
Take him to your bosom; care for him.
It is a man's body we give you;
he was nobly born, look after him. (32)

In this flesh lived a soul created
by the breath of God; in this body

Wisdom, whose head is Christ, had a home.
He who planned and made this man will not (33)

forget him. Cover and protect this
treasure which we now place in your care.
Soon our Father will seek what he gave,
the image of his most divine face. (34)

When that time of justice comes, that time
when God will fulfill all hopes, this grave
will be opened and it will return
the form which today we give to it. (35)

Even though time turned these bones to dust
and that dust became but a handful
of ashes, still the man that he was
will never be allowed to perish . . . . (36)

We will do as you have told us, Lord.
In your defeat of death's blackness you
advised your companion on the cross,
the thief, to follow in your footsteps. (40)

For those who are faithful to your word,
there is a well-lit road to the gates
of Paradise; those who follow you
will enter the garden Adam lost. (41)

I pray you, our Leader, give orders
that your servant, this spirit, be drawn
to you in the place where it was born,
the place from which it went to exile. (42)

We will attend to these buried bones
with sweet violets and green branches;
we will sweeten the stones by sprinkling
precious perfumes on the epitaph. (43)[37]

Pseudo-Dionysius the Areopagite
In the sixth century Pseudo-Dionysius left a commentary on funeral liturgy common to his Syrian Church.[38]

Although practice there differed in liturgical detail from certain customs in the West, one recognizes a common faith and a common understanding of that faith.

In summary, Dionysius describes the funeral as follows. The body of the deceased was brought to the church where the bishop first offered a prayer of thanksgiving to God. Then selections from Scripture about the promise of resurrection were read and psalms on the same theme were sung. When the catechumens had been dismissed, the names of those who have already died in the faith were proclaimed, including that of the deceased in their midst, and all present were exhorted to pray that they themselves might receive ultimate happiness in Christ. Next the bishop prayed over the body and gave the deceased a final kiss of peace; the other ministers and all the faithful follow suit. Then holy oil was poured over the body by the bishop. Finally, after a prayer for all the faithful departed, the bishop laid the corpse to rest in holy ground.

The placing of the corpse in the church, Pseudo-Dionysius explained, mirrored in death one's place in everlasting life as a follower of Christ according to divine justice. It was to celebrate this justice that the bishop opens the funeral liturgy with a great prayer of thanksgiving. Chanting psalms and reading the divine promises signified the kind of happiness and peace awaiting the blessed and also served to exhort the living to pursue that same goal. For Pseudo-Dionysius this liturgy was thus inseparably both symbolic experience and exhortation.

In the prayer that followed, the bishop prayed that God in his goodness would remit all the sins committed by the deceased because of human frailty and assign the dead Christian to the light and the place of the living, the bosom of Abraham, Isaac, and Jacob, where there is no sorrow, sadness, or tears. Once again we recognize here the traditional Christian images of life beyond death as well as the prayer of the Church for the forgiveness of sins.

Pseudo-Dionysius faced the question of how the bishop could ask for the remission of sins when Scripture teaches that one's lot after death is determined by the fruits of one's life (2 Cor. 5.10). His response eloquently reflected on the nature of petition and on the role of the bishop in the Church as revealer of divine promises and divine judgments. Prayer for the dead was compared to any petition which God grants only to the deserving and only when the object is for their good. The analogy is obvious: God in his goodness knows the heart of the deceased, one's strengths and frailties during life, and he will respond to prayer on one's behalf with divine justice. Such prayer, the author argued, was also quite in accord with the bishop's revelatory role. To pray over the faithful dead for the forgiveness of sins and the reward of a place in the company of the patriarchs was to proclaim God's promise of unending life to those who love him.

Pseudo-Dionysius explained the kiss of peace as a desirable Christian gesture toward one who has lived a truly Christian life. The greeting that Christians regularly exchange among themselves was now shared with the deceased, a fitting sign of communion between the living and the dead Christian. Although this kiss was a final gesture toward the body, he insisted that it was not a "farewell," for life in Christ knows no farewell.

Especially significant is his explanation of the anointing with oil in the context of the deceased's initiation as a Christian. At the time of Christian initiation, wrote Pseudo-Dionysius, anointing with oil had called the one to be initiated into sacred combat; now the poured oil proclaimed that the deceased, having fought that sacred fight, died victorious. Thus too the body received an honorable burial among the other faithful departed, for

24

it continued to participate in the glory of the soul. God who joined the body and soul rewards or punishes both as partners in good or evil. This liturgy of burial proclaimed the unity of the Christian person before God.

What Prudentius expressed in poetry Pseudo-Dionysius believed to be celebrated in Christian funeral liturgy. The influence of his writings on the development of Christian thought from Gregory the Great through Thomas Aquinas into the sixteenth century renders his reflections on funeral liturgy an especially significant mirror of liturgical tradition and continuity.

Although ritual practices and prayers continued much the same into the next century, one notes an unmistakable shift taking place in the understanding of how those rites and prayers function in the life of the Church. Canons of local synods and councils regularly mention certain burial practices that were prohibited by ecclesiastical authority.[39] Still very deep-rooted was the practice of giving the eucharistic bread to a corpse. Similarly, altar cloths and other linens used in the celebration of Mass were being used in superstitious rites, either as a shroud or some kind of talisman. The place of burial was also an issue. Interment near the principal altar where the eucharist was celebrated as well as in the baptistry had become widespread. An inordinate desire to be buried there was the occasion for a related practice, the multiple occupancy of one and the same grave site.

All these practices shared a common motivation. They all have to do with securing a protection for the soul of the deceased after death. It is noteworthy as well that all of them focus on the eucharist, whether it be Holy Communion itself, the linens on which the eucharist is celebrated or a final resting place near the altar of celebration. The eucharist as *viaticum* had become the sacrament of protection for the dying; popular preoccupation with the lot of the dead likewise took eucharistic expression. The writings of Pope Gregory the Great embodied the union of this religious mood with evolving liturgical theology—a union that produced medieval funeral liturgy.

Gregory the Great

At the turn of the seventh century the *Dialogues* of Gregory the Great gave a perspective of funerary and commemorative liturgy that reveal a very developed notion of expiation.[40] With Augustine as their most notable master, Gregory and others explained the earlier emphasis on the effectiveness of prayer for the dead. The prayer of the Church, they taught, brought about the liberation of the faithful dead from the purifying fire of expiation for sin. Before long this fire would become localized as "purgatory," and the tradition of prayer for the release of the "poor souls" its complement in popular piety.

Thus the religious sensibility of the times represented the eucharist and prayer for the deceased in a new way. Formerly they were seen as reflecting the Church's evangelical trust in God's mercy toward the faithful departed, according to his promises and mysterious plan. Now this trust was becoming more and more a fear of his judgment. Optimistic faith began to tend toward pessimistic fate. Belief that "the just God is merciful and therefore forgiving" shifted to mean that "the merciful God is just and therefore demands expiation."

This prevailing pessimism about the living thus had its effect on the attitude toward the lot of the dead. With the advent of severe penitential discipline, being Christian became more and more a preoccupation with sin; care for the dead Christian became in turn a preoccupation with the wages of sin. Thus, for Gregory and his contemporaries even the faithful Christian was presumed a sinner whose immediate lot after death was at best one of purification. It was the exceptional saint who escaped. Expiation for unrepented serious sin was believed impossible and punishment for eternity its just desert. Lesser sins of everyday life, however, could be forgiven and the soul could be cleansed through purification by fire, as precious metals in a furnace. It was here that the prayers of the Church, and especially the Mass, were believed to benefit the dead.

Implicit in Gregory's teaching is a new sense of something approaching the automatic, as if by "performing" so many prayers and Masses the release of a soul from the purifying fire would be achieved provided the deceased had earned the right to such help during life. To be sure, Pope Gregory does not specify a *quid pro quo* theology, but such was nevertheless the attitude that soon came to characterize prayer for the dead in the Middle Ages. An example of this attitude is the story that is believed to recount the origin of the so-called Gregorian Masses, a popular practice both throughout the Middle Ages and well into the twentieth century. The story goes that Justus, a monk of Gregory's monastery, fell ill. During his illness it was discovered that the monk had hidden three gold pieces in his cell, contrary to the Rule. In order to teach a lesson Gregory was extremely severe. He ordered that no one offer consolation to the dying monk in his last moments, and furthermore, when he had died, they were to throw his gold pieces into the grave after him crying, "May your money be with you in perdition." Brother Justus died repentant. Nevertheless, for thirty days Gregory refused to allow prayers to be offered for him. Finally he took pity on the deceased monk, whom he described as suffering in the fire, and ordered that Mass be celebrated for Justus on thirty consecutive days. At the end of that time Justus appeared to Gregory and told him that until then he had been suffering, but now he was well because on that day he had been received into heaven. Gregory explains that his release coincided exactly with the Mass on the thirtieth day, clear proof that Justus had been freed through the offering of the Mass.[41]

There is no doubt that the *Dialogues* of Gregory the Great, with such marvelous stories illustrating his theology, widely contributed to the success in the West of the practice of celebrating the eucharist on behalf of the dead. The attitude of those times, which Gregory thus shared and articulated in theology and liturgical practice, revealed the shift away from the ecclesial eschatology of the earlier tradition to an eschatology of the individual. Before long this view attained universal acceptance in the West, and the writings of Pope Gregory remained its most authoritative champion.

Columba the Elder

One last text confirms how thorough was that shift. The hymn *In Praise of the Father*, [42] attributed to Columba the Elder of Iona (+ca. 597 A.D.) devoted its final seven stanzas to the day of judgment, the second coming of Christ, and the deserts of the damned and elect. In those verses one already recognizes the themes and imagery that would take lasting form in the sequence *Dies irae*.

In contrast with the hymn by Prudentius, Columba's work is preoccupied with the lot of the dead approaching judgment. Prudentius took for granted that the just dead included the ordinary faithful Christian for whom final judgment meant life with Christ. Columba, on the other hand, doubted whether anyone could survive the Lord's judgment unscathed. Confidence founded on faith in the resurrection had given way to fear and near despair.

Although there are no indications that his hymn ever belonged to a funeral liturgy as such, the presence of an antiphon in certain manuscripts and a collect in others do suggest that it might have been part of a public office in some churches or communities. In the ninth century a long part of the hymn was incorporated into a longer poem by Rabanus Maurus entitled *Aeterne rerum conditor* (not the morning hymn of the same title by St. Ambrose). Its popularity as a private prayer is attested by a gloss praising its powers that include, among many others, protection "against every death save death on pillow," i.e., death in one's sleep.[43] Such a preoccupation with fear of death and the lot of the dead had thus become a familiar theme in medieval church life.

The day of the Lord,
the most righteous King of kings,

is near. That will be
a day of wrath and revenge,

a day of clouds and darkness,
a day of marvellous thundering

and a day of distress,
of mourning and of sadness.

It will be a day on which will stop
the love and desire for women,

the contentions of all men
and the cupidity of this world. (R)

We will stand in fear
before the tribunal of the Lord

and we will render to him
an accounting of all we have done.

Then will we see
all of our evil deeds.

At this time the records
of our consciences

will be opened in front of our eyes.
Then will we weep the bitterest tears

because no longer will we have
the materials needed for work. (Q)[44]

CONCLUSION

The various opinions gathered in this chapter, despite cultural, geographic, and temporal influences, are elements of the religious treasury of living, believing people. They are not, as it were, entirely isolated and independent logs adrift in a fathomless sea of possible attitudes and expressions of belief. Rather, they continue to affect the living practice of the Church.

In summary, these opinions leave us with two distinct though related attitudes of faith in the face of death. One is hopeful, reflecting what tradition presents as the pristine Christian attitude toward dying as going to Christ. The other is threatening and pessimistic and reveals a shift in attitude, where death is seen as a summons to judgment and inevitably to punishment for sin. Both of these appear to have existed side-by-side in differing degrees of emphasis from earliest Christian times. The first written texts of the funeral services indicate that these same two attitudes of faith still appeared side-by-side. The further history of the development of Christian funeral liturgy in the West is the continuous story of their relationship in tension one with the other.

NOTES

1. Margaret Mead, "Ritual in Social Crisis," in *Roots of Ritual*, ed. James Shaughnessy (Grand Rapids, Mich.: Eerdmans, 1973), pp. 89-90. See also Robert W. Habenstein and William M. Lamers, *Funeral Customs the World Over* (Milwaukee: Bulfin, 1960).

2. Reprinted from J.M.C. Toynbee: *Death and Burial in the Roman World*, pp. 43-51. Copyright © 1971 by J.M.C. Toynbee. Used by permission of the publisher, Cornell University Press. See also Donna C. Kurtz and John Boardman, *Greek Burial Customs* (Ithaca, N.Y.: Cornell University Press, 1971).

3. Toynbee, *Death and Burial*, p. 43. See also Cyril Bailey, *Religion in Virgil* (Oxford: Clarendon, 1935), pp. 287-291. Cf. Virgil, *Aeneid* 6, 212-235 and Homer, *Iliad* 23, 109-256.

4. Tobit 1–2 and 12. The *Babylonian Talmud* teaches that the pious Jew is to follow God's own example in this: "The Holy One, blessed be He, buried the dead for it is written, 'And He buried him in the valley' (Deut. 34.6), so do thou also bury the dead." (Sotah 14a: trans. A. Cohen in *The Babylonian Talmud*, ed. Isidore Epstein [London: Soncino, 1936, p. 73]). Furthermore, this act of fraternal love is said to take precedence over prescriptions of the Law. (B. Megillah 3b: trans. M. Simon in *The Babylonian Talmud*, pp. 13-14, 200.) It is understood that this rabbinic teaching also applies to non-Jewish dead. "Our Rabbis have taught: 'We support the poor of the heathen along with the poor of Israel, and visit the sick of the heathen along with the sick of Israel, and bury the poor of the heathen along with the dead of Israel, in the interests of peace.'" (b.Gittin 61a: trans. M. Simon in *The Babylonian Talmud*, pp. 286-287.)

5. Geoffrey Rowell, *The Liturgy of Christian Burial*, Alcuin Club Collections, No. 59 (London: SPCK, 1977), pp. 3-8. See especially the collection of essays, *Jewish Reflections on Death*, ed. Jack Riemer (New York: Schocken, 1974).

6. Rowell, *Christian Burial*, p. 8.

7. Toynbee, *Death and Burial*, pp. 38-39; Siegfried Morenz, *Egyptian Religion* (Ithaca, N.Y.: Cornell University Press, 1973, German original, 1960), pp. 183-213, 226-231; C.J. Bleeker, *Egyptian Festivals* (Leiden: Brill, 1967), pp. 124-140; J. Zandee, *Death as an Enemy According to Ancient Egyptian Conceptions* (Leiden: Brill, 1960), pp. 102-108.

8. Toynbee, *Death and Burial*, p. 38.

9. Frits van der Meer and Christine Mohrmann, *Atlas of the Early Christian World* (London: Nelson, 1966, Dutch original, 1958), p. 5. Although there will be occasion in the course of this work to refer to many articles and studies on specific topics, three books are indispensable as guides to funeral practices during these earlier centuries. Alfred C. Rush, *Death and Burial in Christian Antiquity*, The Catholic University of America Studies in Christian Antiquity, 1 (Washington, D.C.: The Catholic University of America Press, 1941.) This is an excellent collection and analysis of data available at that time and pertinent to a doctoral dissertation. The work utilizes a comprehensive bibliography of earlier studies that is especially

valuable to the later researcher. Joseph Ntedika, *L'Evocation de l'au-delà dans la Prière pour les Morts: Etudes de Patristique et de Liturgie Latines, IVe-VIIIe S.*, Recherches Africaines de Théologie, 2 (Louvain-Paris: Nauwelaerts and Béatrice-Nauwelaerts, 1971). Particularly valuable for its collection of primary sources as well as extensive indices and a very complete bibliography, this work is most helpful in its treatment of patristic material. With regard to the liturgy, the author's literary method is less appropriately applicable and his conclusions should be used with this in mind. Damien Sicard, *La liturgie de la mort dans l'église latine des origines à la réforme carolingienne*, Liturgiewissenschaftliche Quelle und Forschungen, no. 63 (Münster: Aschendorff, 1978). A fourth work, especially worthwhile for its theological reflection on impressions gathered from earlier Christian times in ecumenical context, is Bruno Bürki, *Im Herrn entschlafen*, Beiträge zur praktischen Theologie, 6 (Heidelberg: Quelle & Meyer, 1969).

10. Van der Meer–Mohrmann, *Atlas*, pp. 47-55. For further details concerning structure, layout, and types of burial places, see Toynbee, *Death and Burial*, especially for Christian cemeteries, pp. 234-244.

11. Van der Meer–Mohrmann, *Atlas*, pp. 48-49.

12. Ignatius, *Ep. ad Ephesios*, 20, trans. Maxwell Staniforth, *Early Christian Writings. The Apostolic Fathers* (Baltimore: Penguin, 1972), p. 106. See also Irenaeus, *Adv. Haer. IV* 18, 5 (PG 7, 1029).

13. For example, the funeral crown, the *planctus* and *nenia* of the pagan wake and procession, mourning garments, cremation, the pagan *vale*. See Rush, *Death*, pp. 133-149; 163-186; 187-235; 238-242; 254-256; and Toynbee, *Death and Burial*, pp. 39-64.

14. Aristides, *Apology*, 15, ed. J. Armitage Robinson, *The Apology of Aristides*, Texts and Studies 1 (Cambridge: The University Press, 1893; rpt. Nendeln, Liechtenstein: Kraus, 1967), pp. 49-50. See also J. Ntedika, *L'Evocation*, pp. 24-25.

15. Cyprian, *De Mortalitate* 1; 20-21, trans. Roy J. Deferrari, *Saint Cyprian: Treatises*, The Fathers of the Church, Vol. 36 (New York: Fathers of the Church, 1958), pp. 199, 215-216.

16. Eusebius, *The History of the Church* 7, 22, trans. G.A. Williamson, *The History of the Church* (Baltimore: Penguin, 1965), pp. 305-306. Although allowing for exaggeration, the subsequent comparison with the pagans, who are said to have abandoned their dead out of selfish fear, reveals the author's belief in the Christian ideal.

17. Van der Meer–Mohrmann, *Atlas*, pp. 58-172.

18. Van der Meer–Mohrmann, *Atlas*, p. 71.

19. The chancel mosaic of S. Apollinare Nuovo, Ravenna, is a good example of the identical theme set in the context of the eucharist—food for eternal life. The reader is urged to compare the plates collected in Van der Meer–Mohrmann, *Atlas*, pp. 58-172. See especially p. 132.

20. Ambrose, *De Bono Mortis*, 12, 57, ed. and trans. William T. Weisner, *S. Ambrosii De Bono Mortis*, The Catholic University of America Patristic Studies, 100 (Washington, D.C.: The Catholic University of America Press, 1970), pp. 152-153.

21. Augustine, *De Civitate Dei* II, 9, trans. Gerald G. Walsh and Daniel J. Honan, *Saint Augustine: The City of God*, The Fathers of the Church, Vol. 24 (New York: Fathers of the Church, 1954), pp. 277-278:

"For, the souls of the faithful departed are not divorced from Christ's kingdom which is the temporal Church. If they were, we should not be mindful of them at God's altar in the communion of the Body of Christ. . . . Why do we go to all this trouble if the faithful departed are not still Christ's members . . . ? We conclude, therefore, that even now, in time, the Church reigns with Christ both in her living and departed members. 'For to this end Christ died,' says St. Paul, 'and rose again, that he might be Lord both of the dead and of the living' (Romans 14.9)."

22. In his oration at the death of his brother Satyrus, Ambrose refers to the grief of those present as a consolation, as saving tears that wash away sins. That kind of grief looks beyond the sorrow of death and heals the pain of present sorrow with the richness of perpetual joy. *De Excessu Fratris* I. 5 (CSEL 73, p. 212).

23. In Sermon 172, 1 Augustine taught that Paul, in his Epistle to the Thessalonians, did not admonish us "not to mourn," but "not to mourn as others who have no hope." The full impact of Augustine's Latin can only be felt in the original: *Constramur ergo nos in nostrorum mortibus necessitate amittendi, sed cum spe recipiendi. Inde angimur, hinc consolamur: inde infirmitas afficit, hinc fides reficit: inde dolet humana conditio, hinc sanat divina promissio* (PL 38, 936).

24. Ambrose, *De Obitu Theodosii*, 36, ed. and trans. Mary D. Mannix, *Sancti Ambrosii Oratio de Obitu Theodosii*, CUAPS, 9 (Washington, D.C.: The Catholic University of America Press, 1925), pp. 56, 75.

25. Ambrose, *Explanatio Psalmi*, Ps. 38.11 (CSEL 64, p. 192).

26. *De Excessu Fratris* II, 101 (CSEL 73, p. 305). See also Augustine, *De natura et origine animae* IV, 16.24 (CSEL 60, pp. 403-404). A popular summary of the rendering of the image "bosom of Abraham" in medieval art is found in T.S.R. Boase, *Death in the Middle Ages* (New York: McGraw-Hill, 1972), pp. 26-36 (Figs. 17, 18, 21, 24). See also *The Flowering of the Middle Ages*, ed. Joan Evans (New York: McGraw-Hill, 1966), pp. 203-244.

27. *Confessiones* IX, 3.6 (CSEL 33, pp. 200-201).

28. "Prayer for one who is dead and is to be carried forth," *Euchologion*, 18 (Brightman), ed. F.E. Brightman, "The Sacramentary of Serapion of Thmuis," *The Journal of Theological Studies* 1 (1900), 268, 275-276; trans. John Wordsworth, *Bishop Serapion's Prayer-Book* (Hamden, Conn.: Archon, 1964; rpt. 1923² revised), pp. 79-80.

29. Augustine, *Confessiones* IX, 11-12 (CSEL 33, pp. 220-223). Chrysostom, on the name "cemetery," PG 49, 393. Jerome, *Epistula* 77, 11 (CSEL 55, p. 48): *Sonabant psalmi, et aurata templorum tecta reboans in sublime alleluia quatiebat*.

30. *De cura pro mortuis gerenda*, 6-7; 22 (CSEL 41, pp. 629-633, 658). See also Ntedika, *L'Evocation*, pp. 1-45.

31. For example, Romans 14.10 and 2 Corinthians 5.10. *De cura pro mortuis gerenda*, 2 (CSEL 41, pp. 622-623); *Enchiridion* 110 (CCSL 46, 108). Augustine's prayer for Monica, *Confessiones* IX, 13, 35 (CSEL 33, p. 224).

32. *De cura pro mortuis gerenda*, 6; 22 (CSEL 41, pp. 629-630, 658-659); *Enchiridion* 110 (CCSL 46, pp. 108-109): *Non enim omnibus prosunt; et quare non omnibus prosunt, nisi propter differentiam vitae quam quisque gessit in corpore? Cum ergo sacrificia siue altaris quarumcumque eleemosynarum pro baptizatis defunctis omnibus offeruntur, pro valde bonis gratiarum actiones sunt; pro non valde malis propitiationes sunt; pro valde malis etiamsi nulla sunt adiumenta mortuorum; qualescumque vivorum consolationes sunt. Quibus autem prosunt, aut ad hoc prosunt ut sit plena remissio, aut certe ut tolerabilior fiat ipsa damnatio.* This reference to Augustine would become very popular in medieval spirituality, as we shall see.

33. *Enchiridion* 110. See note 32 and also *De civitate Dei* XXI, 24 (CCSL 48, 790): *. . . sicut etiam facta resurrectione mortuorum non deerunt, quibus post poenas, quas patiuntur spiritus mortuorum, inpertiatur misericordia, ut in ignem non mittantur aeternum.*

34. J. Ntedika well summarizes and documents the development of Augustine's thought: *L'Evocation*, pp. 88-103. See also his bibliography and earlier articles.

35. *Aurelii Prudentii Clementis Carmina*, ed. M.P. Cunningham, CCSL 126 (Turnholti: Brepols, 1966), pp. 35-50; Liber Catherinon X: Hymnus circa Exequias Defuncti. This work is described as "a kind of daily hymnbook, consisting of twelve sacred poems for private use," according to A.S. Walpole, *Early Latin Hymns* (Hildesheim: George Olms, 1966; Reprografischer Nachdruck der Ausgabe: Cambridge, 1922), p. 115. For the full text and English translation see Harold Isbell, trans., *[The] Last Poets of Imperial Rome* (Baltimore: Penguin, 1971), pp. 198-203.

36. Walpole, *Hymns*, p. 140. Note also the many parallels with Horace, Ovid, Virgil, Lucretius, *et al.*

37. Excerpts taken from pp. 198-203 of *[The] Last Poets of Imperial Rome*, translated by Harold Isbell, Penguin Classics, 1971. © Harold Isbell, 1971. Reprinted by permission of Penguin Books, Ltd.

38. *Ecclesiastical Hierarchy* VII, Funeral Rites; PG 3, 551C-584D (based on the 1634 edition by B. Cordier and including the thirteenth-century paraphrase by G. Pachymera). See also the English translation prepared by Thomas Campbell for his un-

published dissertation, "Dionysius the Pseudo-Areopagite: The Ecclesiastical Hierarchy," Catholic University of America, 1955.

39. A classic reference work in which the reader can locate the texts of these canons is: Carlo de Clercq, *La Législation Religieuse Franque de Clovis à Charlemagne* (Louvain-Paris: Bibl. de l'Univ.-Sirey, 1936), *passim*.

40. Gregorius Papa I, *Dialogorum Liber* IV, 38-60; PL 77, 389C-429A; trans. Odo J. Zimmerman, *Saint Gregory the Great: Dialogues*, The Fathers of the Church, Vol. 39 (New York: Fathers of the Church, 1959), nn40-62, pp. 244-275. This translation follows Moricca, and thus has a different system of paragraph numbering than the PL: both will be indicated in the notes. See also J. Ntedika, *L'Evocation*, pp. 105-110.

41. *Dial*. IV, 55 (PL 77, 421C): . . . *res aperte claruit quia frater qui defunctus fuerat per salutarem hostiam evasit supplicium*. See full context: *Dial*. IV, 55 (PL 77, 420A-421C; trans. Zimmerman, pp. 267-270; ed. Moricca 57).

42. The hymn *Altus prosator* comes down to us from Irish tradition as a song of praise in honor of the Blessed Trinity. Both tradition and the consensus of modern students of Irish history and hymnology attribute the authorship of this alphabetical hymn to St. Columba the Elder, not to be confused with his younger contemporary, Columbanus. The text of the *Altus* has been preserved in, among other sources, John H. Bernard and Robert Atkinson, eds., *The Irish Liber Hymnorum*, HBS 13-14 (London: Harrison, 1898), Vol. I, pp. 62-83; Vol. II, pp. xxvi-xxix, 23-26; 140-169. See also F.J. Kenney, *The Sources for the Early History of Ireland*, Vol. I (New York: Octagon, 1966), p. 264. For the full text and English translation see Isbell, *Last Poets*, pp. 275-277.

43. F.J.E. Raby, *A History of Christian-Latin Poetry from the beginnings to the close of the Middle Ages* (Oxford: Clarendon, 1973^2), p. 134.

44. Excerpts taken from pp. 275-276 of *[The] Last Poets of Imperial Rome*, translated by Harold Isbell, Penguin Classics, 1971. © Harold Isbell, 1971. Reprint by permission of Penguin Books, Ltd.

Chapter Two

The Rite of Funerals: Formation and History

Our data from the past impress upon us that care for the deceased was an integral part of the daily Christian life from the beginning. Earlier literature and iconography especially mirror the faith that found expression in an ever-developing Christian liturgy surrounding death and burial. It is no wonder, therefore, that one discovers formularies for funeral liturgy among the oldest extant manuscript witnesses to Western liturgical practice.

These earliest extant examples of funeral formularies mark the beginning of a "rite of funerals." They were descriptions of and guides to "what Christians do" at funerals, that is, the practice of the Church. At some point around the time of Pope Gregory the Great Christians began more and more to set down in writing specific aspects of their funerary practice. Sometimes these were based on a "model funeral" from the past, sometimes they gave a pattern to be followed by a cathedral chapter or were the means of teaching appropriate procedures to scattered and often uneducated clergy. While it would be anachronistic to consider such early manuscript witnesses of funeral liturgy to be normative in any modern sense, nevertheless they reveal a great deal about the developing Roman *Rite of Funerals*.

Coincidental with the first stages of writing out rites there existed a movement toward consolidation of practices according to the liturgical usage of the church at Rome. Thus our first extant witnesses to a written rite of funerals already mirrored both local funerary customs and what was considered authoritative Roman church practice. Moreover, monastic life that was beginning to

37

flourish about the same time, was already having its effect on funeral liturgy and on what was written out. Those early extant manuscript witnesses thus represent an amalgamation of these three sources of influence.

The basic pattern of Christian funeral care and the two principal motifs of the faith noted in Chapter One were common to all three contributing influences. Our early liturgical manuscripts point to some of the different ways that ritual was being molded on the eve of the Carolingian reform. They show how a model rite of funerals eventually emerged that would guide ritual development down to the present.

These manuscript witnesses differ in shape and in size. Some are simply brief collections of prayers with a rubrical title that indicates their position in the funeral liturgy: this type is found as part of early Sacramentaries. Others consist only of rubrical directions and first-word indications of liturgical pieces such as prayers, psalms, and responses: this type is found among the so-called *ordines*. Still others are more elaborate and include further rubrical details as well as the full text of prayers, responses, and the like. All three represent different stages of development and, by the time they are available to us in extant sources, they are already an amalgamation of liturgical usages from different churches at different times and places. Apart from several outstanding exceptions, all appeared during the eighth century and came to be widely disseminated as time went on. The first five centuries of this history constitute a formative era for what was to become the Roman funeral liturgy. That period closes about the year 1250 with the appearance of a rite of funerals that became, through the coincidences of history, the model for subsequent Roman funeral practice. Its influence is noticeable both in Tridentine reforms and in the present revised *Rite of Funerals*. Those five hundred years from the eighth to the thirteenth centuries constitute the first stage of our survey of developing funeral rites. The other sections of this chapter will take us from the thirteenth century to Trent and from Trent to the present.

FUNERAL LITURGY IN FORMATION

In the ninth century several different influences are represented in funerary sources. Terms such as Roman, Gallican, Visigothic and the like constitute broad designations for differing liturgical traditions. Taken together they enable us to describe the most significant characteristics of the Christian funeral in the West during the first period of documented liturgical history. The period opens on the eve of the Carolingian reform, and its sources are the earliest extant manuscript witnesses of funeral liturgy. It is not our purpose to isolate specific traditions, such as the pure Roman liturgy of burial, but to discern what Christian funeral liturgy was like in those first typical liturgical documents. We are interested in the way in which the specific marks of Christian faith and hope in face of death manifest themselves when, for whatever purposes, rites of the Christian funeral began to be written out.

First, one is aware that funerals would have varied greatly from place to place at that time. A city funeral might have been a solemn affair with cathedral clerics and chanters on hand, whereas in the country funerals were necessarily much simpler. Likewise, the funeral of a bishop, civil dignitary, priest or monk was certainly much more elaborate in general than that of a layman. Each local church followed its own customary liturgical usage; no general set of formularies existed. In fact, it is far from clear whether at that time every deceased Christian was buried with liturgical rites. Subsequent Carolingian legislation placed such emphasis on the priest's duty to see that no Christian was left to die without *viaticum* that we can hardly expect him to have been more available to bury the dead than to administer the sacraments before death.

Secondly, comparative liturgical study suggests that our earliest extant manuscript witnesses of a developing rite of funerals in the West represent an amalgamation of *two* basic forms and several different content traditions. It is helpful to sketch the structural patterns briefly; as to the variant prayer traditions, it will suffice here to review principal themes and the faith dimension they express. For, when these witnesses were first committed to writing, there existed a manifest unity of faith cast in a variety of traditional usages.

The simplest basic pattern is reflected in the *ordo* of the so-called Phillipps Sacramentary.[1] It consisted of the preparation of the body in the home, a funeral procession with the body to the church, and burial there. One notes here a continuation in Christian context of the basic burial pattern of classical antiquity. It was faith and the liturgical expression of that faith that makes the Christian funeral different from that of pagan and barbarian neighbors. It was faith that saw to the preparation of the corpse in a setting of prayer; it was faith that expressed itself in psalms during the procession with the body; it was faith that rendered the church and its immediate surroundings the Christian place of burial *par excellence*.

This pattern was characterized by two principal locations of liturgical action: home and church. We can think here of "church" as church compound—a broader architectural notion than today. These two liturgical services were joined by the traditional funeral procession. The church compound functioned symbolically as the heavenly Jerusalem, toward which the deceased drew near, entered, and remained. And in the Christian community it functioned as the place where prayer was offered for the deceased and the body laid to rest. There does not appear to have been any separate liturgy in the church apart from the service of burial. That consisted in a solemn entrance, prayers for the deceased, and burial. Interment took place within the church compound, for example, along the wall, in the church floor, in the atrium, or along the cloister walk.[2]

Another principal pattern of funeral liturgy—probably representing Roman usage more closely—is attested in several manuscript sources. For purposes of description we follow the rite of burial contained in the Sacramentary of Rheinau.[3] This document, like the Phillipps manuscript, dates from about 800. Its funeral service is a compilation of the older Roman *ordo defunctorum* and the liturgical formulas of a "Gelasian Sacramentary of the Eighth Century." Other early manuscript witnesses also serve to verify and complete the scene.[4]

This basic pattern shared with the Roman usage the same procedures of preparation of the body in the home and burial in the church compound. Different was the practice of keeping the body of the deceased in the church for an extended wake. This wake was a liturgical service in the church separate from the service of prayer and burial. In this pattern the transfer of the body from the home to the church seems to have been part of the preparation for the liturgy in the church rather than a solemn procession as such. The procession from the place of the wake to the place of burial within the church compound was the traditional funeral procession.

In both patterns the liturgy consists of consecutive shorter services or units which are distinguished by reason of the place where they are carried out. Both began *in the home* or place of death and presented liturgical rites to mark the dying person's last living moments as well as those immediately after death.[5] Then the body is *brought to the church*, during which time antiphons and psalms are sung. A prayer service follows *in the church* where the body is buried immediately or kept until burial. Finally, the *transfer to the cemetery* (where necessary), again

41

accompanied by antiphons and psalms, and the *service at the grave* conclude the funeral. Let us now review the liturgical content of these services and processions.

The Service in the Home

This first unit, when compared to the rest of the service, stands out as the longest component. For convenience we may divide it into the "commendation of the Christian" (the administration of *viaticum* and the *commendatio animae* before and after death) and the washing, vesting, and laying out of the corpse on a bier in preparation for transfer from the home.

It is significant to note that this early funeral rite did not begin with death but with *viaticum*, the Church's sacrament for the dying Christian.[6] The liturgy here proclaimed that the eucharist, the sacrament of the Christ-life, was administered to the dying person as the pledge of Christian faith in Christ's promise of victory over death. Although this eucharistic emphasis was soon to shift in practice to the time of a last anointing (extreme unction) and thus leave all later funeral rituals to begin with death and the deceased, pastoral care today is recovering something of this earlier Christian emphasis on a continuity between liturgy for the dying and that for the dead. While the focus still tends to shift at death from the dying person to the family or bereaved, it is not difficult to direct that focus to the continuity of the Christ-life for both the deceased and the living. In that way the funeral liturgy both proclaims Christian faith and founds its consoling hope on the resurrection of Jesus. This continuity is surely what the liturgy of the early medieval *ordo* intends with the directive that the eucharistic communion will be for the dying person "a defense and a helper at the resurrection of the just, for it will raise him up."[7] Eucharistic life embraces even human death. Thus the *ordo* directed that communion be given as soon as one sees that the sick person was approaching *exitus* or departure. This notion of *exitus*

42

was the central theme of the service in the home. Psalm 114, "When Israel came out of Egypt," was recited at death and indicated how this key moment was understood: the deceased was indeed leaving this life, but, just as the Israelites had been led out of Egypt into Canaan, he or she was crossing over to the Promised Land. After the administration of *viaticum* the pre-death commendation consisted in readings from the Lord's Passion. One version of the *ordo* appropriately recorded Psalm 42, "As the deer longs for running waters," a litany, and a concluding prayer of commendation. In other versions of the *ordo*, Psalm 42 occurred at the transfer from the home to the church. This mobility of formulas within a basic order appeared from the beginning and points to the ritual freedom enjoyed. Yet certain formulas and combinations of formulas already began to appear as constants within the larger funeral context.

The moment of death was immediately recognizable from the short service designed as its accompaniment. It consists in a responsory and versicle, an antiphon and psalm and finally an oration "as contained in the Sacramentary." The formulas are familiar:

Saints of God, come to his (her) aid!
Come to meet him (her), angels of the Lord!

Receive his (her) soul and present it before
the face of God the Most High.

May Christ, who called you, take you to himself;
May angels lead you to Abraham's side (bosom).

May the choir of angels welcome you, and with
Lazarus once poor may you have eternal rest.

Psalm 114: When Israel came out of Egypt. . .

The concluding oration, just as the Sacramentary from which it was prayed, remains as yet unidentified, but its tone was surely one of commendation. Together these formulas early formed an independent unit in this station in the home, and they would have some part in the Catholic funeral down to the present. They were well suited to the moment of death, completing the *exitus* theme of the service in the home. Images that stood out so clearly in the earlier tradition remained here in constant continuity: going to Christ, the communion of the saints, and Abraham's bosom. Later we shall see how the same symbolism of the moment of death comes to characterize other moments of the funeral as well. Psalm 114 with its Exodus theme is the only principal formula of this short service in the home that would fall into disuse during the coming centuries. Nevertheless, its presence during the final commendation at the funeral of Pope Paul VI reveals that its appropriateness would not be forgotten.

After this commendation immediately upon death, the body was prepared for burial. While the body was washed and placed on the bier psalms were sung, and before the deceased was carried from the home, a final prayer closed the service. This *ordo* thus attests the widespread custom of washing the corpse before burial, with this difference: here it was placed in the ritual framework of the Church's care for her dead. We can assume that those caring for the body and those present would pray during this service. Obviously this would have been very simple in the ordinary Christian household and far more elaborate in clerical and monastic houses, as several versions of the *ordo* indicated. Although the liturgical formulas of the *ordo* derived more from the latter setting than from the ordinary Christian home, they do indicate the faith dimension expressed at that special moment. Present-day funeral liturgy, searching to recover ways in which the faith might express itself at times like the final arranging of the body or at the first opening of the casket, may find here a source of inspiration.

44

Common to this kind of dual action was the chanting or recitation of antiphons or psalms. One apparently favorite antiphon noted in this position by the early *ordo* prays, "You formed me from the earth, you clothed me with flesh; Lord, my Redeemer, raise me up on the last day." Its biblical themes (Ps. 139; Job 10.8-12; 19.25) spoken, as it were, by the deceased, rendered the physical preparation of washing and dressing of the body a hymn of faith. Calling to mind God's wondrous deeds for the deceased (*anamnesis*), the Church prayed in confident trust for the fulfillment of God's promise (praise and petition). The faith dimension of this antiphon itself cannot have been very far removed from earlier liturgical usage. This antiphon was joined with two favorite psalms that accompanied the action of washing, vesting, and laying out the deceased: Psalm 93, "God is king, robed in majesty," and Psalm 23, "God is my shepherd, I lack nothing." Although Psalm 93 took up the clothing theme, focusing on God's steadfastness and his robe of glory, presumably awaiting the deceased, it is Psalm 23 that best extended the theme of preparation. Its double allegory, seeing God as shepherd and host, and its Christian interpretation pointing to baptism and eucharist, symbolized that reality beyond death which the deceased Christian both lived sacramentally and prepared for in faith and hope. Just as the deceased was once led to baptism (washing and dressing) and fortified throughout life by the eucharist (eucharistic life and finally *viaticum*), he or she is now prepared through the faith of the community to walk fearlessly through death's threatening shadows to the eschatological banquet in the Lord's house forever. On the lips of the community every verse of this psalm of trust appropriately proclaimed paschal faith and consoling hope. It was a perfect complement to the Exodus theme of this *service in the home*. From that simple liturgical action where the symbolic language of its biblical antiphon and psalm alone expressed all that needed to be spoken, one learns that good liturgy speaks for itself—that it is transparent. This *ordo* at the root of all future Roman funeral liturgy can help to sensitize us to the importance of verbal restraint in present-day funeral liturgy.

The Service in the Church

A short prayer concluded this *service in the home*. When the body was ready, it was carried to the church while the singing or reciting of psalms continued. No special emphasis is given this transfer in the more generally extant early *ordo*. Although antiphons and psalms were sung on the way, taking the deceased to church became part of the preparation for the wake in the church and for the burial rites to follow. The subsequent transfer of the body from its position in the church to the place of burial (often likewise in the church) had become the principal funeral procession. It is the role of the church building and the wake service that developed there that marked the most significant Christian change in the traditionally cultural rites of burial. By the time our earliest manuscript witnesses of the Roman *ordo* appeared, the wake was already traditional. Nevertheless, the rites in the church remain the most perplexing of the entire *ordo*. That continual ritual development was taking place at this point in the funeral liturgy is abundantly clear from analysis of the manuscripts. In these documents the complexity and movement within the *service in the church* reveal the early stages of ritual elaboration that would one day bring the entire focus of the Catholic funeral to center in the church. Nevertheless, through all that complexity, one discovers what must have characterized the earlier vigil service before burial. That is the simple rubric, the only item common to all versions of the *ordo*, that the mourners sing "psalms and responsories (intermittently)."[8]

It is possible that this rubric is all that survives of the earlier Christian wake when complicated vigils and even the celebration of Mass were not yet part of the funeral liturgy itself. Augustine's earlier account of celebrating eucharist at the grave of his mother before burial exemplifies a different and exceptional tradition.[9] The newer *service in the church* that the extant manuscript versions of the *ordo* already show took shape through confrontation with new liturgical desires, especially those of monastic life, as we shall see. According to this reading of the earliest extant witnesses, the deceased was simply layed out in the church and a watch was held near the body. Psalms and responses were sung intermittently until the time of burial.

The Funeral Procession
When all was ready the body was carried in solemn procession to the grave or tomb. Most often the place of burial would have been located in the church compound itself, as we saw above. Here and there subterranean cemeteries, not unlike earlier catacombs, remained in use well into this period. The body was preceded by wax tapers and incense. Lighted tapers or candles continued earlier pagan usage to which Christians had given their own meaning. Incense at the funeral was something Christians likewise retained from pagan custom. It apparently had no particular religious significance. And even when Roman Christians had not yet adapted the Eastern practice of burning incense as a symbol of praising God and of prayer, it was burned at funerals in the West. Gradually the use of incense as a sign of honor was applied to the deceased, undoubtedly by analogy to its use in honor of the relics of the martyrs.[10]

The singing of psalms and antiphons accompanied the procession. Three antiphon–psalm sets stand out as significant in the early funeral *ordo*. First, Psalm 25 recurred: "To you I lift up my soul." It was again a prayer of trust that God will lead the deceased through the dangers of death to shelter in him. Nearly all its verses are especially appropriate to the funeral procession. The familiar chant *In paradisum*, already present at this point in the funeral, was noted as an antiphon with Psalm 25. Although scholars continue to discuss whether it was of Roman origin or not, one thing is certain: this chant has been an element of the funeral procession, either as an antiphon or later as an independent response, from the beginning of written funeral rites. The text as translated today reads:

May the angels lead you into paradise;
May the martyrs come to welcome you
and take you to the holy city,
(the new and eternal) Jerusalem.

Both the opening clause, "May the angels lead you into paradise," and the final verse, "and take you to the holy city Jerusalem," served to make this chant appropriate for the funeral procession. For while the Christian community carried the body of a dead member to its earthly grave, the liturgy saw the community of saints and angels accompanying the deceased into the eschatological kingdom. Even when later funeral orders, including the new *Rite*, recommend its use as a recessional chant after the funeral Mass (today the only surviving remnant of a funeral procession in the United States), this ancient symbolism remains valid. This is especially so when pastoral care is taken to make this short movement from the sanctuary to the waiting hearse a true procession. It is well to remember that, due to the proximate location of graves, the procession noted in the older *ordo* would frequently not have been much longer than the recessional of today's funeral. It is not length but a sense of movement with the deceased as liturgical action that creates a "funeral" procession.

A second traditional antiphon–psalm set that was common to early *ordo* combined the Hebrew processional Psalm 118, "Give thanks to the Lord, for he is good," with the Roman antiphon taken from the psalm itself. Verse 19 is the proper antiphon: "Open for me the gates of holiness, I will go in and praise the Lord." Using this set of funeral chants for the procession with the body, the Church embraced all the paschal imagery from the "Hosannas" of a triumphal entry into the heavenly Jerusalem to the Easter acclamation, "This is the day the Lord has made." The funeral liturgy proclaimed again the Church's faith and hope in face of death. Those who shared this faith with the deceased now joined him or her in this hymn of praise and thanksgiving for the promise of victory over death in Christ.

No, I shall not die, I shall live
to recite the deeds of God;
though God has punished me often,
he has not abandoned me to Death.   (Ps. 118.17-18)

This kind of funeral liturgy, beginning with the Exodus *Hallel* (Ps. 114) and ending with the last *Hallel* of Easter (Ps. 118), left no room for doubt or pessimism. Rather, a faith-filled realism permeated the funeral procession found in this early *ordo*.

One final antiphon–psalm set noted for the funeral procession deserves mention. It is Psalm 42, "As the deer longs for running waters," with verse 4b of the psalm serving as antiphon, "I will go to the glorious shrine of God, to the dwelling place of my Lord." An obvious processional choice because of its sense of longing for and movement toward the "house of God," this psalm likewise expressed the reality of the confusion and fear of death. No one can pray Psalm 42 in the context of a funeral procession and not recognize its symbolism. The psalm's "levite in exile" longing for the house of the Lord becomes the Christian who, freed from the exile of sin, now goes to meet the Lord. Where there is sorrow, the psalm counters with hope both for the deceased and the community:

Why so downcast my soul,
Why do you sigh within me?
Put your hope in God: I shall praise him yet,
My savior and my God.   (Ps. 42.5-6)

In closing these remarks on the funeral procession as outlined in the *ordo*, it is pastorally important to note that the new *Rite of Funerals* has restored the funeral procession, where opportune, including appropriate chant pieces. Among the antiphon–psalm sets proposed are the three just observed in the earlier *ordo*. The chant *In paradisum* is the only exception, in the new *Rite*, where it serves as a recessional antiphon. Although the funeral procession as such is no longer common in the United States, the appropriate symbolism and long tradition of these psalms deserve pastoral attention. For example, at the cemetery these may serve as accompaniment for the short walk with the casket from the hearse to the grave or cemetery chapel—often an awkward moment that has lost every semblance of the simple yet meaningful procession it might be. The image language is available, if we will but allow it to speak again.

The Service in the Cemetery
Burial itself, finally, was likewise set in a liturgical context, not unlike that of the service in the home. First, there was the laying of the corpse in the grave or sarcophagus with accompanying psalms and a prayer by the priest "before covering." Psalms suggested for this moment, while the mourners have a last opportunity to look upon the body of the deceased and take their leave, include Psalm 51, "Have mercy on me, O God," the recurring Psalm 42, "As the deer longs for running waters," followed by its complement Psalm 43, "Defend me," and finally Psalm 132, "God, remember David,"

with verse 14 serving as its proper antiphon: "Here I will stay forever, this is the home I have chosen." Standing before the open sarcophagus or grave the Christian community looked beyond even the harsh reality of burial to the all-embracing reality of their faith. With the deceased even now they could pray:

Save me from death, God my Savior,
and my tongue will acclaim your righteousness;
Lord, open my lips, and my mouth
will speak out your praise.   (Ps. 51.14-15)

Looking beyond the apparent permanence of the grave to the eternal city of David the antiphon of Psalm 132 took on special meaning at the open grave or tomb in the church compound:

For God has chosen Zion,
desiring this to be his home.
Here I will stay forever,
this is the house I have chosen.   (Ps. 132.13-14)

A familiar antiphon–psalm set also accompanies the covering. Psalm 118, "Give thanks to the Lord," with the antiphon, "Open for me the gates," is a powerful statement of faith while the grave or sarcophagus is being covered.

No mention is made in the *ordo* of any further ritual gestures. Only two prayer formulas are specifically noted at burial. One is the Frankish invitation to prayer (*praefacio sepulturae*) before covering the grave. The new *Rite of Funerals* has incorporated it as an introduction to the final commendation where the English adaption reads:

With faith in Jesus Christ,
we reverently bring the body of our brother (sister)
to be buried in its human imperfection.
Let us pray with confidence to God,
who gives life to all things,

that he will raise up this mortal body
to the perfection and the company of the saints.

May God give him (her) a merciful judgment
and forgive all his (her) sins.
May Christ, the Good Shepherd,
lead him (her) safely home
to be at peace with God our Father.
And may he (she) be happy for ever
with all the saints
in the presence of the eternal King.   (no. 46)

The original text of this exhortation, earlier used at the open grave or tomb (before the notion of "bringing" was added), is obviously still appropriate and meaningful in today's liturgy. Pastorally, when planning funerals, this invitation to prayer might thus serve better when the final commendation and farewell is to be celebrated in the cemetery.

Finally, the simple *ordo* closed its funeral rite with a prayer of final commendation that would also characterize Roman funeral liturgy down to the present. Much like Psalm 51, it takes the sinful weakness of the deceased into the liturgy of hope and asks God's forgiveness. Simply and to the point this prayer proclaims God's justice while never doubting his mercy and his desire to save. The English text included in the *Rite of Funerals* reads:

We commend our brother (sister) N. to you, Lord.
Now that he (she) has passed from this life,
may he (she) live on in your presence.
In your mercy and love,
forgive whatever sins he (she) may have committed
through human weakness.
(We ask this) through Christ our Lord.   (no. 192)

The five centuries between these first extant manuscript witnesses to funeral liturgy and the crystallization of the Roman rite of burial in the thirteenth century saw the spread of this *ordo* across Western Europe. Comparative study of liturgical manuscripts shows beyond doubt that this *ordo* served as a basic model for the developing rite of funerals. Both ritual form and liturgical expression have their roots there. Even where shifts in emphasis are noted, the constancy of a strong and respected model perdures. Thus these five centuries of gradual, spreading influence of the *ordo* tell a story of both fidelity to the Roman tradition behind the simple rite and further amalgamation with local Frankish practices. The earlier process of subtle amalgamation gave way during this period to explicit adaptation. The one force most responsible for adapting the rite of funerals and for giving direction to its future was the medieval monastery.

Monastic influences had already had an effect on the earliest extant witnesses of the *ordo*, as we noted above. No wonder, for it was the monastic *scriptorium* that provided copies and monks' liturgical books that preserved for posterity the developing story of the medieval funeral. Some form of monasticism held a predominant place in both secular and spiritual life for all those five centuries. One recalls, for example, the new importance accorded the Frankish monasteries during the reign of Charlemagne and his sons, and still further monastic influence under the reform abbots of Cluny and affiliated foundations. During the eleventh and twelfth centuries it was the religious houses of the Augustinian canons, and to a lesser degree the Cistercian abbeys, that succeeded the Benedictine monasteries in meeting many of the religious and social needs of an expanding society. So too the mendicant friars, particularly the

Dominicans and Franciscans, took on the new ministry demanded by the needs of the emerging cities of the thirteenth century. The "modern" religious family of St. Francis in fact became the channel most responsible for spreading the results of contemporary liturgical adaptation.

The simple Roman *ordo* had thus been absorbed into monastic and cathedral life. Because initially these centers already enjoyed traditional burial practices of their own, old and new ritual patterns merged, and practice dictated the result. That result was a funeral liturgy whose new basic pattern had as its normal setting the monastery with its style of life, its church, and its cemetery. Liturgical content too underwent the influence of ritual fusion, and here too practice dictated how the various formularies of differing traditions were to function in the emerging rite.

Some manuscript sources bear witness to the result of this evolution in its full monastic or cathedral setting, others in less elaborate circumstances. No extant sources are known, however, that preserve explicitly the far simpler practice of the village pastor. Although one reads in earlier synodal decrees and similar documents that the parish priest is expected to have a manual of celebration for such services, no such "rituals" survive from prior to the twelfth century, and even those are monastic in their elaboration.

Nevertheless a formulation of the newer rite did emerge in a ninth-century manuscript that bridges the elaborate monastic rite and what must have been parochial practice. This apparently cathedral version of Roman burial liturgy, coming from Paris (St. Denis), can have served bishop and parish priest alike as a realistic model, quite adaptable to differing local needs and customs.[11] Gradually this newly composed Carolingian funeral rite established itself on the local scene and entered the further formative process in its own right. During the two and half centuries after 1000 A.D. it merged again with still other expressions of the earlier Roman tradition and thus influenced the redaction in the thirteenth century of the burial rite of the Roman curia that would dominate subsequent Roman funeral liturgy. Just as some monastic burial usages which owed their formulation to this period of development were to perdure in the rites of religious orders independent of the spreading Roman ritual, so too this simple Carolingian rite was destined to preserve ancient customs in the liturgy of local churches, some still common in modern times.

Thus the monks' way of life, the role that death played in monastic spirituality, and the ever more significant place enjoyed by liturgy in the monastery—especially under the inspiration of Cluny—concurred to make the monastic funeral an elaborate liturgical occurrence. This elaboration of the rite occasioned the introduction of new elements into the earlier burial tradition. Some of these elements were "new" in that they represent a new use of formulas within a basic pattern. Others were entirely new additions to the structural pattern of the ordo, to the traditional pool of liturgical formulas or to both.

Service in the Church

The emergence of the station in the church as the focal point of monastic funeral liturgy is the most important consequence of ritual development during this five hundred year period. Nevertheless the dominant motif that lay behind the development of an extended station in the church was common to the medieval funeral generally. That motif focused on supplication for the deceased. Early on, Mass offered for the dead had already become the most effective expression of such prayer. What could be more natural than that religious, whose life centered around the monastery or convent church, would begin to bring deceased brothers and sisters to their church for prayer and especially for the sacrifice of the Mass on their behalf. By the time this practice found its way into written orders of service, it is very elaborate, and the church edifice had become the focal station of the monastic funeral. The body was brought to the church after preparation and remained there until removed for burial. During this time the community offered its daily Office as well as the Office of the Dead and special vigil prayers for the deceased. This wake ordinarily concluded after Mass in the morning.[12]

Because these monastic rites represented religious sensibilities of the times and had such an influence on liturgical life generally, what took place in the monastery would have had its parallel in cathedral and parochial life. Furthermore, despite variations, proper local customs, concomitant folkloristic practices and the like, here we have to do with recorded funeral liturgy in which the Church experiences and recognizes itself at prayer in face of death. This station in the church was therefore not an isolated ritual practice but, as liturgy, stood in a living tradition—the tradition of celebrating one's passage through death to Christ that joined earlier Christian funeral liturgy with the emerging medieval rite of funerals.

Those elements that specifically constituted the station in the church as a new ritual unit were twofold: the celebration of Mass as a specific part of Christian funeral rites before burial and the short service of suffrages at the bier after Mass. Included also is the effect this new unit had on the funeral procession.

The Funeral Mass
The key to understanding the meaning and development of the station in the church is found in the celebration of the eucharist. The Church's oldest memories of Christians caring for their dead included, as we saw in

Chapter One, the celebration of the Lord's Supper. When that celebration took place, and how it was understood in the funeral context, are matters which vary in those earlier sources. Nevertheless, the Mass as part of the liturgy before the burial was not yet part of the tradition represented by the *ordo*, despite textual corrections in the manuscript. The new situation thus included a "funeral Mass" (to use later terminology) that analysis shows must have been a new composite formulation drawn from Masses of other contexts. [13] One can best describe the novelty as an attempt to incorporate a rubric about the celebration of Mass into a text that did not originally include such a rubric. The result was a new version of the *ordo*. This updated version intended to describe, among other things, an already existing and apparently widespread practice whereby the bodies of the dead were kept in the church for some time as part of the funeral and, secondly, that Mass was offered for the deceased during that stay in the church. History attests that the wake in church was already customary for persons of some dignity and for clerics. [14] The second reflects the evolving situation, noted in Chapter One, where the celebration of Mass came to be considered the prayer *par excellence* to effect the forgiveness of sins and therefore to be offered on behalf of the deceased *as part of the liturgy of burial*. Funeral liturgy itself was becoming a rite to implore God's forgiveness for the deceased. The ideal was therefore to keep the body until Mass could be celebrated. Because offering Mass had come to be reserved to a morning hour, any monk or nun dying after noon would be kept until the following morning when possible. There is no evidence to indicate that the celebration of Mass was anything other than one of the morning Masses of the monastic day.

A process of adapting existing prayer texts as well as readings and chants for Mass before burial would lead, through liturgical practice and further adaption, to proper "funeral Masses." One of those was the familiar

Requiem Mass. Historically it was the presence of this Mass in the thirteenth-century funeral liturgy of the papal court that put it in the mainstream of later Roman liturgical tradition. The *Requiem* became thereby the normative funeral Mass for adults in the Tridentine *Missale Romanum* (1570) and this characterized Roman Catholic funeral liturgy until the revised Missal of Pope Paul VI.

It is likewise in the liturgical books of the twelfth and thirteenth centuries that one sees signs that the funeral Mass celebrated for the deceased before burial had come to be a Mass other than one of the scheduled eucharistic celebrations of the day. Rubrics began to refer to the celebration of the funeral Mass at a time that is opportune, meaning, of course, a morning hour. Rather than keeping watch by the body until the scheduled morning Mass, a *special* Mass became part of the funeral itself.

Both the development of specific Mass formulas for the dead, such as the *Requiem*, and the introduction of the celebration of the funeral Mass as part of the funeral liturgy separate from the daily eucharist of the local church, furthered the already diminishing ecclesial sense of the Christian funeral. Late medieval funeral liturgy thus took little account either of the liturgical year or of the ecclesial community as such. All of this went hand in hand with the fearful eschatology of the individual that came to characterize the medieval funeral liturgy. Time was right for innovations such as the sequence *Dies irae* and the offertory chant asking the Lord to deliver all the faithful departed from the pains of hell, from the deep pit, from the lion's mouth, and so on. Although the liturgy preserved a certain traditional balance of hope even in these chants, the "waning of the middle ages" was close at hand and it would leave its macabre mark on the expression of faith in face of death.

In this context it is pastorally important to note that the growing practice in recent years of bringing the deceased to the church for a wake service and to retain the body there overnight offers an excellent opportunity to highlight the ecclesial dimension of the revised *Rite of Funerals*. Furthermore, that practice logically points to the fuller ecclesial celebration whereby one of the daily parish Masses would become the funeral Mass. Not only would the funeral liturgy thereby retain greater contact with the revised liturgical year, with its Christocentric and paschal focus, but the funeral would also have a greater place in the life of the parish. Modern liturgical renewal has thus brought the Catholic funeral full circle, from an exaggerated medieval individualism that survived in the former Roman rite of burial to an invitation to partake again in the best of earlier ecclesial traditions. The faith that once brought the eucharist into the funeral liturgy itself now offers Christians, through the revised funeral liturgy, ever new eucharistic opportunities to proclaim paschal faith and eschatological hope.

Once customary, the station in the church before burial became an occasion for even further elaboration. That elaboration would in turn be the occasion of still newer elements and go on to affect the further development of written orders. One of the first effects of this new emphasis on a station in the church was to encourage duplication of elements within the earlier pattern of the rite of burial. Notably among these there are two. First, as indicated above, the funeral procession now became two processions or transfers, with the second one to the site of burial generally taking precedence as the more solemn one. Secondly, the service after Mass, concluding the station in the church, duplicates the suffrages for the dead that immediately followed upon death in the earlier tradition.

The Funeral Procession

One of the most important traditional units of Christian burial is, as we saw in Chapter One, the funeral procession. Where burial in the church compound followed immediately upon a short service of prayers at the church, the procession from home to church compound was the only procession associated with burial. Whatever short prayer service took place in the church, it was part of the whole funeral and not an independent unit as it was to become in the monastery. In the tradition of the earlier *ordo* the rubrics simply indicate that, upon arrival in the church, all pray for the deceased. When interment followed immediately, this would have been a brief occasion for final prayer, surely not unlike the prayers indicated in the sacramentaries.[15] Already in the earliest extant witnesses, however, expansion pointed to a longer vigil, the celebration of Mass and an Office of the Dead before interment. Younger manuscript witnesses even go on to include fully elaborated written formularies for the all-night wake services in the church.[16] When the body came to remain in the church for a longer time (even over night), then the procession from the home also took the church with its long wake service as its *terminus*. Thus the later transfer from the church to interment became the procession traditionally associated with burial, that is, the funeral procession.

The Absolution Service
Entirely new to the earlier tradition of the simple *ordo* is the introduction of suffrages for the deceased after the celebration of Mass and before removing the body to the place of burial. This new short service, later called the *absolutio* and presently perduring as the final commendation and farewell, followed the model of the formulas assigned in the rite for the moment of death, i.e., responsories and prayers. In fact, ninth- and tenth-century sources almost without exception repeat the principal responsory of those earlier suffrages, "Saints of God," with the verse, "May Christ who called you," as the first formula of the new service. The other elements

vary from source to source, but a basic pattern can be seen to emerge as a constant: an exhortation and/or prayer introducing one or more responsory–verse sets, each followed by short litanic prayer and the Lord's Prayer and concluding with a closing prayer. This pattern was common to the suffrages which during the same period were beginning to play a greater role in the monastic celebration of the hours, especially the Office of the Dead.

At the appropriate time, and when everything prescribed for the deceased had been accomplished, the monastic community and other faithful would be called together for the procession to the place of burial. A transition to this solemn, traditional moment of Christian burial was evidently found wanting. Suffrages, familiar from the opening moments of the *ordo*, were apparently the most fitting formularies at hand. Just as these suffrages placed the moment of death in a faith context, so too now they sealed the celebration of eucharist and offered a transition to the solemn funeral procession.

This short service at the bier, being one of the newest elements of the funeral liturgy, was the scene of the most radical shift toward medieval fear and pessimism in face of death. First of all, whatever the intention of its original incorporation early in the Carolingian era, it soon became the moment above all others in the funeral liturgy to insure God's good favor and forgiveness of the deceased. It was the responsories of the service that best mirror the shift. Initially, in the first Carolingian witnesses to the practice, it was a simple service nearly identical to that at the moment of death. Responsories such as "Saints of God" and the Frankish formula, "You knew me, Lord, before I was born, for you made me in your likeness; now I return to you my soul, for you are my maker," reflect the scriptural emphasis of trust. It is with that trust that the second clause of the latter responsory also prayed: "My sins, Lord, make me afraid, and bring me shame; do not condemn me when you come in judgment" (no. 188).

It is quite a change when, in the twelfth century, another tone emerged in the responsory, "Deliver me, O Lord, from eternal death," and from then on dominated the service at the bier after the funeral Mass. A recent English version reads, "Deliver me, Lord, from everlasting death in that awful day, when the heavens and the earth shall be moved, when you will come to judge the world by fire. Dread and trembling have laid hold upon me, and I fear exceedingly because of the judgment and the wrath to come. O that day, that day of wrath, of sore distress and of all wretchedness, that great and exceeding bitter day, when you will come to judge the world by fire."[17]

Comparative studies of this responsory and its contemporary, the sequence *Dies irae*, suggest that the latter piece was composed from later tropelike verses of the responsory.[18] In any case the popularity of both reveal how church poets and thus undoubtedly the faithful as well interpreted this liturgical moment. The emphasis is on the horrendous expectations of the last day, applied both to the living and the deceased. Poetic descriptions of the last day coupled with the theme of the worthlessness of human and wordly achievements led into prayerful pleas that the just would be preserved from eternal damnation. Fear and insecurity dominated, as if the last day will be so terrible that even the just will run the risk of falling and be deserving of damnation.[19] The mood was apparently such that this final service before the funeral procession served as a *momento mori* to the living while they prayed fervently to secure protection for the dead through forgiveness of sins, lest they who no longer could help themselves be abandoned to such horrible fate. It is this emphasis on purification that extended the use of incense and holy water to this service. Again it is not until the twelfth century that this addition is noted in liturgical manuscripts. The prayer of the Church for forgiveness gave the service its Latin title *absolutio*. Certain monastic practices during this period tempt one to interpret the prayer formulas of this short service as if they implied sacramental absolution or the granting of plenary indulgences to the deceased. Scholars agree, however, that nothing more was intended than the intercession of the Church on behalf of the deceased. Nevertheless this new mood stands out sharply in contrast to earlier, more subdued propitiatory formulas. Those were clearly no longer considered effective expression of the current mood. Yet, apparently, neither did they seem to be convertible, which indicates that the earlier spirit was not transformed or misunderstood. Quite simply the new medieval spirituality viewed Christ's coming in judgment as a cause for fear, whereas formerly it was a source of consolation. Just as primitive Christian art expressed this latter mood, it is not surprising to find the emergence of the medieval frescoes and paintings of the Last Judgment coinciding with liturgical pieces such as the chants *Dies irae* and "Deliver me, O Lord, from eternal death."

Finally, comparative study of the absolution service throughout those first five hundred years of documented ritual development reveals the service to be associated inseparably with the funeral Mass. Even where, for example, Mass was not celebrated before burial due to the hour of the funeral liturgy falling after noon, the *absolutio* remained with the Mass. If the funeral Mass was celebrated next day, the *absolutio* followed Mass just as if the body were present. This conception of the service would perdure *via* the Tridentine Ritual to the twentieth century. Pastorally, therefore, one notes a significant difference in the revised *Rite of Funerals* where the new final commendation and farewell is seen to relate directly to the deceased and burial. Thus even when, for whatever reason, Mass is not celebrated, the revised commendation rite is always part of the funeral liturgy. This change in emphasis follows from the totally new role the final commendation and farewell has been assigned in Catholic funeral liturgy. These detailed pages on the medieval *absolutio* remind today's funeral minister where the Church has been so recently, and how serious is the pastoral obligation to discern the new emphasis and its meaning for people today. It was unfortunate, for example, that one commentator covering the funeral of Pope Paul VI continued to refer to the liturgical action of this new commendation rite as "purifying the body."

Other New Adaptations

Besides the absolution service other elements that appeared in the expanding medieval *ordo* were the blessing of the grave, the sign of the cross, and a final absolution over the deceased. The blessing of the tomb or grave emerged as still another element that was not part of the earlier tradition. Yet, already in the ninth century the use of holy water and incense at the site of burial was accompanied by a prayer with the title *benedictio sepulchri*. This novelty was conspicuously absent in Carolingian services. Although not familiar in that tradition, and uncommon in the pontifical usage that influenced the Roman rite, this practice eventually found its way into the *Roman Ritual* of 1614 and perdures in the revised *Rite of Funerals*.

Similarly, the sign of the cross over the grave after burial appeared as a new element in the tenth century. Although rubrics noting this concluding gesture of blessing were rare in medieval liturgical books, they did occasionally appear. The sign of the cross was a common liturgical gesture of blessing by the High Middle Ages and undoubtedly took place often, without specific rubrics, in conjunction with certain formulas. That it became the final element in the Tridentine *Roman Ritual* of 1614 shows it enjoyed a certain popularity, at least in local traditions if not in that of the Roman curia. Closely

64

related, to be sure, was another practice that was new to the earlier *ordo* but not uncommon in medieval burial rituals. This was a prayer of absolution over the deceased after burial.

Although hardly significant elements in the longer development, the sign of the cross and some sense of absolution for the deceased were nevertheless important to the popular medieval concept of burial rites. *The Song of Roland* (twelfth century) attests this well. The anonymous troubador, recounting the King's lament upon finding Roland and his army dead, described burial as follows:

And then spake Naimon: Bid us search the field
And find our friends who fought and died for us.
That we may pray for them, and bury them.
He raised his hand. The horns of all the host
Rang loud. The Franks dismounting, sought their friends
And brought them to the King, and tonsured priests
Absolved and signed them with the cross of God,
And burned sweet myrrh and spices. So they laid
Their comrades in one grave, and left them there
In Spain. Alas! There was no other way.[20]

The Model Funeral Liturgy
A brief description of the funeral liturgy that, through the influence of the papal court and Franciscan pastoral practice, became the model for future Roman usage closes this first era and sets the stage for reviewing the later centuries of ritual history. Following the curial rite appended to the Franciscan Breviary of 1260 one has a guide to Franciscan funerals and the pastoral funeral usage of the mendicant friars for whom the new Breviary was a *vade mecum* of ritual practice.[21] Recalling the obvious adjustments that would have been necessary in the Christian family, one can form an idea of pastoral practice, using the friar's funeral as a model.

As death approached, the brothers gathered around the dying confrere to pray with him and support him in his agony with psalms and litanies—in short, the service later called the "commendation of the soul." Although the rite began before death, Holy Communion as *viaticum* was no longer part of this rite; a separate order for communion of the sick now preceded the rite for the dying. It would not be long before all these last liturgical moments before death too would become part of a separate short rite. Certainly in the growing cities and widely dispersed villages and manors, the priest's presence even at death itself was far less frequent now. Yet, the Franciscan model still opened with the priest at the death bed, despite presumed earlier arrangements for *viaticum*. At death the same traditional suffrages were offered, the responsory and verse, "Saints of God" and "Christ who called you." A concluding prayer followed—now, however, introduced by a short list of versicles. The prayer, "To you, O Lord, we commend,"[22] as well as the above responsory illustrate that a commendation of the deceased upon death remained part of the rite of funerals.

Next the body was washed by the brothers whose charge it was to care for the dead; it was dressed for burial, and laid out on a bier. The rite then indicates a selection of prayers and added versicles followed by Vespers, apparently to be prayed when the body is laid out. Thus it appears that the actual preparation for burial in this rite no longer took place in a liturgical setting. Those prayers and psalms came rather to constitute a kind of wake service after preparation before the body was taken to church. This was another shift away from earlier customs, and one that corresponded surely with changed circumstances surrounding care for the dead.

At the appointed time the friars, chanting the familiar responsory and verse, "Saints of God" and "Christ who called you," carried the body into the church. Of the many different traditional chants marking the transfer to the church this set is found among the earliest Carolingian customs (rite of St. Denis); it survived *via* this Franciscan rite and the Roman Ritual down to the twentieth century. The present revised *Rite of Funerals* includes it among alternative entrance formulas. Once the body had been laid out in the church, the friars chanted Vigils (Matins) followed by short versicles for the deceased. During the concluding prayers the priest and ministers are said to have prepared for solemn Mass, if the time was opportune. In context, this implies an early morning hour: either one of the regular daily Masses or a special early morning funeral Mass after Matins might be intended here.

In any case, after Mass the friars gathered in a circle around the bier. The priest, standing at its head, opened the service with an invitation to prayer, and three sets of suffrages followed. Each was composed of a responsory and verse (during which the priest incensed the body), versicles, the Lord's Prayer, and a concluding prayer. Despite the multiplication of formulas, one recognizes immediately the structure that would characterize this service for the next 700 years; even when the service would become the revised final commendation of the present *Rite*, the same basic structure would stand. As to content, *both* those responsories already traditional to this service, such as "Saints of God," and the more recent composition, "Deliver me, O Lord, from eternal death," appear side-by-side. Whereas the latter alone would come to characterize the suffrages in the Tridentine rite of burial, earlier traditional responsories like "Saints of God" would serve as the new "song of farewell" in the twentieth century *Rite*. Thus both in form and content the short service after the funeral Mass in this Franciscan rite of 1260 would have an influence on the way Catholics in the twentieth century take leave of their dead. Just as the thirteenth-century rite expressed the faith in both old and new ways that were appropriate to late medieval Christians, so too does the revised *Rite of Funerals* serve the needs of people today. In the service after the funeral Mass, for example, the new *Rite* transformed the medieval service of suffrages to accord with the ancient Christian tradition of commendation. Similarly, what once took place at death and had become lost has thus been restored to the *Rite* in a new position.

After the final set of suffrages the friars carried the deceased to the grave singing, "May the angels lead you into paradise" and "May the choir of angels. . . ." This distance from church to grave was apparently not far in the community where this version of the rite was drafted. When all arrived there and the antiphons were completed, the priest recited the prayer that in some other twelfth-century rites bore the title "blessing of the tomb":

Lord God, we give you thanks and praise
for you created the earth and the heavens
and set the stars in their places.
When mankind was caught in the snare of death
you set us free through baptism.
In fulfillment of your will
our Lord Jesus Christ
conquered death and rose to life
to bring salvation and resurrection to those who belong
    to him by faith.
We ask you, Lord, to bless this grave.
Give our brother (sister) peace and rest,
and on the day of judgment
raise him (her) up to eternal life
with all your saints.   (no. 194)

There followed a list of six traditional funeral psalms with antiphons, closing with the Canticle of Zechariah and its antiphon from Lauds, "I am the resurrection." These, the rite noted, are sung *in persona defuncti* and apparently accompanied the actual interment. Meanwhile, in curious medieval style, the priest was directed to recite a series of traditional funeral prayers. At the close of this solemn burial rite, the priest blessed the grave or tomb with holy water and said the Lord's Prayer. After several closing prayers, including the invocation, "May his (her) soul and the souls of all the faithful departed through the mercy of God rest in peace," all returned to the church singing another responsory from the Office of the Dead ("Remember me, O God, because my life is like a wind; no longer shall I be seen by men.") There the priest concluded the liturgy with the commendation prayer, "To you, O Lord, we commend. . ." (cf. no. 192).

THE MODEL BECOMES NORM

The next era, leading to the *Roman Ritual* of 1614, has little effect on the model funeral liturgy described here. What it does reveal, however—and what makes it worthwhile reviewing—is the way this liturgy was understood and celebrated in local churches throughout Europe. By the end of the period many of those traditions would accompany later settlers and immigrants to the New World and there too be the context within which the Tridentine rite of burial would become the norm for funeral liturgy after the seventeenth century.

During the nearly four centuries between the initial influence of this Franciscan–curial model (1260) and the Ritual of 1614 events in Europe were far too complex to permit easy generalizations about funeral ritual. This was the era of such images of mortality as the Dance of Death, and most of the funerary customs one usually identifies with this era (for example, prayers against sudden death, elaborate cemeteries and sepulchral monuments and the like) were expressions of popular piety surrounding the liturgy. Nevertheless, the funeral liturgy itself was not entirely static. Existing diocesan and Roman formularies were apparently respected as models which local churches adapted according to spe-

69

cific needs. These mostly exhibited a trend toward simplification of the station in the church for the ordinary funeral and an elaboration of graveside rites. Unfortunately these adaptations are scarcely indicated in extant ritual books. Even where the need for new parochial manuals was met, the funeral liturgy incorporated there followed earlier standard models with minor variations.[23] Adaptations of the model formularies seem to have been a matter of local tradition, and it was apparently not considered necessary to write them out, even where the prohibitive cost of recopying manuscript rituals could be afforded.

For our purposes the best approach to this diverse history, for which little direct liturgical documentation has survived, is to compare earlier patterns of ritual development with the large body of liturgical data that becomes available after 1500. With the invention of printing many dioceses were able to reproduce ritual books that had worn out through centuries of pastoral use. Some of these "manuals," as many were called, reproduced old diocesan funeral liturgies; others, especially in the immediate context of Tridentine reform legislation, took the opportunity provided by printing to update their rites in light of current pastoral practice and conciliar decrees. Such updating at the time new books were produced was common throughout liturgical history. Printing added considerable efficiency to the process. As in the past, the result remained a witness both to ideal rites *and* to the incorporation of changes that were already part of current practice. Together, ideal and actual use constituted the diocesan model. Thus diocesan rituals from the early sixteenth century mirror for us both earlier and contemporary funeral usage.

Still another kind of ritual book appeared for the first time during the early sixteenth century. This was a general pastoral manual not intended for any one diocese or region. Its purpose was the pastoral education of the clergy in general. This kind of ritual was thus didactic in approach and, in our context, sought to teach the ideal Roman funeral liturgy. One of these works stands out as a valuable witness for our purposes, the *Sacerdotale Romanum* edited by the Dominican Albertus Castellani in 1523.[24] This book enjoyed the explicit approval of Pope Leo X, who died, however, shortly before it appeared in print. Its popularity and influence is attested by the work's sixteen editions during the sixteenth century alone.

The final special witness to this era of ritual life is a unique, encyclopedic work that Julius Cardinal Sanctorius produced during the last quarter of the sixteenth century. This *Rituale Sacramentorum Romanum*,[25] originally intended to be the Ritual of the Council of Trent, was judged too impractical for pastoral use. Nevertheless, it is valuable for our purposes, for its funeral liturgy brings together the many sources, both old and recent, which the scholarly Cardinal considered representative of the Roman tradition. His guiding principle that the best of the past is the ideal for the present produced a distinct kind of encyclopedia of ritual that would have been impossible prior to the advent of scientific historical scholarship in the same sixteenth century.

Whereas the earlier diocesan manuals provided pastoral guides to existing local funeral usages, both the general manuals and the Sanctorius Ritual were written in a didactic and normative tone reflecting the spirit of reform that caused the Council of Trent to order uniform liturgical books for the entire Roman Catholic Church.

The liturgical scene around 1500 was far more diverse than this brief sketch suggests. Funeral liturgy often revealed even greater diversity and vitality. Thus together with reform principles and normative liturgical manuals, it was ultimately the familiar, living liturgical practice that determined the final character of the funeral rite

71

incorporated in the *Roman Ritual* of 1614. We note, therefore, the importance among our witnesses of, firstly, the general manual; secondly, the Sanctorius *Ritual*; and finally, ritual books reflecting the burial practice of churches whose usages also served as models for the editorial commission of the *Roman Ritual* of 1614. It will be for the final section of this chapter to review briefly the Rite of Burial in that *Ritual* and the role it played in Roman liturgical practice in the subsequent three hundred and fifty years before Vatican II.

Rite of Burial in the General Manuals
Our witness to the new general manuals appearing in the sixteenth century is the *Sacerdotale Romanum* edited by Castellani in 1523. A first noteworthy difference between this and earlier extant books is that here we have a Ritual that presented separate rites for the burial of clergy and of lay adults.

That the ordinary parochial funeral in the Middle Ages was simpler than that of the clergy and religious as celebrated in cathedrals and monasteries is beyond doubt. In the *Sacerdotale Romanum* there is a new feature—the juxtaposition of these separate rites of adult burial. Something that had been taken for granted was now set down in print. Yet, the order of burial for laymen was nothing other than an abridged version of the clerical order. One may wonder, however, whether something different was happening here than the mere writing out of an existing burial order. Something about it is too antiseptic, too clean-cut for it to be a mirror of true-to-life burial usage. The nature of Castellani's manual itself confirms the accuracy of our intuition. The Rites of Burial presented there are first and foremost models to be followed for proper liturgical celebration according to the Roman tradition. Nevertheless, these are models within a tradition and as such can be presumed to represent contemporary experience of that tradition. The solemn clerical rite of burial that Castellani incorporated as his ideal followed minutely the prototype of the medieval rite in the Franciscan Breviary of 1260. In other words, the order which Castellani presented as the ideal for contemporary burial practice is nothing other than the clerical funeral liturgy which the Franciscans adapted from the thirteenth-century Pontifical of the papal curia.

Not only did Castellani find this thirteenth-century order predominant among his sources, but he recognized there the prototype of the rite of burial for clergy in his day. What better rite to follow as a clerical model? Furthermore, its venerable Roman tradition and direct roots in the papal curia gave it an aura of authority that was influential indeed during the troubled 1520s.

The situation of the lay funeral was different. Contemporary experience of the Roman tradition in parochial funerals differed widely, often even from parish to parish. In formulating his burial rite for laymen Castellani clearly allowed himself to be guided by certain existing simplified forms of burial orders, especially with respect to the basic form and liturgical content. There is nonetheless an obvious direct dependence of Castellani's rite of burial for laymen on his ideal Roman model for the burial of clerics.

The thirteenth-century Franciscan order of burial is familiar to us from the preceding section, and we have already indicated that Castellani followed that order scrupulously. His order for the burial of laymen differed from the longer clerical version only in two moments of the rite. Both were liturgically significant moments: first, the *absolutio* before removing the body from the church for burial and, secondly, the chanting of psalms and antiphons during the service at the rite of burial itself.

At the absolution, where the pontifical model presented the traditional threefold suffrages, the simpler rite showed two. Recalling the history of the development of these suffrages, one recognizes here the preservation of an earlier simplicity. An even simpler form of the *absolutio* characterized the diocesan orders of burial for laymen, as we shall see. Increasing the number of suffrages was a medieval way of adding greater solemnity to the funeral, especially of a bishop, pope, or other dignitary, a practice which continued into modern times. (The funeral of Pope Paul VI in 1978 closed that era and demonstrated dramatically how great can be the solemnity of a noble simplicity.)

Similarly, during the cemetery service before burial, the funeral order for clerics in the *Sacerdotale Romanum* preserved the chanting of a series of antiphons and psalms *in persona defuncti* (as if the deceased himself were offering the prayer). These we recognize from medieval rituals as traditional chants at burial. There too one recalls the wide choice of psalms and antiphons. All these antiphons and chants, except one set, disappeared from Castellani's simplified lay order, and even that one became the last of the processional chants, possibly as the community reached the grave.

The nature of the change here appears to be one of simplification by means of systematic abridgment. Following his authoritative thirteenth-century model Castellani seemingly formed the burial order for laymen by removing from his model two traditionally self-contained segments: the middle set of suffrages and the psalms before burial. Put in another way, those elements which in his experience and/or research showed themselves to be specifically proper to the burial order were retained.

In the absolution service two sets of responsories, "Saints of God" and "Deliver me, O Lord, from eternal death," had become constant elements. They show how the liturgy absorbed the new piety of dread while preserving the hope implied in the heavenly welcome awaiting the deceased. That the middle set was the one omitted apparently had nothing at all to do with its content. Compared with the other two suffrages, this set might be excised without seriously altering contemporary expression of funeral piety. Yet this logical excision removed more than just a given set of liturgical texts. It eliminated in the new model order of burial for laymen precisely one of those moments in the service where local traditions preserved a variety of expression. Our comparative study of sources reveals that, while the first and third set of suffrages became more or less fixed and proper, the middle set remained variable, showing different responsories and collects representative of Christian burial tradition and faith.

Similarly, what Castellani apparently judged to be a most significant element in the cemetery service was the chanting of the canticle *Benedictus* with its antiphon "I am the resurrection," since it is the only chant set he retained there. We can assume that chanting the full set of traditional psalms and antiphons, followed by the canticle set, was certainly infrequent in medieval parochial practice. Nevertheless, other Rituals did preserve these venerable burial psalms and antiphons so that one or more would have been chosen on occasion. Castellani's choice of the canticle *Benedictus* undoubtedly rested on his experience with other current usages. But by preserving *only* this fixed chant set, Castellani's model limited the traditional options in a new, deliberate way. The result also separated the canticle set "I am the resurrection"–*Benedictus* from its original context of Psalms 148–150. What was itself a remnant of a morning Office once added to the traditional burial psalms had now been reduced to the canticle and antiphon alone. Not only had ancient psalms thus been removed from the cemetery service for laymen, but the new element itself was to lead a life of its own. Already in the *Sacerdotale Romanum* this canticle and antiphon functioned differently in the rite for clerics from their role in the new rite for laymen. Soon they would become a proper

Roman chant for the funeral procession. Thus while attempting to form his authoritative thirteenth-century model into a new burial order for laymen, Castellani employed a principle whereby elements which he judged representative and constant were identified as essential and necessary. But when only "constant" elements are retained to the exclusion of variants—often every bit as "necessary"—a traditional means to a variable expression of faith is cut off as well. That which is "constant" then becomes rigidly fixed and essential.

What is most distinctly different here is not ritual development itself. The process whereby priority comes to be accorded certain liturgical elements while others are removed to the background or disappear entirely is commonplace and familiar to us. Rather, in this situation a reformulation seems to have been imposed from outside the normal pattern of ritual development. In the more normal situation, reformulation of rites usually served to bring liturgical books into line with already changed practice, and was far less radical. Liturgy is not as much a matter of logic as Castellani's work implied. Ordinarily reformulation involves changing emphasis, and custom on the local scene determines practice. In such a natural process, changes such as those noted in the *Sacerdotale Romanum* do occur, but only after indications of emphasis in earlier ritual books show that the practice in question has in fact fallen into disuse. As our comparison with contemporary diocesan manuals will show, this is not the case with either variant suffrages at the absolution service or with the traditional psalms at burial.

Castellani's was a praiseworthy effort to reduce liturgical chaos in the early sixteenth century and to educate the clergy in the proper celebration of Roman liturgy. Nevertheless, by constructing this abridged version of the Roman rite of burial for parochial use, he set precedent for reform that would contribute to an ever more

76

impoverished, rigid liturgy of Christian burial in the years to come. Thus, the seed was implanted whereby the new burial liturgy itself would be far more responsible for the subsequent rigidity of the rite of burial than any influence from conciliar decrees and papal bulls, as some mistakenly assume concerning liturgy after Trent.

The Rite of Burial in the Sanctorius Ritual
In addition to the published edition of the Ritual of Cardinal Sanctorius the Vatican Library preserves the annotated manuscript from which the final edition was produced.[26] There Sanctorius explained his ritual reforms and noted the sources that support his reasoning. In the funeral liturgy he followed the thirteenth-century models and Castellani almost *verbatim*. His notes justified that choice as most in accord with the ancient and current Roman usage. It is only by way of exception that Sanctorius incorporated a simpler rite for the burial of laymen. He explained that this is a novelty in the long Roman tradition where, in contrast to other liturgical usages, no distinctions were made in the funeral of clerics, religious, or lay Christians. Thus he urged pastors to celebrate the complete funeral liturgy, including the full Office of the Dead, for all deceased. Only truly bona fide custom (two hundred years or older) or very serious pastoral reasons, such as multiple funerals, were considered sufficient to justify the shorter rite. For use in those cases Sanctorius followed Castellani's rite for the burial of laymen as the most opportune. Unfortunately for us he did not comment on the structure of the rite for laymen or on its actual use. The implication is that it was rarely found in practice.

Both Sanctorius' strong protests and the constant presence of Castellani's rite in subsequent ritual books, however, indicate that the shorter rite was not at all infrequent in pastoral practice. Despite the worthy Roman liturgical tradition of not distinguishing between persons in the liturgy of their funerals, in practice that liturgy itself had outgrown the tradition and become too complex for general use. The simple version of funeral liturgy was here to stay. However, it would take the reforms of Vatican II and Paul VI to return to the Roman simplicity of celebrating the same funeral liturgy for all the baptized. The funeral of Pope Paul VI was itself the best exemplification of Sanctorius' principle of liturgical equity in the liturgy of Christian burial. Meanwhile, from the sixteenth century to the present the funeral liturgy for laymen according to Roman ritual books would bear the marks of Castellani and the influence of Sanctorius. Happily the editorial committee for the *Roman Ritual* of 1614 consisted of pastors as well as scholars who followed the influence of existing diocesan practice as much as the didactic norms of Castellani and Sanctorius. Thus it is to this third group of sources for the *Roman Ritual* that we now turn.

The Rite of Burial in Diocesan Rituals
This kind of ritual, prepared for use in a specific diocese or province and authorized by the local ordinary, reflects the variety of local liturgical usages reminiscent of the Middle Ages as well as the desire and concrete attempts at local reform. This is not the place nor is it our intention to provide an exhaustive study of these manuals. We are interested rather in a cross-section of documented information concerning diocesan rites of burial. A study of such manuals from some twenty-five dioceses across sixteenth-century Europe reveals a wide variety of expression within the traditionally familiar pattern. One observes ritual types or families that stand in a direct ancestral line with earlier medieval tradition. Others reflect "modern" trends such as those in the *Sacerdotale Romanum*. We concentrate our attention on the former group, those preserving a type of parochial burial rite not yet influenced by an ideal Roman model such as Castellani presents in the *Sacerdotale*.

Witnesses of this type give us an impression of the variety of traditional liturgical expression that was preserved in contemporary diocesan rites of burial. Assuming that such manuals, often recently updated, intend to express the faith of the contemporary Roman Catholic Church teaching, one may examine the variety of expression preserved there as an indication of that faith. In other words, these burial orders preserve for us genuine forms of faith expression which the ideal Roman rite of burial (according to Castellani and successors) relegated to the library shelf.

The Absolution Service

At first glance one is struck by the predominant place held in these burial orders by the responsories "Saints of God" and "Deliver me, O Lord, from eternal death" at the absolution. Without a doubt these two responsories had become an integral part of Christian burial during the Middle Ages. Together these responsories summarized the two major emphases of medieval prayer for the dead: an earlier Christian hope that the deceased will be received by God (*Subvenite*) and the subsequent fear of judgment and damnation (*Libera me*). That was the thirteenth-century "solution" which Castellani preserved. Diocesan manuals following a solution different from the Roman–Franciscan model and not influenced by Castellani's reformulation reflected different approaches.

The most striking is that noted in some sixteenth-century French manuals that preserved intact an earlier absolution service dating to the Carolingian model of ninth-century Paris (St. Denis).[27] In these rituals the earlier type of suffrages revealed a realistic Christian hope as their dominant motif. In addition to the responsory "Saints of God" one finds the richly scriptural responsory "You knew me, Lord, before I was born" (no. 188). Its accompanying verse, as we saw above, confessed one's sinfulness and prayed not to be condemned, thus reflecting Christian realism regarding judgment where trust in God's mercy was the prevailing tone rather than fear of hell.[28]

These manuals support the assumption that a simple form of the absolution service had been preserved in parochial rituals. Moreover, they kept alive the spirit and balance of the Christian tradition incorporated in the St. Denis model—a tradition closer to Roman origins than that preserved in the later Roman model of the thirteenth century.

That the responsory "Deliver me, O Lord" and the fearful faith it expressed had won the day is beyond doubt. In fact, there are indications in some diocesan manuals that even the almost universally traditional practice of chanting the responsory "Saints of God" at the absolution could be surpassed. This most hopeful of chants, praying for a safe passage through death and reception in eternity by Christ himself, unconditionally trusted God's mercy and forgiveness. For the still medieval Christian of the sixteenth century on the threshold of troubled times, fear colored such a trust, and fearful prayer for an almost unhoped-for mercy seemed far more urgent. Castellani's absolution service thus remains a reflection of traditional faith and late medieval religious sensibility. Although his model rite of burial limited the formulas of expression in the absolution, it preserved a sense of the traditional balance. Nevertheless, the shift in emphasis is apparent. For we encounter burial orders not only where the responsory "Saints of God" is seen to disappear altogether from these suffrages, but where its counterpart, "Deliver me, O Lord," becomes the one and only responsory.[29] It is clear that the transition to the absolution service that would be included in the *Roman Ritual* of 1614 has already taken place. Further simplification would finally reduce the expression of faith at the absolution to the responsory "Deliver me, O Lord" alone.

Interment Services

The model Roman rite of burial for laymen formulated by Castellani presented a cemetery service that was little more than an outline of liturgical actions, chants, and prayers proper to burial. The liturgical action consisted of a procession with the body to the place of burial, followed by interment and a final rite of sprinkling with holy water. The chant pieces "May the angels lead you" and the Canticle of Zechariah with the antiphon "I am the resurrection" are indicated to accompany the first action while a short service including the Lord's Prayer, some short versicles, and a prayer constituted the rite of sprinkling.

Among diocesan manuals that continue the same Roman tradition as Castellani, some are seen to have preserved only the longer rite of burial (Castellani's rite for clerics, probably abbreviated in practice) while others printed an actual shorter version. The latter are of greater direct interest for our purposes, for they provide indications as to how the simpler rites functioned in past oral practice.

The Ritual of the diocese Toulouse (edited in the year 1514 and possibly unchanged since the 1476 edition) provides an even earlier example of a shorter Roman interment service. This cemetery service recorded a practice which had preserved some very ancient liturgical elements. One notes there, for example, Psalm 114, "When Israel came out of Egypt," as processional chant with the traditional antiphon *In paradisum*. Here too, as in Castellani's order, the traditional list of burial antiphons and psalms no longer played any role at all. The three morning psalms (148–150) with the antiphon "Let everything that has breath praise the Lord. . ." were included, however, here clearly among the processional chants. Upon arrival at the site of burial after a blessing of the grave and an alternate antiphon with the canticle *Benedictus*, one notes also the antiphon "I am the resurrection." The redactor of this diocesan rite could take for granted that local custom determined when interment took place. We can assume that burial preceded the rite of final blessing and thus seems to have occurred during the chanting of this New Testament canticle with its antiphon. In this Toulouse Ritual we witness a shorter interment service that is older than Castellani's model. It appears therefore that precedents existed for the liturgical content of Castellani's abbreviated cemetery service. What remains interesting, however, is the difference of pastoral manner between the two approaches to the same liturgy. Some later sixteenth century manuals[30] also indicated that the antiphon "I am the resurrection" and canticle *Benedictus* accompanied burial itself. Taken together these diocesan manuals revealed, however slightly, the living context within which the reform of Castellani and Sanctorius ought to be observed. Moreover, they pointed clearly to the pastoral tradition which the funeral liturgy of 1614 would stabilize for the universal Roman Church.

Similarly, some longer diocesan rituals faithfully preserved the tradition of psalms at burial, again dating from the ninth-century Carolingian model of St. Denis.[31] One Paris version corresponded almost identically to its ninth-century prototype. Its one additional rubric pertained to the custom whereby the priest threw some earth onto the casket while the antiphon–psalm set "Of earth you formed me" and Psalm 139 were chanted. One observes this practice for the first time in the monastic service of the twelfth century where ritually covering the grave at earth burial became the parallel usage to closing the sarcophagus or tomb that was familiar in earlier medieval witnesses. This gesture was very popular indeed. Many diocesan rituals after Trent continued it and thus offer a good example of how post-Tridentine books continued to preserve in practice significant local liturgical customs even after 1614.

Finally, one of the most influential diocesan pastoral rituals to exemplify this ongoing process is the famous *Pastorale* of Mechelen (Malines). Its first three editions (1589, 1598, 1607) contributed much to pastoral renewal throughout northern Europe in the decades between the council and the promulgation of the Roman Ritual in 1614. This work has likewise been identified as one of the sources of pastoral directives used to produce that Ritual.

The cemetery service proper to the Mechelen diocese reveals a sound articulation through liturgy of the way Christian faith gave meaning to the essential cultural action of laying to rest and leave-taking. Its widespread use outside Mechelen shows that this funeral liturgy was also common elsewhere. A brief sketch can assist American funeral ministers today both to appreciate similar funerary customs among certain ethnic groups and to recognize the potential for liturgical action in the interment process itself. One will note the contrast between the all-too-common antiseptic rites of the American cemetery that sometimes bespeak little faith or hope and the down-to-earth truth of this diocesan rite. In many Belgian and Dutch parishes it still proclaims paschal life where only death is apparent.

The chants *In paradisum* and *Chorus angelorum* accompanied the funeral procession. Upon arrival at the grave the body was laid to rest and sprinkled with holy water as the celebrant proclaimed, "Today may your resting place be in peace and your dwelling in holy Sion. Through Christ our Lord. Amen." Taking the processional cross the celebrant signed the grave three times, "I sign this body with the sign of the holy cross so that on the day of judgment it may rise and possess everlasting life. Through Jesus Christ our Lord. Amen."

Then followed the older custom noted above of throwing earth onto the casket with the words adapted from Psalm 139 and Job 10 and 19: "Of earth you formed him (her); you wove him (her) with bones and sinews, O Lord: raise him (her) up on the last day. Through Jesus Christ our Lord. Amen." A short litany, versicles and prayers followed. Finally the grave is sprinkled again as the celebrant says: "May God shower you with dew from heaven in the name of the Father and of the Son and of the Holy Spirit. Amen." The cemetery service closed with the note that where customary the participants return to the home of the deceased "unto the glory of him who descended to the dead and returned." Where this rite is observed today, relatives and friends often sprinkle the grave or throw a handful of earth or a flower onto the casket as they pass by one final time before leaving—a sign of the constancy with which such a tradition bridged the Roman Ritual and perdured in contemporary liturgical usage.

Funeral Liturgy for Children
Toward the end of the Middle Ages liturgical manuscripts began to reveal additional formularies entitled "for the burial of children." The origins of the practice of celebrating a separate funeral liturgy for baptized children remain shrouded in medieval history. By the time formularies began to appear in written form the practice had taken the same shape as the adult funeral but had developed a content of its own. Such a rite for the burial of children was familiar to Castellani and Sanctorious from, among other sources, a fifteenth-century manuscript Ritual from Capua and the general *Libellus catechumenorum* (Brescia, 1511). These represented two distinct liturgies, and it was the Capua version, apparently more representatively Roman, that won the day. With very slight variants, that burial service for children appeared in Castellani's *Sacerdotale Romanum* (and other later general manuals), the Sanctorius Ritual, a wide

variety of sixteenth-century diocesan manuals, and finally in the *Roman Ritual* of 1614.

This funeral rite itself was thoroughly scriptural, except for the prayer formulas. These exemplified the tendency of the times toward theological expression in the liturgy. The predominant tone was one of joy and thanksgiving; the absence of reference to the pain of untimely death strikes the modern reader as harsh. The antiphons, psalms, and canticles accommodated biblical texts about children to the funeral setting. For example Psalm 113, "You servants (Vulgate: children) of God, praise, praise the name of the Lord," set the opening tone. Psalm 24, "To God belong the earth and all it holds," dwelt on innocence, here that of the deceased child. In procession to the cemetery all chanted Psalm 148, "Let the heavens praise the Lord," using verse 12 as antiphon, "Young men and girls, old people and children too—let them praise the name of the Lord. . . ."

The prayers, on the other hand, proclaimed theologically the absolute dependence of all, even children, on the infinite goodness of God. They taught the effects of baptism and reminded the living of their commitments. Few of the surviving prayers represented the theological balance with which St. Thomas Aquinas had described the celebration of Mass for deceased children. Emphasizing of course that Mass for baptized children was never celebrated for the remission of sin nor for the increase of grace (a debated position), explanations citing St. Thomas taught that such celebrations consoled the living, proclaimed the mystery of our redemption, offered gratitude for dead children innocent before God, and demonstrated that they belong to the mystical body of Christ.[32] These latter four purposes, taken together with the first, proclaiming the effects of Christian initiation, apply beautifully to the spirit of funeral renewal after Vatican II. In the sixteenth century they were still too overshadowed by late medieval preoccupations with the sinner's death to find complete fruition even in the funeral liturgy for children.

Pastoral instructions published with the various rites reveal that the question of Mass for deceased infants and children before the age of reason was a real issue. All insisted that *Mass for the Dead* was not to be celebrated for them because they had never committed sin—a clear commentary on how the funeral Mass was understood. Sanctorius hesitatingly allowed that such a Mass could be celebrated *on the occasion* of their funeral but *for* their deceased adult relatives or others. Most other sources recommended one of the votive Masses in honor of the Trinity, the Holy Spirit, or the Angels. Occasionally a suggestion appeared favoring the Mass of the day, especially if it were a feast, including a commemoration of the dead child. Among the diocesan manuals studied by this author only one incorporated a special set of Mass formularies for the funeral of children, and even they disappeared in the next edition of the book.[33] Editions of the *Roman Ritual* of 1614 were silent about Mass on those occasions, but the practice of choosing one of the votive Masses became the custom. The Mass of the Angels was considered the most appropriate. From this would follow the unfortunate association that referred to deceased infants as "little angels before the face of God" and marked off their special part of the cemetery with infant cherubs.

A very different matter indeed was the funeral of children who died without baptism. Across the entire spectrum of witnesses to funeral liturgy for children before Trent, priests and faithful were explicitly forbidden to mark the burial of the unbaptized with any Christian ceremony whatsoever. Such children were to be buried in a plot outside the cemetery and often in the evening. The liturgy of the Church offered neither prayer for them nor consolation to their parents. The most frequently cited authority for this harsh but logically consistent attitude was a canon of the second Council of Braga (ca. A.D. 560) that forbade both the celebration of Mass and the chanting of psalms for "catechumens who died without the redemption of baptism."[34] They were compared with suicides by the Braga Council.

Despite the matter-of-fact tone of our sources, the faithful undoubtedly experienced this to be painfully severe. Reactions led to abuses. Sanctorius commented, for example, on the practice by some ignorant priests and women of burying such unfortunate infants under the eaves of churches in the superstitious hope that rain water running off the roof would "baptize" them.

Although the *Roman Ritual* of 1614 did not explicitly prohibit funeral liturgy for non-baptized children, the custom of burial without rites continued well into the twentieth century. As infant mortality became more and more rare, the loss of a child came to cause even greater pain, and Christian parents felt ever more deeply the silence and seeming rejection on the part of their Church. The revised *Rite of Funerals* would offer them new hope at such a turn of events. In the meantime, however, reform movements after Trent attempted to soften the blow by revising the language of the prohibition. Yet, only a revised theology and renewal of liturgy could affect the kind of change embodied by the new *Rite of Funerals* of 1969.

FUNERAL LITURGY FROM THE ROMAN RITUAL (1614) TO THE RITE OF FUNERALS (1969)

Already the history of funeral liturgy up to this final turning point has shown that the so-called Tridentine rite of burial was no stranger when it appeared in the early seventeenth century. Likewise, by this stage of our survey it will not be a surprise that funeral liturgy would continue to develop locally much the way it always had since the beginning.

One major difference, however, was the normative character which Roman liturgical books were given by order of the Council of Trent and by the popes who promulgated them. Although Pope Paul V allowed greater freedom in his promulgation of the *Roman Ritual* of 1614, there is no question that it was regarded as normative in practice. The post-conciliar years, the period of the Counter Reformation, was an age in need of norms. The more such an attitude came to be coupled with the growing centralization of ecclesiastical jurisdiction in the papal curia, the more the *Roman Ritual* became in fact a normative manual. Its official interpreter was likewise the recently founded Congregation of Rites. The "peaceful coexistence"[35] between authorized diocesan rituals and the *Roman Ritual* which Pope Paul V apparently had intended to achieve could not prevent the decline of the diocesan rituals because of the subtle forces aligned against them, i.e., the authority of Rome and the prestige of Roman norms among clergy and people. Although the *Ritual* of 1614 itself professed to respect other genuinely revered traditions, its tone was unmistakably normative, and contemporaries understood that it meant to be the general norm for the universal Roman Catholic Church. Even the titles of those diocesan books that continued to maintain genuine local traditions spoke of "accommodation to the *Roman Ritual*," e.g., later editions of the familiar manual of Mechelen bore the title *Pastorale Rituali Romano Accommodatum*. It was thus a normative age with two consequences for funeral liturgy: not only did the rite of burial in the *Roman Ritual* become the norm, but local rites were made to conform to the Roman norm, with the result that liturgy was becoming a matter of correctly executing appropriate rites. Consequently, funeral liturgy became more and more divorced from the harsh experience of death and from the pastoral care for the dying and the bereaved. It became far more a reliquary of Christian faith, expressed in a very one-sided late medieval way, than a proclamation of a living paschal faith that believes in everlasting life through Jesus dead and risen and can give real hope to the bereaved in Christian community. This is not to say that such faith did not exist. Faith was indeed alive, but it concentrated its attention on the lot of the deceased in purgatory, mirrored in the funeral liturgy, and expressed its vitality more in popular devotions than in the liturgy. Novenas, pious practices like visits to the Blessed Sacrament and the rosary, as well as an emphasis on indulgences gained "for the poor souls" meant more to the faithful than the funeral liturgy. It was in this context too that even the Mass was "applied" for the release of souls from purgatory. By this point in ritual history, "saying Mass" had come, by way of late medieval piety, to mean performing the ritual of the order of Mass correctly so that the fruits of Calvary could be applied to the living and the dead. In the same way funeral liturgy including the funeral Mass came to be performed for the repose of the soul of the deceased.

When this rubristical attitude began to predominate in ecclesial life, it is fortunate that those responsible for drafting the rite of burial for the *Roman Ritual* of 1614 had for their consultation a dozen or more pastoral sources, like the *Pastorale* of Mechelen, and that they preserved a sense of the longer funerary tradition as documented and popularized by men like Castellani and Sanctorius. Above all we can be grateful for those men themselves who relied more on pastoral practice of living liturgy than on their personal theological propensities for their reformulation of the funeral liturgy according to the principles of Trent. However one-sided in its emphasis on the fearful lot of the deceased, the post-Tridentine rite of burial did sufficiently enshrine the tradition to preserve an essential balance between confident hope and realistic prayer for forgiveness. How that rite and its "balance" was experienced varied a great deal from the seventeenth to the twentieth centuries. One can imagine the effect of many influences, such as the late Baroque period, the rise and spread of Protestantism, missionary expansion to the Orient and Americas, the age of reason, political revolutions and independence, Neo-Gallicanism, Jansenism, Romanticism, two world wars and so on. After reviewing the rite, which itself remained virtually unchanged during all those changing times, we shall comment briefly on the rite in its world context.

The Funeral Liturgy in the Roman Ritual of 1614
The *exsequiarum ordo*[36] opened with the parish priest and ministers going to meet the body at the home of the deceased. There the deceased was sprinkled with holy water and Psalm 130, "Out of the depths I cry to you, O Lord," was recited. Although this psalm of trust in God's mercy preserved a tone of Christian hope through many centuries of funeral liturgy, late medieval spirituality concentrated on the image of the opening words "Out of the depths." The proper antiphon (verse 3), "If you, O Lord, mark iniquities, Lord, who can stand?" indicates the attitude with which the psalm was prayed. This was quite a shift from the earlier spirituality that suggested the antiphon *In paradisum* with Psalm 130. When the body was brought out of the house, the priest intoned in a serious tone (*gravi voce*) the processional antiphon, "They will rejoice in the Lord (the bones that you have crushed)" with Psalm 51, "Have mercy on me, O God. . . ." Here again the antiphon (verse 8) carried the promise of rejoicing and yet dwelt on the negative, rendering this once hope-filled psalm a somber penitential plea in the funeral liturgy. The common earlier antiphon used with Psalm 51 during this transfer read "Lord, grant that the soul you have taken up from its body may rejoice with your saints in glory. . . ." This antiphon has been reinstated in the new *Rite.* The English version adapted the body–soul language as well as the meaning of the last phrase to read, "Lord,

may our brother (sister), whom you have called to yourself, find happiness in the glory of your saints" (no. 149). This rite of transfer was identical to local usage in the diocese of Brescia whose pastoral manual served among the sources of the *Roman Ritual*.[37] This is a good example of how local liturgical usage found its way into the universal practice of the post-Tridentine Church. Moreover, it was understandable that the 1612 editorial committee would have looked to a diocesan ritual for the liturgy of this transfer. Neither general manuals, like that of Albertus Castellani, nor the Roman pontifical versions represented current practice in this matter. Among the committee's respected diocesan sources, the *Ritual* of Brescia presented a practical pastoral solution to the transfer that was sufficiently Roman in its tradition and enjoyed the authority of the reform-minded Bishop Bollanus of Brescia. Whatever else contributed to their choice, surely considerations such as these played a role.

In addition to Psalm 51 others are indicated for those occasions when the distance between home and church was long. Upon arrival at the church door the antiphon was repeated in full. Then, with the entrance of the body into the church, the service continued along the lines set forth in most contemporary manuals. In cases where long distances were involved, it is evident that the transfer from the home was already a matter for the laity themselves to look after. The parish priest would have met the procession at the entrance to the town or sometimes at the church yard.[38]

When the body entered the church the post-Tridentine rite, following the widespread practice of the time, presented the responsory, "Saints of God," with its appropriate verse. Traditional directives for arranging the body in the church and for the chanting of the Office of the Dead followed. After *Benedictus* and its antiphon, "I am the resurrection," was completed, a short service of versicles and a prayer of absolution closed Lauds of the Dead. During Lauds the priest was directed to prepare for the solemn celebration of Mass, if the hour was opportune. Later editions of the *Roman Ritual* would make alternative provisions. Even in the 1614 edition the presumption seems to be that the body remained in the church until Mass could be celebrated next day. This was quite explicit elsewhere, for example in the Salisbury (Sarum) *Manuale Sacerdotum* of 1610[39] that appeals to its "ancient Catholic tradition" and in the practice of the *Pastorale* of Mechelen, a neighbor to Douai where the English Catholic exiles printed the Sarum text of 1610. The Mass to be celebrated was that of the recently published *Missale Romanum* (1570), i.e., the *Requiem*. After Mass the priest and ministers were directed to gather at the bier. The rubrics here are explicitly clear, undoubtedly the work of a rubrical stylist. The absolution service that followed revealed an attempt again to be both pastoral and Roman.

Taking the reform even beyond Castellani, the editorial committee followed an absolution service that was already in use elsewhere, for example, in the diocese of Verona.[40] As indicated above pastoral practice seems to have preserved only one set of suffrages, i.e., a prayer, the responsory "Deliver me, O Lord, from eternal death" with its verses, followed by versicles, the Lord's Prayer and a closing prayer. The opening, no longer an invitation to prayer, but since the thirteenth century a prayer formula, read:

"Do not enter into judgment with your servant, O Lord, for in your sight no man shall be justified, except that you grant him remission of all his sins. Do not, therefore, permit, we beseech you, your sentence of judgment to weigh heavily upon him, for his true petition of Christian faith commends him to you. But by the help of your grace may he deserve to escape the judgment of vengeance, he who while he lived was sealed with the sign of the Blessed Trinity: who lives and reigns forever. Amen."

This typically Mozarabic text that became commonplace in the Roman funeral liturgy exemplifies how Catholic faith was preserved in medieval prayer while the emphasis revealed the preoccupations of contemporary piety. There is little wonder that the present *Rite of Funerals* did not choose to retain this prayer. In the late medieval context of 1614, however, it set the tone well for the responsory to follow, "Deliver me, O Lord, from eternal death." During the singing of this responsory incense and holy water were prepared and afterwards, while the Lord's Prayer was prayed (silently except for intonation and closing), the priest incensed and sprinkled the deceased. Versicles followed, and the closing prayer of the absolution was read:

"O God, whose nature it is to be merciful and to pardon, humbly we beseech you for the sake of the soul of your servant, *Name*, which today you ordered to depart this world. Do not deliver it into the hands of the enemy nor forget it at the end [of time], but order it to be taken by the holy Angels and brought to the fatherland of paradise, so that because it hoped and believed in you, [this soul] may not suffer the pains of hell but possess everlasting joy. Through Christ, Our Lord. Amen."

This translation has been kept literal in order to communicate the emphasis of the original Latin on the lot of the soul alone as well as on the image of God as vengeful judge. Once again, faith in the just God who is *merciful* has indeed been preserved, while the prayer speaks most to the merciful God who demands *justice*.

The final note of this absolution prayer looked ahead to the antiphon indicated for the recessional with the body, the very traditional processional chant, "May the angels lead you into paradise." Here the companion chant, "May the choir of angels," was joined with *In paradisum* to form one recessional piece, a musical anomaly because they had been sung traditionally in two different chant modes, the seventh and eighth, respectively. Apparently, as the manuscript of 1613 reveals, the text of the rite of 1614 was drafted without considering the musical quality of these (or any) chants. Because the antiphons *In paradisum* and *Chorus angelorum* had for centuries followed each other as alternate processional chants, the Tridentine editors may have been the first to combine them. Most of their sources, such as Castellani and Sanctorius as well as the diocesan *Rituals* of Brescia, Mechelen, and Verona referred to them as distinct *antiphonae*. More than likely, however, the practice of chanting *In paradisum* and *Chorus angelorum* together was probably not uncommon, and the *Ritual* of 1614 simply reflected such a usage. Nevertheless, this author's study of sources has not uncovered that hypothetical model. Whoever was responsible, the result was that these two traditional chants, *In paradisum* and *Chorus angelorum*, were treated as one *antiphona* by Roman funeral liturgy for the next three hundred and fifty years.

That these chants became more and more part of the service in church and less processional antiphons as such is apparent from the shift of emphasis in later editions of the *Roman Ritual*. In 1614, for example, one was directed to omit the responsory *In paradisum* when the body was not taken directly to the grave, just as the blessing of the grave was omitted when it had already been blessed. Later editions of the nineteenth and twentieth centuries revealed, however, that in such cases the combined antiphon was to be sung all the same *in eodem loco* (in the same place). Thus the *processional* antiphon *In paradisum–Chorus angelorum* of the earlier tradition would become inseparable at Catholic funeral liturgy *in the church*. It would not be difficult for the twentieth-century drafters to place it in a similar interim position as recessional chant, even where the funeral procession as such no longer exists. The latter solution, where the chant accompanies at least the initial movement of the body toward its last resting place, certainly corresponds better to the theme "May the angels lead you into paradise."

The *Roman Ritual* of 1614, just as its model sources, did not conceive of a long distance from church to grave. Burial in church or adjacent churchyard was still the implied practice. Upon arrival, after singing or reciting the processional chants, the grave was blessed (if necessary) using the following prayer that the new *Rite* also preserves in an adapted English translation:

Lord God, through your mercy
those who have lived in faith
find eternal peace.
Bless this grave
and send your angel to watch over it.
Forgive the sins of our brother (sister)
whose body we bury here.
Welcome him (her) into your presence,
and with your saints let him (her) rejoice in you forever.
(We ask this) through Christ our Lord. Amen.

(no. 193)

Despite the different local traditions that had developed and lasted as Christian grave-side rituals, such as the one from Mechelen reviewed above, the Tridentine funeral liturgy was stark by comparison. In this it was even more austere than the earlier traditional Roman cemetery service with its psalms during interment, covering and the like. Reform influence such as that of Castellani was probably more responsible for this than Roman austerity.

When it was time for burial, the priest was to sprinkle the body and the grave with holy water and to incense them. Without further mention of interment or other disposition, the *Roman Ritual* next presented the New Testament canticle *Benedictus* with its antiphon "I am the resurrection." Practice differed as to whether burial took place before, during, or after this canticle. Even where churches preserved local burial customs of throwing earth or covering, signing with the cross, etc., some inserted these before and some after the assigned chant *Benedictus*. However appropriate to the final cemetery action this johannine antiphon might have been, the *Roman Ritual* remained vague as to its specific function. Something of the arbitrariness of Castellani's short rite remained here. This is noteworthy when one compares it with the explicit, almost exaggerated, detail of the absolution rubrics. Such differences point up the rite's priorities.

The familiar funerary versicles and the Lord's Prayer were a preparation for the final prayer that the editors of 1613 found to be a popular closing prayer in their sources (e.g., Verona, 1536). They prescribed it as conclusion to the cemetery service, and the present *Rite* retains it (in an adapted English version) in the same position.

Lord,
listen to our prayers for our brother (sister).
As he (she) always desired to do your will,
so in your mercy forgive
whatever wrong he (she) may have done.
By his (her) Christian faith he (she) was united
with all your believing people.
Now, in love and mercy
give him (her) a place with your angels and saints.
(We ask this) through Christ our Lord. Amen.   (no. 56)

For more than a thousand years this prayer has preserved the balance of the practical theology of Catholic funeral liturgy: faith, church, community of saints, divine mercy and forgiveness and a joyful life everlasting.

This is realistic liturgy that is founded on paschal faith. It neither denies human weakness and sin nor exaggerates fear of God's vengeance—it neither denies the paschal mystery nor exaggerates resurrection without death. After this prayer the rite of 1614 provided an antiphon–psalm set to be recited while returning to the church (or sacristy). Although this was more than likely a clerical directive, it stood in a long tradition of maintaining a prayerful unity from beginning to end of the funeral liturgy.

Finally, two corrections in the cemetery service of the 1613 manuscript text deserve our attention. One was the addition of a rubric connected to the Lord's Prayer to the effect that the priest was to sprinkle the body with holy water. This obvious duplication in short succession, clearly by analogy with the absolution service, heightens one's awareness of the starkness and lack of tradition in this recently abbreviated Roman interment liturgy. Secondly, and more significantly, the editor at work added a rubric to the manuscript that emphasized the independent liturgical role the New Testament canticle and antiphon *Benedictus–Ego sum resurrectio* (with accompanying versicles and prayer) had acquired. The rubric specified that this service was never to be omitted (*quod numquam omittitur*). Thus in context even when the body was not to be taken to burial, not only the chant *In paradisum–Chorus angelorum* but now also the canticle and antiphon *Ego sum resurrectio–Benedictus* would be sung or recited in the church. The reform tendency of Castellani *et al.* seems to have won the day. In the *Roman Ritual* of 1614 certain formularies, chants, and gestures had been made to constitute the rite of burial. When they were carried out according to the rubrics, whether or not in correspondence with their meaning (for example, processional chant, burial formulary, or the like), that was considered funeral liturgy. The "rubrical funeral" of the *Roman Ritual* was to become in the years ahead more a context for personal expression, both devotional piety and secular pomp, than vital liturgical expression. When it no longer mattered whether liturgy really meant what it said or did (as praying over an empty catafalque), then other practices emerged to express the piety and sometimes the superstition of the faithful. When liturgy is divorced from life, devotional practices and folklore tend to replace liturgy altogether rather than co-exist in the natural symbiosis of faith expression.

Funeral Liturgy After Trent
To have even a hint of liturgical life at the time when the *Roman Ritual* was published we might imagine ourselves with one foot in the late Middle Ages and the other in the emerging "modern" era. In some ways the twentieth-century experience of "future shock" is quite similar. Liturgically, basic form and content changed very little after Trent. In fact the Council's liturgical goal was to preserve and protect that form and content in face of direct opposition to Catholic liturgical forms. Funeral liturgy especially was an explicit target of Reformation eschatology. As the form and content of funeral liturgy remained virtually unchanged, the context within which that liturgy was performed changed with the cultural patterns of a world that was developing economically, technologically, and internationally. The ethnic web of European cultures expanded both East and West. Through all that, the Tridentine rite of burial remained a clerical liturgy whereby parish priests in old Europe as well as missionaries to Japan and the Americas laid their dead to rest while the faithful stood by and watched.[41]

Piety after Trent has been characterized as didactic, pragmatic, and aliturgical.[42] Some of the concerns we meet in the pastoral manuals on funeral liturgy confirm this general judgment. Considerable emphasis was given, for example, to explaining for parish priests the rites and practices of the liturgy so that they might teach their people its meaning. This was especially apparent in those churches surrounded by Reformation communities and their teaching against public liturgy on behalf of the dead.[43]

Popular piety outside the liturgy too taught its lesson. Tolling church bells at the time of a funeral, for example, not only honored the deceased and called all to pray for the dead, but was a recurring reminder of faith in the immortality of the soul. So-called death planks carved with skulls and symbols of death were frequent reminders of death in villages and at countryside crossroads. Inscriptions on cemetery gates taught the passerby: What you are now, so once was I; what I am now, soon you will be. Even the funeral liturgy itself served as a *memento mori*, and prayer for the deceased was not totally untainted by concern for one's own death.

One widespread exception to accommodation to and gradual adoption of the *Roman Ritual* after Trent stands out in the "Neo-Gallican" dioceses of France. During the seventeenth and eighteenth centuries one saw there the creation of rituals that contained thorough pastoral directives pertaining both to funerary care and theology and to new liturgical rites. Although many of these differed from earlier diocesan traditions and from the *Roman Ritual*, they stood in continuity with the longer tradition generally. The best example of such a book was the influential and widely used *Ritual* of the diocese of Alet (1667). More interesting than the funeral liturgy it presents is its companion, *Instructions of the Ritual*.[44] Arranged in question and answer form, this pastoral manual explained Catholic liturgy and the faith it expressed in easily understandable language. With regard to the funeral, it took up questions of the tradition (why does the priest go to meet the deceased? why do Christians burn candles at funerals?) as well as issues of contemporary concern (why offer Mass for the dead? why do prayers imply that the deceased is still going to meet

God when he or she has already died?). Throughout the fifteen pages devoted to the funeral one notes a concern for a biblical emphasis and a reserve about unchristian pomp. In other times the fruit of this pastoral approach to the liturgy would be appreciated. In the wake of Trent, however, it appeared but one national barrier to the new universal ecclesiology.

The explicit didacticism of liturgy during the later Enlightenment built upon these tendencies and sought to channel their potential to achieve ever greater results for the betterment of society. Typical of this approach was a proposal for a new ritual in the diocese of Constance (1806). It was intended as a guide to better pastoral use of the *Roman Ritual*. Its section on funeral liturgy was laced with vernacular hymns, prayers, and a closing exhortation. One rubric insisted on the use of the vernacular for the words: "Remember man, you are dust. . . " The rest was in Latin. The priest's final exhortation at the cemetery exemplified the "edification theology" of the Catholic Enlightenment in Germany. Aware of the grief that is present at funerals, the text spoke of how death makes one think of the needs of this world and teaches truth, virtue, and devotion. Reflection on death was not to sadden the Christian but to strengthen courage and to give consolation and relief under the burdens of life.[45]

The funeral after Trent was generally characterized by greater pastoral attention on the part of the clergy, whatever their pastoral theologies at different times, than by inner liturgical reform. Where pastoral care touched the liturgy, it was often as an appendage to the *Roman Ritual*. For example, one finds model words of consolation and encouragement in the vernacular appended at the conclusion to the rite of burial in many diocesan books. In the same way an insert with formularies for centuries-old local usages, at the cemetery

100

for example, are bound in their proper place but clearly as a supplement to the universal *Ritual*.

Together with authoritative Roman commentaries like that by Hieronymus Baruffaldo (1735),[46] local books such as the French and German manuals just mentioned illustrated the way in which Catholic funeral liturgy between the sixteenth and mid-twentieth centuries was experienced. Immigrant churches in America were no different, except that ethnic traditions even at funerals soon gave way entirely to the universal *Roman Ritual*, especially during the nineteenth century.

Despite all the pastoral emphasis surrounding it, the rite of burial remained something the Church performed *for* the deceased. Similarly, it was not funeral liturgy as such that responded to the emergence in the twentieth century of the modern way of burial customs. As recently as 1952 one American commentary superbly continued the pastoral effort to place the Tridentine rite of burial in its best light,[47] but the rite itself read as if almost nothing had changed since 1614 and before. In practice, however, the *Roman Ritual* was accommodating itself to growing cities, remote cemeteries, the prominence of the funeral home, embalming and the like. The *English Ritual* of 1964 marked the end of a process, already well established by the time of the first edition of the *Ritual* of 1614, whereby rites surrounding the funeral Mass became "telescoped" around the church. In the United States, funeral liturgy in 1964 ordinarily began at the entrance to the church. Similarly, due to distance, weather, and other inconveniences, it likewise not infrequently absorbed into the closing rite of absolution the *Canticle of Zechariah* and its antiphon "I am the resurrection" from the cemetery service.

The year 1964, three hundred and fifty years after the promulgation of the *Roman Ritual*, also marked the beginning of a process of liturgical renewal promulgated by the Second Vatican Council the previous December. The next chapter will study the first fruits of that renewal for the liturgy of Christian burial. After this long journey through funerary and ritual development one will understand that the revised *Rite of Funerals* is itself but a beginning of renewal of Roman Catholic funeral liturgy according to Vatican II. It offers us a vastly restored proclamation of faith, and is the culmination of a process that we have followed from its beginnings.

NOTES

1. *Incipit de migratione animae*: Berlin, Offentliche Wissenschaftliche Bibliothek, codex 105 (Phill. 1667), fol. 173^v-174^r. An edition of this *ordo* is available in the dissertation of Rev. Damien Sicard. Thanks to the generosity and hospitality of Father Sicard, this author had the privilege of studying the dissertation in manuscript form. This work has recently been published as *La liturgie de la mort dans l'église latine des origines à la réforme carolingienne*, Liturgiewissenschaftliche Quelle und Forschungen, no. 63 (Münster: Aschendorff, 1978).

2. Pre-Carolingian ecclesiastical statutes are frequently concerned with the place of interment in the church compound. Superstition concerning the place of interment was apparently very widespread. See C. de Clercq, *La Législation Religieuse Franque de Clovis à Charlemagne* (Louvain-Paris, 1936).

3. *Orationes super defunctis vel commendatio animae*: Zürich, Zentralbibliothek, codex Rh 30, fol. 152^v-155^r, Anton Hänggi and Alfons Schönherr, eds., *Sacramentarium Rhenaugiense,* Spicilegium Friburgense, No. 15 (Freiburg i.d. Schweiz: Universitätsverlag, 1970), pp. 273-276.

4. The other most representative manuscript sources are: *Ordo qualiter agatur in obsequium defunctorum*: Rome, Biblioteca Vaticana, codex Ottob. 312, fol. 151^v. M. Andrieu, ed., *Les Ordines romani du haut moyen âge* I, Spicilegium sacrum lovaniense 11 (Louvain, 1931), pp. 529-530.
Ordo defunctorum qualiter agatur erga defunctum a morte detento: Cologne, Dombibliothek, codex 123, fol. 80^r. G. Haenni, "Un

'ordo defunctorum' du Xe siècle," *Ephemerides Liturgicae* 73 (1959), pp. 433-434.

Qualiter erga infirmum morte detentum agatur: Paris, Bibliothèque Nationale, B.N. lat. 1240, fol. 16^r-16^v. Studied in Paris manuscript by this author; see Damien Sicard, *La liturgie de la mort*, p. 18.

5. Here the Rheinau manuscript is completed by the other parallel sources.

6. See Alfred C. Rush, "The Eucharist: The Sacrament of the Dying in Christian Antiquity," *The Jurist* 34 (1974), pp. 10-35.

7. *Communio erit ei defensor et adiutor in resurrectione iustorum. Ipsa enim resuscitabit eum* (according to Ms. Vat. Ottob. 312).

8. *Psallant psalmos vel responsoria (per) mixt (. . .)* according to all the manuscript witnesses indicated above. See notes 1, 3-4.

9. See Augustine, *Confessiones*, 9, 12. Also, Damien Sicard, "The Funeral Mass," in *Reforming the Rites of Death*, ed. Johannes Wagner, Concilium 32 (New York: Paulist, 1968), pp. 45-52.

10. Tertullian's references to the burning of incense at funerals are familiar: *Apol.* 42, 7 (CCL 1, p. 157); *De idol.*, 11, 1 (CCL 2, p. 111); cf. *De res. carnis* 27. See C. Atchley, *A History of the Use of Incense in Divine Worship*, Alcuin Collection 13 (London, 1909).

11. *Incipiunt orationes agenda mortuorum*: Paris, B.N. lat. 2290, fol. 160^r-165^r. Edition with *incipits*: E. Martène, *De antiquis Ecclesiae ritibus* III (Antwerp, 1763), pp. 385-386.

12. See for example *Regularis Concordia*, ed., T. Symons (London: Nelson and Sons, 1953), p. 65 and *Decreta Lanfranci*, ed., David Knowles, *The Monastic Constitutions of Lanfranc*, (London: Nelson and Sons, 1951), pp. 127-129.

13. See Sicard, "Funeral Mass."

14. See Rush, *Death*, pp. 154-162; 170-186.

15. For example: *orationes antequam ad sepulcrum deferatur* or *orationes ad sepulcrum, priusquam sepeliatur* (according to Vat. Reg. 316), i.e., "prayers before the deceased is carried to the tomb" or "prayers at the tomb before the deceased is buried."

16. For example, the ninth-century funeral manual, found in the Vatican Ms. Pal. Lat. 550, fol. 2^r-24^v, presents decades of psalms to be recited during the long wake.

17. *Saint Andrew Bible Missal* (Bruges: Biblica, 1962), p. 1152.

18. Clemens Dreves and Guido Blume, *Analecta Hymnica Medii Aevi* 49 (Leipsig, 1906; Repr. Johnson Reprint Corporation, New York and London, 1961), pp. 369-389.

19. Dreves–Blume, *Analecta* 49, pp. 377-378. For a different view, see Joseph Szoverffy, *Die Annalen der Lateinischen Hymnendichtung: Ein Handbuch* II (Berlin: E. Schmidt Verlag, 1965), pp. 220-224, where the author argues in favor of a good balance in the sequence *Dies irae* between hope and fear, anticipation and tension, and refers to it as ultimately a "chant d'esperance."

20. Reprinted with permission of Macmillan Publishing Co., Inc. from *The Song of Roland*, translated by Frederick B. Luquiens. Copyright 1952 by Macmillan Publishing Co., Inc.

21. Stephan J.P. van Dijk, *Sources of the Modern Roman Liturgy. The Ordinals of Haymo of Faversham and related documents (1243-1307)*, II (Leiden: Brill, 1963), pp. 385-397.

22. See above, pp. 43-44. Cf. *Rite*, no. 192.

23. See for example K. Ottosen, N.K. Rasmussen, and C. Thodberg, eds., *The Manuals from Notmark* (Gl. kgl. Saml. 3453, 80/14th c. on vellum), Bibliotheca Liturgica Danica, Series Latina, I (Copenhaven: G.E.C. Gad, 1970), pp. 97-108, and A. Franz, "Zur Geschichte der gedruckten Passauer Ritualien," *Theologischpraktische Monats-Schrift* 9 (1899), pp. 75-85; 180-185; 288-299 (including comparison of the 15th c. Ritual of Passau).

24. *Liber Sacerdotalis* (Venetiis: M. Sessam–P. de Rauanis Socios, 1523), capita 21-31.

25. *Rituale Sacramentorum Romanum Gregorii Papae XIII Pont. Max.* (Romae, 1584). See Bruno Löwenberg, *Das Rituale des Kardinals Julius Antonius Sanctorius. Ein Beitrag zur Entstehungsgeschichte des Rituale Romanum* (Diss. 1937), Teildruk (München: Druk der Salesianischen Offizin., 1937).

26. Vat. lat. ms. 6116. The author wishes to express his gratitude to Rev. Damien Sicard who introduced him to this manuscript and who generously shared his microfilm copy of it until it was possible to consult the work itself in the Vatican Library.

27. B.N. lat. ms. 2290. Edition with *incipits*: E. Martène, *De antiquis Ecclesiae ritibus*, III (Antwerp, 1763), pp. 385-386. Among these are Rituals of the churches of Meaux (ed. 1546), Paris (ed. 1552), and Rouen (ed. 1587).

28. See above, pp. 61-62.

29. Already in 1536 a Manual of the diocese of Verona presents the following absolution service:

Oratio: *Non intres*
Resp.: *Libera me, Domine, de morte*
VV.: *Tremens, Dies illa, Requiem*
     Kyrie. . . Pater. . .
Oratio: *Deus cui omnia/indulgendo. per*

30. For example, those of Yper (ed. 1576), Bordeaux (ed. 1588), Madrid (1595).

31. These include among others the *Institutio Catholica* of Paris (ed. 1552), the Manuals of Meaux (ed. 1546) and Rouen (1587).

32. See among others the Ritual of Reims (ed. 1621): *Missa celebratur pro parvulis baptisatis, non quidem ad remissionem culpae, nec ad augmentum gloriae, sed ad solatium vivorum, et ad commendandum redemptionis nostrae mysterium, ad gratiarum actiones pro eis et ad ostendendum quod pertinent ad corpus Christi mysticum.* (4 d. 4 L.fi.). See Sancti Thomae Aquinatis. . .*Omnia Opera*, P. Fiaccadorus, ed., XXV (Parma, 1852-1873; repr. New York, Musurgia, 1949), p. 330 (=Index reference).

33. See the Cambrai manuals of 1562, 1606, and 1622.

34. *Item placuit, ut catechumenis sine redemptione baptismi defunctis, simili modo, neque oblationis commemoratio neque psallendi impendatur officium: nam et hoc per ignorantiam usurpatum est.* Ioanne Baptista Martin and Ludovico Petit. See Giovanni

Domenico Mansi, ed. *Sacrorum conciliorum nova et amplissima collectio* (Paris: H. Welter, 1900–1927), IX, pp. 779-780. (Although referred to as the "first" Council of Braga in our Rituals and by Isidore and the earlier Jesuit collection in Paris, the council in question has been shown to be in fact the second. See Mansi, IX, p. 779, no. 1.)

35. Term used in this context by Balthasar Fischer. See "Das *Rituale Romanum* (1614-1964): Die Schicksale eines liturgischen Buches," *Trierer Theologische Zeitschrift* 73 (1964), pp. 257-271.

36. The following brief description is based on the final manuscript version of the *Rituale* (1613) that belonged to the Barnabite priest J.A. Gabutius (member of the commission) and used with the kind permission of Professor Dr. Balthasar Fischer, Liturgisches Institut, Trier.

37. *Rituale Sacramentorum* authorized by D. Bollanus, Bishop of Brescia, 1575. This Ritual served as a model for both Sanctorius and the Tridentine commission of editors.

38. For example, *Rituale Sacramentorum* of Geneva under Bishop Francis de Sales, 1614.

39. A.J. Collins, ed., in *Henry Bradshaw Society* XCI, 1958 (1960), ms. p. 296.

40. *Liber catechumenorum*, Verona, 1536.

41. See, for example, the Japanese Ritual, *Manuale ad Sacramenta Ecclesiae Ministranda*, D. Ludovici Cerquerira Japonensis Episcopi opera ad usum sui cleri ordinatum cum approbatione et facultate (Nangasaquii: Collegio Japonico Societatis Jesu, 1605) and the Ritual of Peru, *Rituale seu Manuale Peruanum*, L.J. de Ore (Naples, 1607).

42. Aloys Schrott, "Die Trienter Reform im Spiegel der nachfolgenden Andachsliteratur," in G. Schreiber, ed., *Das Weltkonzil von Trient*, I (Freiburg i.B.: Herder, 1951), pp. 349-350.

43. For example, the *Rituale Sacramentorum* of Francis de Sales (Lyons: J. Charvet, 1614). See also, Rowell, *Christian Burial*, pp. 74-98.

44. *Les Instructiones du Rituel du diocese d'Alet* (Paris: A. Des Hayes, 1719).

45. *Entwurf eines neuen Rituals von einer Gesellschaft katholischer Geistlichen des Bistums Constanz* (Tubingen: J.F. Heerbrandt, 1806).

46. Hieronymus Baruffaldo, *Ad Rituale Romanum Commentaria* (Augsburg: J.C. Bencards, 1735).

47. Philip T. Weller, *The Roman Ritual*, II (Milwaukee: Bruce, 1952), pp. v-xviii; 2-37.

The Reformed Rite of Funerals

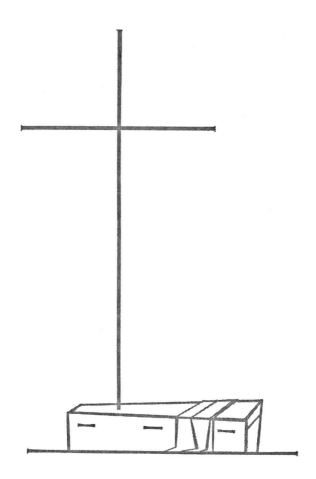

Chapter Three

The Rite in General

On August 15, 1969, the Sacred Congregation for Divine Worship published for the universal Roman Catholic Church the official Latin version of the *Ordo Exsequiarum, Rite of Funerals*.[1] This publication marked the end of the most extensive authorized program of guided liturgical experimentation up to that time in the post-Vatican II revision of the liturgical books. It likewise heralded the imminent appearance of proper funeral Rites for the United States and Canada that would include the results of the American contribution to the work of revision. Thus, when one speaks of "the Rite in its present form" both the model or typical edition in Latin and the culturally adapted editions in the vernacular of regional churches are included in the term. In English-speaking North America, for example, the Canadian version of the *Rite* differs in some cultural detail from the edition used in the United States; yet, both versions represent the Roman *Ordo Exsequiarum* in its present form. Although this chapter is primarily concerned with the *Rite* as approved for use in the United States, its general commentary will apply to the Canadian *Funeral Rite* as well. Moreover the "pastoral notes" from that *Rite* are included in Appendix II. In both these churches the work of ritual revision and initial cultural adaptation went hand-in-hand.

Already in November 1970 the Bishops' Committee on the Liturgy had received the approval of the Holy See for the complete list of adaptations that have since come to characterize the Catholic *Rite of Funerals* in the United States.[2] All who took part in the various stages of developing, testing, and evaluating the "experimental funeral rite" recognized in this version the fruit of some five years of work. Not a few American liturgists expected that this work would have appeared in the typical edition as well, but the Congregation for Divine Worship opted for a more general universal model. Dioceses such as Atlanta, Chicago, Green Bay, and St. Louis were pioneers among those designated to work on the pastoral revision of the *Rite*. It was above all the adaptation of the Roman experimental rite prepared by the Commission on the Sacred Liturgy in the Archdiocese of Chicago between 1966 and 1970 that became the American model. Those parts that now correspond most to Catholic funerary customs in the United States bear the distinctive marks of Chicago's experimental *Rite of Christian Burial*.[3] By the summer of 1971 published editions of the new Roman *Rite of Funerals*[4] for use by Catholics in the United States appeared. On November 1—only two years after the Vatican's typical edition—Catholic churches across the United States began to make their own the *Rite of Funerals* in its present form.[5]

The *Rite* in its present form thus has a "personal" story as well as the long history sketched in Chapters One and Two. Thus such a *Rite* stands in the living tradition of Catholic faith expressing itself in worship. Such rites cannot be created in the experimental laboratory of liturgical scholars; they can only be born. In the process one manner of expressing death in the rituals of faith gives way almost organically to the next. Scholars and liturgical commissions can serve the worshiping faith community by discerning, understanding, and appreciating the result of this process.

The rite thus born and embraced as one's own by the worshiping community will have its further history as well. It will grow and develop and take on a personality, a character of its own. Thus it becomes not merely a set

112

of rubrics for disposing of a corpse, ~~but truly a human and Christian symbolic language that allows death and the grief of loss their rightful articulation in a living faith community.~~ When we turn to the *Rite of Funerals* in its present form, therefore, all these aspects of ritual behavior are likewise inseparably part of our considerations.

THE RITE OF FUNERALS

The name itself, a translation of *Ordo Exsequiarum*, suggests a notion of "funeral" that embraces more than a single rite of leave-taking. Colloquially Americans use the term "funeral" mostly to mean only such a ritual. "Going to a funeral" usually implies attending a "farewell service" of some kind either in a place of worship or a funeral home. Sometimes this includes accompanying the body of the deceased to a cemetery or crematorium, where a final ritual of leave-taking closes the "funeral." The Roman Catholic *Rite of Funerals* embodies a broader understanding of *exsequiae* or "obsequies" where the term includes all the rituals with which human death is surrounded from the time of death itself until the last leave-taking and Christian consolation are completed.

This Catholic usage is not surprising when one considers the place the present *Rite of Funerals* holds in the longer tradition. In Chapter Two we saw, for example, how at one time even the moment of death itself was considered part of the liturgy for the dead and how the procession was so central to the obsequies to have left us the very term "funeral" (*funus*). Thus the *Rite of Funerals* provides basic patterns for funeral liturgy that pertain to all aspects of Christian attention to their dead. In this way the *Rite* both continues the thread of Christian funerary tradition and offers the opportunity for churches everywhere to allow that tradition to become a liturgical expression appropriate to their own people and rooted in their own cultures.

THE INTRODUCTION

The Vatican typical edition of the *Rite* opens therefore quite soundly with introductory notes (*praenotanda*) that can be termed a "general instruction on the liturgy of funerals." Those few pages are, pratically speaking, more important even than the ritual patterns and proposed texts that constitute the rest of the work. This pastoral instruction summarizes contemporary Catholic teaching about death, about the mystery of death and resurrection and about the manner of giving ritual expression to this faith in the world today. Without such an understanding all that follows in the body of the *Rite* can remain empty gesture and mere ritualism. Thus it was essential that the national liturgical commissions translate and adapt this pastoral instruction into a form that would embody its teaching in their language and culture. Clergy, educators, funeral directors, and Catholic people generally would thus have a means to make their own the renewed understanding of the faith in face of death and its articulation in liturgy where the primary emphasis is the paschal mystery of Christ.

The *Rite* for the United States adopted almost *verbatim* the translation of these *praenotanda* that had been prepared by the International Committee on English in the Liturgy (ICEL) as an official English language version of the Latin edition. This approach followed quite literally the established Roman guidelines for the translation of liturgical books but left to others the work of adaptation itself. The result, while a faithful rendering of the Latin *praenotanda*, remains just that, a translation of a universal document in Roman curial style. Although many parish priests and others responsible for funeral liturgy may have once read this instruction, few have been inclined to give it the attention and study it deserves. A more creative and pastorally written American version of this Introduction, including pastoral suggestions for the best possible implementation of the *Rite*, would be a welcome change in any future revised edition. For example, Frederick McManus' pastoral commentary on the *Rite*, which appeared early in 1972, treats the kinds of issues one would expect to find in the Introduction itself.[6] In fact, the Introduction (21, 5) declares that the material contained in it should be adapted and supplemented so that "the ministers will fully understand the significance of the rites and celebrate them effectively."

Three good examples of a national adaptation of this "general instruction" are available in the editions of the *Rite* prepared for the dioceses of France (1972), for those of Canada (1973), and West Germany (1973).[7]

The Introduction is preceded in the liturgical editions of the *Rite* by a Foreword for the dioceses in the United States, which we reprint in Appendix I. The body of this chapter is a commentary on the pastoral Introduction to the *Rite of Funerals* and as such a commentary on the *Rite* itself. To facilitate serious study of the *Rite* the paragraph headings of this chapter offer an outline of the Introduction. For the text of the Introduction, see *The Rite of Funerals* in *The Rites*, Volume One, Pueblo Publishing Co.

THE FUNERAL OF CHRISTIANS (NOS. 1-3)
The Rite opens with an indication of what is specifically Christian about the Roman Catholic funeral. Essential to everything that follows is the assertion that in the Christian funeral the Church celebrates the paschal mystery of Christ. This emphasis is stylistically visible in the Latin text where the very first words read *Paschale Christi mysterium*.

Paschal Mystery
One of the most profound insights of the liturgical movement in this century is the central place held by the paschal mystery of Christ in Christian life. It was with great wisdom that the *Constitution on the Sacred Liturgy*

115

(n. 81) established the paschal character of Christian death as the principle of reforming the Catholic rite of burial. The Church confesses in faith and practice that Christian life is life born of the paschal mystery—life that proclaims the message and the meaning of the death and resurrection of Jesus. It is through living out in practice its faith in the paschal mystery that the Church bears witness to the kingdom of God, both present and to come.

There is no greater threat to faith in the paschal mystery than the phenomenon of death. In face of human death to proclaim life founded on the death and resurrection of Jesus is one of the Church's strongest affirmations of faith in that Christ-life, for there is nothing in the experience of death itself that even hints at the viability of such a faith. It is for this reason that the Christian funeral is above all else a celebration of the paschal mystery.

Sacramental Life and Eschatology
Death for a Christian is thus inseparable from the faith context of the paschal mystery. The death of a Christian is not an isolated event—however significant—ending a person's life; it is rather an event, a moment that relates indispensably to every other moment of life by virtue of one's incorporation into the risen, living Christ. Sacramental life at once proclaims, celebrates, and nourishes that paschal faith. It is sacramental incorporation into the paschal mystery of life transformed by Jesus' death and resurrection that constitutes the making of a Christian (Christian initiation). It is the paschal mystery sacramentally actualized in the bread and wine of the Lord's Supper that is the anamnetic motive for eucharistic life. The celebration of the eucharist is the liturgy *par excellence* of the paschal mystery. The paschal mystery is what every sacramental sign of the Christian life proclaims for all the world to witness. The Roman Catholic funeral is above all else a proclamation in word and

sacrament that the Christ-life of the paschal mystery, begun with Christian initiation, not only does not end with human death but now for this Christian finds its fulfillment in the eternal present of God's kingdom beyond death. This is the kerygmatic truth that the Introduction to the *Rite of Funerals* asserts in its opening sentence. Translated more closely to the original, it reads: "It is the paschal mystery of Christ that the Church confidently celebrates in the funerals of her children, for those who through baptism have been incorporated into the body of Christ dead and risen [will] pass with him through death to life—their souls purified and taken into heaven with the saints; their bodies meanwhile awaiting the blessed hope of Christ's coming and the resurrection of the dead." (No. 1) This faith statement, combining the language of both theological reflection and biblical imagery, expresses unequivocally the characteristic mark of a Christian funeral.[8]

It is this fundamental insight of faith that constitutes the touchstone for discerning a specifically Christian response to all the other concerns involved in the funeral. This is what renders the Christian funeral an act of thanksgiving for the Christ-life of the deceased as well as an occasion of prayer for the "repose of his/her soul"; this is what determines the preference for *Alleluia* chants rather than the theme and tone of the sequence *Dies irae*; this is what enables the Christian funeral to be a source of true consolation to the bereaved, for not only this death, with all its human sorrow, but the whole past and future life of the deceased has been given meaning through the gift of Jesus' risen life—life that not even death can hold in its power. This is death touched by the paschal mystery of Christ, a mystery that does not remove any of the human sting but is yet a mystery that allows Christians to call even the funeral "celebration."

"Paschal mystery" and "everlasting life" are thus not merely images that provide Christian content to the coping rituals and grief therapy of people who happen to call themselves Christians. These are images that proclaim the very bedrock of the Christian faith. The sooner Christians recognize that the therapeutic value of their funeral rites rests on this bedrock of faith in Jesus dead and risen, the sooner will their funerals once again become both authentically Christian and genuinely human ritual with an appropriate therapeutic value of their own. With these opening words, therefore, the Introduction invites Catholics of today to an unknown new experience of their faith—an experience few generations have realized in the same way since the dawn of the Middle Ages.

Spiritual Help and the Consolation of Hope
Paragraph 1 thus states how Roman Catholic funeral liturgy spells out in worship the Christian faith at the center of the life–death experience. It affirms that the paschal mystery involves both the living and the dead as the community of Christ. The eucharist takes first place in such a celebration and in the second place, prayers and suffrages. Both are modified by the phrase "for the dead" and yet both are described as being "a consoling hope" to the living as well as "spiritual help" to the dead.

The *Rite of Funerals* certainly does not intend to define theologically here the effects of eucharist and prayers/suffrages *for* the dead. Neither is this statement to be taken out of context of the consolation of hope that these same liturgical expressions of the community of Christ offer the bereaved.[9]

Mass for the Dead
"The Church," continues the Introduction, "therefore celebrates the eucharistic sacrifice of Christ's passover for the dead." Two points deserve attention.

118

First, it is the essential truth of faith relating the death of a Christian to the paschal mystery of Christ that is presented here as the reason for the Catholic practice of celebrating the eucharist when a Christian dies. The choice of the conjunction "therefore" and the description of the eucharist as "eucharistic sacrifice of Christ's passover" both stress the teaching that the eucharist is the liturgy *par excellence* of the paschal mystery[10] and therefore of the Christian funeral. Chapters One and Two have shown how this same faith and practice are rooted in early, specifically Christian reactions to death, and contemporary usage continues the long tradition of celebrating the eucharist both in the context of the *Rite of Funerals* and on certain customary anniversaries.

Whereas all Christians profess the relationship of one's death and personal salvation to the paschal mystery of Jesus' death and resurrection, liturgical celebration and especially eucharistic celebration of this belief remains specifically Catholic.[11]

The second point concerns the way contemporary American Catholics understand "offering the eucharist for the dead" (*offerre . . . pro defunctis*).[12] We saw above how this practice and its theology developed in history, and thus we recognize the tradition behind these words in the Introduction. From early Christian times the presumption of faith has been that the deceased in need of atonement benefits from the celebration of eucharist. This belief is still very much alive in Catholic pastoral life and thus also continues to be a distinguishing mark of Roman Catholic faith in life after death.

Roman Catholics today understand the practice of offering Mass for the dead in a traditional way, yet not without a sensitivity to the liturgical and theological renewal of Vatican II. Two attitudes appear operative simultaneously in the faith life of American Catholics. Both proclaim the belief that through the paschal sacrifice of

Jesus, God has reconciled the world to himself[13] and, true to his promise, has offered that forgiveness to this faithful Christian now dead.[14] Both accept the traditional Catholic teaching that this merciful God is nevertheless a just God who in his justice requires atonement for the evil consequences of the sins that have been forgiven. For the ordinary Christian, atonement after death implies a state of purgation, traditionally termed purgatory.[15] Both current attitudes also continue to reflect the way Catholic teaching about purgatory assimilated to itself the earlier Christian practice of including the faithful dead in the celebration of eucharist.

It is precisely here that the two attitudes toward Mass for the dead differ. One conceives the Mass primarily as an *act of worship* that is celebrated as an end in itself. Its strength rests on Vatican II and post-conciliar documents as well as on the renewed liturgical books. The other attitude views the Mass primarily as a means of worship and a *channel of grace* applicable to other ends. It is rooted in late medieval theology about the value of the Mass and looks to Trent and post-Tridentine practice for its verification. Presently, varying blends of these two views are common, and those responsible for pastoral–liturgical ministry with bereaved families and friends face them almost daily. The importance of *eucharist for the dead* in the *Rite* calls for a brief comment on each of these attitudes.[16]

By its very nature the Mass is an action—an act of worship of God by the Church through and with the risen Christ. It consists in the sacramental representation in praise and thanksgiving of the paschal mystery of Christ through which universal salvation was achieved once and for all. Just as the paschal sacrifice was thus universally effective for salvation and at once an act of worship totally and completely acceptable to the Father, so too does the eucharistic commemoration of this paschal mystery actualize sacramentally the saving passover of

Christ and his perfect sacrifice of praise. It is this primary understanding of the eucharist as an *action* of the risen Christ together with the faithful assembled as Church that post-Vatican II documents recognize to be the model or the "normative Mass" today. [17] Eucharistic liturgy is thus first and foremost an end in itself: worship.

When the eucharist in this sense is offered for a deceased Christian, that person is remembered as one of the baptized who died faithful to the promise of the paschal mystery and whose personal passover the community now celebrates, even if somehow not yet realized in its fullness. The Church continues to reckon among "the faithful" the Christian who during his life followed the way of conversion and of faith in Jesus dead and risen. Just as that life was lived in eucharistic community, so too does it continue to enjoy the concern of that eucharistic community after death. The name of the deceased is mentioned in the intercessions and the proper prayers of the Mass. These prayers profess the Catholic belief that the blessed who are with God, the faithful dead in a state of purgation, and the Church living in time are all united in worship (the "communion of saints"). They recognize that the living Christians can offer atonement vicariously for the punishment due the past sins of the dead who suffer in that interim state. These prayers do not, however, spell out a theology of judgment or punishment, of heaven, hell, or purgatory. Mass for the dead and the *Rite of Funerals* demonstrate most clearly in practice that the liturgy is not limited in its expressions of the faith to theological explanations. The liturgy takes place in time, but it reaches beyond time into God's eternity. In the Mass for the dead the community thus utters its hope for the deceased in the mode of God's now. There are prayers for forgiveness of sins that speak in the first person on behalf of the deceased Christian standing before God. There are prayers asking God's mercy while atonement for the evil of sin

121

is suffered. There are prayers looking forward to the final resurrection and fullness of life in the kingdom.

In the eucharistic celebration these prayers of the Church that characterize the continuous movement of praise and petition are joined with the worship of the risen Christ. As such they cannot remain unheard by God who always accepts the perfect worship of his glorified Son; as human prayer, however, their effect depends on the faith and devotion of the petitioner. This conviction of faith rests on the very nature of eucharistic worship that is at once the action of Christ and of his Church. This point of faith, together with the very mystery which the eucharist commemorates— the *paschal mystery*—is why prayer for the dead as part of the eucharistic celebration has always been accorded a special efficacy.[18] Pope Paul VI asserts firmly in his apostolic constitution on Indulgences: "Our loving mother the Church, always concerned for the welfare of those believers in Christ who have died, declares that every time the Mass is offered the fullest possible intercession for the dead is made . . . ."[19]

According to this first attitude, therefore, the Church offers the eucharistic sacrifice for the faithful dead, not as a means of effecting the salvation or ameliorating the purgatory of the deceased, but rather to proclaim in faith that Jesus' death and resurrection has reconciled this Christian with God. Thus the community celebrates the deceased's personal passover from the power of sin and death and, taking to itself some of the hardship of the desert passage through purgation, anticipates in hope his or her entrance into the fullness of the promised kingdom of everlasting life in Christ.

The other predominant attitude toward Mass for the dead conceives of the Mass as having ends apart from the act of worship itself. According to this view celebrating eucharist ("saying Mass") has an objective value. To explain this view of the value of the Mass, Catholic theology since Duns Scotus has employed the model of "the fruits of the Mass." In our case, one applies the so-called special fruits of the Mass to a deceased person according to the intention of the priest celebrant.[20] Thus one offers Mass "for the repose of the soul of so-and-so." Popularly this means that the sacrifice of the Mass is offered to God as the greatest of all prayers on behalf of the deceased in question. God then applies the fruit of the Mass to his or her specific situation.

Such an application of the Mass is secondary to the essence of the eucharistic celebration.[21] It derives from a theology that gives equal significance to all four "ends of the Mass" (adoration, thanksgiving, petition, and expiation). In pastoral practice an emphasis on petition and expiation continues to characterize requests that "Mass be said *for*" a certain deceased person. This interpretation of the Tridentine canons on the Mass[22] sees the Mass itself as a means to these ends.

This view of the Mass is certainly the way most Catholics, including many of the clergy, conceive what "happens" when Mass is offered for a deceased Christian on the occasion of a funeral or at other times. A random comparison of parish bulletins across the United States supports this conviction not to mention certain pastoral (canonical) manuals.[23] One is tempted to interpret the reference in paragraph no. 10 of the Introduction according to this same theology. Pastorally one is advised to study Catholic liturgical theology after Vatican II in the full context of *all* the pastoral instructions that were promulgated together with the new Rites. There one finds the balance of a teaching Church in touch with both the old and the new of its faith.

Prescinding from further discussion about the priority of either theological opinion, one danger deserves mention. That is the misunderstanding caused by *confusing* a secondary effect of the eucharist with its primary meaning. This occurs when one argues that the value of the

123

Mass as the worship of Christ is infinite (primary) and that it is therefore useless to offer more than one Mass for any given deceased person (secondary). The error here is to apply the infinite value and infallible acceptance by the Father of the worship of Christ sacramentally actualized in the Mass to either intercessory prayer on behalf of the dead or to Mass itself as propitiatory prayer for a particular intention. The hoped-for effect of such prayer depends on the dispositions of the petitioner and of the one to receive the favor rather than on the gift itself. Although more than one Mass for the deceased is consistent with contemporary theology of prayer, exaggerations in either direction are obviously out of place. On the one hand, multiplication of Masses for a dead Christian that is based on a quantitative, quasi-magical view of prayer fails to take into account the primary nature of eucharist as well as the nature of propitiatory prayer and God's providence.[24] Discouraging the faithful from requesting special remembrance of a deceased person at a given celebration of eucharist fails, on the other hand, to recognize the place of the faithful dead in the eucharistic celebration of the paschal mystery of Christ according to the ancient tradition of the Church. Sensitivity to genuine eucharistic faith— even when that faith is in need of pastoral correction— remains the only proven approach to fostering the kerygmatic Catholic truth expressed in the words of this Introduction: "The Church therefore celebrates [offers] the eucharistic sacrifice of Christ's passover for the dead . . ." (no. 1).

Prayers for the Dead
Prayers and petitions offered for the dead "bring spiritual help to them" according to the Roman Catholic tradition that the living can aid the faithful dead who find themselves in a state of atonement. Although the exact nature of this "spiritual help" is beyond definition, the presumption of the faith is that God accepts the

124

devotion poured out in prayer by the living on behalf of the dead, that is, in atonement for the evil effects of the deceased person's sins.

No distinction of effect is intended by listing the eucharistic celebration and prayers separately in the Introduction. The distinction is rather a liturgical one. The *Rite of Funerals* presents the eucharist as the sacramental celebration of the Christ-life in face of death. Besides this proclamation of the paschal mystery on behalf of the deceased, the *Rite* includes still other prayers and petitions asking God to accept the devotion of the Church so that the deceased may enjoy the fullness of the paschal truth being celebrated in the eucharist.

Consolation of Hope

The celebration of the eucharist and prayers for the dead bring consolation to the living. Not just any consolation but the "consolation of hope" or "consoling hope."

Here one more specifically Christian note is struck, and the Introduction sets it in a peculiarly Catholic context. Christian faith in the Christ-life through which one shares the risen Christ's victory over death has always been a source of consolation to the bereaved Christian, as we noted historically above. This is not the consolation of the skeptic who refers to death as consoling because it frees one from the misery of life. Neither is it the empty consolation of mere religious sentiment— saccharine pictures and funerary mood music. The consolation of hope (*spei solacium*) or consoling hope is consolation founded on the certainty of Christian faith in the eschatological promise of Jesus. This hope does not stand alone or suddenly make its appearance at a funeral. This is the hope Christians proclaim and celebrate in every eucharist—the divine pledge of everlasting life. This is the hope that Catholics spell out even further in every commemoration of the dead at Mass and in every profession of the Nicene Creed: "I believe . . . in the communion of saints, the forgiveness of sins, the resurrection of the dead and the life of the world to come." This is no new hope; it is the hope at the very heart of Christianity grounded in the paschal mystery itself. It is a "consoling hope" to the bereaved not because it takes away or lessens the pain of loss but because it enables the believer to see this death with all its pain in the grace-filled context of Jesus' saving death and victorious resurrection. It is a consoling hope because it gives the bereaved a conviction of life where there is nothing but death, and that life is risen life. It awaits only the perfection of complete personal fullness in an eschatological kingdom where somehow even the body now dead will also be transformed. Whatever is meant by this biblical image of the resurrection of the body—whether literal or more than literal—it too speaks of consoling hope to the bereaved. However grief-laden the thought of human decomposition or calcification, the believer can look beyond the grave's time to God's now where even this most final law of physical nature has no validity. This is not "cheap hope" for its proclamation is far too absurd for anyone but a true believer in Jesus dead and risen to even dream. The "resurrection of the dead" is a source of consoling hope, for it states unequivocally the force of Jesus' pledge of everlasting life to those who believe and live the Christian life. It at once emboldens and gives courage, confidence, and security. All of these flow together in Tertullian's classic profession of resurrection faith: *Resurrectio mortuorum fiducia christianorum* (De Resurrectione Mortuorum, 1).

FAITH AND CULTURE (NO. 2)
After asserting the paschal character of the *Rite of Funerals*, the *Constitution on the Sacred Liturgy* (no. 81) states, as second guiding principle, that funeral rites "should correspond more closely to the circumstances and traditions found in various regions." Commentaries on the conciliar debate reveal the importance this prin-

ciple enjoyed among the Fathers. Not infrequently, it has been suggested that the great variety of circumstances and traditions surrounding burial make anything like a Roman *Rite of Funerals* quite impossible. As a matter of fact the opinions of the Council Fathers mirrored an already existing adaptation of Roman ritual to regional differences. To discover the actual practice and the needs in different countries was one of the first tasks of the subcommittee that prepared the draft version of the *Rite*. Their consultation revealed a much greater variety than one would ever suspect from merely reading the earlier *Roman Ritual*, as Chapter Two indicated. Nevertheless, all this variety pointed to a threefold set of ritual patterns that became the three plans of the revised *Rite*. In this way the new *Rite* would offer a model that preserved the essential tradition and its doctrinal implications as well as respected the principal cultural practices of the universal Church.[25]

Hope in Eternal Life—Rooted in Present
In paragraph no. 2 this second principle of the Constitution is incorporated into the pastoral instruction of the *Rite*. It states the most difficult ideal of the liturgical renewal: the union of worship with life. Yet this principle is meant to guide each and every Catholic funeral. It is not merely a description of what the compilers of the *Rite* tried to achieve; its force did not cease with the publication of the *Rite* in English. This is precisely the kind of pastoral guiding principle that allows the *Rite* to come alive as liturgy. The minister's attitude toward the deceased and his or her family must always be expressed in the context of faith and with pastoral sensitivity. This means that not any and every wish of the family must be carried out. Contemporary feeling and local custom are not meant to dictate the faith proclamation of our funeral liturgy; feeling and practice are rather the context for the funeral message—the touchstone of receptivity. These words of the Introduction caution the

minister to avoid getting trapped in all-too-frequent situations of which the following are two extremes. Genuine Catholic people often complain either that such and such a funeral was canned "resurrectionist pietism," completely out of touch with the existential state of the bereaved family, or that it was overly concerned with the emotional and religious state of the family, afraid to celebrate the very faith they most wanted to affirm. This caution pertains both to ministerial practice as well as to personal feeling and offers a bridge to the next point.

Family Tradition, Local Customs: Accepted or Adapted
One might be tempted to pass over this point as if it applied only to so-called mission lands. The American Catholic would do well to discern whether what one often takes for granted in American funeral custom really deserves the full Christian respect and acceptance it seems to enjoy. Does the standard American funeral offer the kind of ambience Christians want in their celebration of the paschal mystery? This is not a criticism of the funeral industry; it is, however, a challenge to American Catholics. This author's experience with a cross-section of American funeral directors indicates that they are first of all business people who desire to serve and to satisfy the customer. The most recent study by the Federal Trade Commission (June 1978) is a strong move to eradicate those pockets of malpractice that still plague the industry.[26] As a good business person in the service of the public at large, the professional funeral director can be expected to do everything possible to give the consumer the funeral he or she desires. That is simply good business. On the other hand, we may well ask, what might Catholics in America request of the funeral industry in order to celebrate more authentically the paschal faith and proclaim the spirit of the gospel?

Principle: Paschal Faith and the Spirit of the Gospel

Paschal faith proclaims risen life through death. This implies an acceptance of the death that has occurred, and it is also the concern of the grief therapist to foster such acceptance on the part of the bereaved. Denial of death, encouraged by whatever means, is unacceptable to Christian funerary care as well as to sound psychology. Obviously this too is an area where great pastoral sensitivity is needed. What could be death-denying for one person or family (for example, viewing the body laid out, "restored to a lifelike appearance," as the phrase goes) might be a clear recognition and acceptance of death for others.[27] The same can be said for the closed casket funeral or immediate disposition of the body followed by the funeral liturgy. The pastoral minister must be alert to just about any combination of possibilities. To assist people in this process is part of the context of proclaiming paschal faith. Except for sudden, unexpected death, the process does not, of course, ordinarily begin with death. The relationship between pastoral care for the sick and dying and funeral ministry is obvious, yet scarcely practiced.[28] Where a minister comes to the funeral with the experience of having stood with the deceased and the bereaved in faith during the dying process, there is greater hope for a funeral that proclaims a paschal faith. Cooperation between funeral counselors, a service not uncommon in funeral homes today, and the parish team could help Catholic families better integrate their life and faith needs at such a critical time.

Similarly, the spirit of the gospel suggests Christian priorities that reputable funeral directors would honor if requested. Several values stand out in particular: community, prayerfulness, and simplicity.[29] Existing funeral parlor arrangements differ considerably from region to region in the United States, but most facilities do remain generally flexible and multipurpose. There is little that would prohibit viewing arrangements that serve both to support the bereaved and facilitate times of prayer. Christian community requires an arrangement of casket and chairs that best suits the gathering of people as a community of faith and prayer. Christian simplicity demands rooms and furnishings that serve their purpose in good taste and yet do not draw attention to themselves. The stereotype of viewing parlors and mortuary chapels does not correspond to these values; it has emerged in response to different priorities, some of which honest Christians cannot help but question. Where, for example, the plush and plastic interior of a funeral parlor does more to distract than to aid the purpose for gathering there, it is serving to mask the reality of death. Christians can demand the kind of space that serves the recognition of death. In the same way there are extravagances in the application of the cosmetic art that do not serve the Christians' purpose. A good mortician can use the same "code of beauty" to retain the simplicity of the dead while still providing for reverent viewing.

This raises the question of embalming. Christians who wish to provide the opportunity for family and friends to view the deceased as they pay their respects and pray together are, at the present time, practically speaking, obliged to choose embalming. Parish ministry teams owe it to their people to be knowledgeable about the embalming requirements of their state[30] and alternatives to embalming, e.g., preservation until burial by freezing. Embalming and the cosmetic restoration of the body are not one and the same thing. However, because the embalmed corpse without make-up is experienced by most Americans as a grotesque and distasteful sight, some cosmetic work is recommended. Many morticians recommend it even for a closed casket funeral, if only to ease the brief moment when members of the family or personal friends come to view or identify the body.

Nevertheless, the family (or the deceased before death) has the consumer's prerogative to arrange whatever embalming and cosmetic services they desire. In those states where freezing the corpse is permitted as an alternative to embalming, some may wish to choose this as the simpler process, requiring less surgical handling of the body. For reasons of simplicity some Christians may prefer freezing for the closed casket funeral. At the present time concern for condensation, giving the appearance of perspiration, renders the freezing process less amenable where a period of viewing is planned. Whether one chooses embalming or freezing, cosmetic restoration remains a matter of further choice and also deserves consideration on the basis of Christian values. In short, for the Christian whatever cosmetic work that is performed ought to contribute to the proclamation of paschal faith and the spirit of the gospel rather than be guided merely by the principle of restoring the body to a lifelike appearance. For the Christian the funeral proclaims life through death and not through the appearance of life.

Today funeral directors are recommending that families pre-plan their funerals. While this is a business promotion for the industry, it offers Christians an excellent opportunity to present their values to the funeral director and to request the kind of arrangements that correspond to them. Such funeral planning sessions can help the funeral director better understand the *Rite of Funerals* in a practical way and help Christian people better understand the services provided by the funeral home. Together priests, ministers, and funeral directors can pursue ways in which Catholic funeral liturgy can best serve the faith. Adaptations can be studied and planned, such as the wake with the body in the parish church, the evening funeral, the evening wake without the body in the home of the deceased (to mention several already in process). This is a practical way to carry out the discernment implied by the Introduction when it speaks of keeping traditions that are good and of changing whatever is alien to the gospel.

Respect and Prayer in the Interval Between Death and Burial (no. 3)

For the Christian the interval between death and burial is a time when both the reality of death and faith in eternal life are very present. It is a time when one's personal faith takes on a special meaning, for it is then that this faith becomes inseparably entwined with human suffering and grief. It is a time of very special need, and the human psyche has found an outing for those needs in cultural customs of grieving and condoling. The *Rite of Funerals* was not created for its coping value. It grew out of the life situation of Christian people through the centuries. Thus it provides for the faith a context within which the believing Christian begins the process of coping—of adapting to the new situation created by the loss of the deceased.

Many of the needs that sociology and psychology identify as operative in this process find space for some resolution in the faith context of the *Rite*.[31] Grief therapists describe, for example, the need for social support during this time. The *Rite* is founded on the principle of Christian community. This implies, of course, that its liturgy is celebrated at times when it is convenient for people to attend, and such other practical pastoral considerations. Far more important, however, is the genuineness of that community life. "Going to a funeral" can be every bit as hypocritical as skeptics insist, if Christians indeed fail to build a community of genuine support. The *Rite* depends on such a community and thus implies, as do all the new rites, a renewal of ecclesial life. Empty ritualism is far less due to the failure of the *Rite* than to the failure of Christians to have a faith life to ritualize.

Coming together during this interval for prayer and fellowship with the bereaved bespeaks a kind of support that one can count on in the lonely weeks and months ahead. Far from reading social psychology into the *Rite*, this understanding flows from the very nature of Christian liturgical life. In faith, that life both expresses Christian community and causes it to happen ever more really. This is another facet of the contemporary mandate to Catholic pastoral renewal, another challenge to present priorities.

Psychologists also point to the need at this time to actualize the loss and to express sorrow. The *Rite* offers an opportunity to respond to this too in a faith context.

Respect, Not Pomp or Display
The *Rite* notes the importance Christians place on holding the body of the deceased in respect and honor. Whether one chooses to have the body available for viewing or prefers the casket to be closed during the reception times for family and friends, the same point is made: this dead body is important. One can hardly show Christian honor to the body of a loved one without beginning at least to face the reality of what has happened, the reality of loss. The recommended prayer services during this time suggest themes, psalms and other scriptural texts and prayers that make the reality of loss very actual indeed. The psalms especially give the bereaved, in the midst of a supportive community, an opportunity to make their own some deeply human expressions of loss, sorrow and grief, but at the same time of hope and trust in God.

For the bereaved to take part—however passively—in these services is one means of telling others and oneself that the deceased is gone. It is a ritualized statement that gathers into prayer the harsh reality of loss; it puts on the lips of the bereaved words that cannot avoid owning, however barely at first, the emotions flowing from the loss. What begins in liturgy will often overflow into conversation with others and personal expressions of sorrow.

It is this faith context, this special expression of sorrow and hope that is the Christian way of taking leave of the dead and facing the loss. Human needs and Christian faith flow as a unified life experience. In face of death the faith does not have its own separate grief therapy, but it brings to the grieving process the values of the Christ-life. Thus the *Rite* respects the customs and choices of the bereaved with regard to laying out the deceased, viewing or not, condolences and the like, but it urges Christian discretion of gospel simplicity. Honor and respect are due the deceased because this body was so recently alive with the life of God's grace (temple of the Holy Spirit). The faithful Christian whose body lies in death now lives life victorious over death, in whatever state of fulfillment. The person awaits only the future perfection of that Christ-life to which this body too somehow looks forward. Yet, the same mystery that requires honor and respect for the body leaves no room for pomp or empty display.

The final respect ("last respects") paid the body is an American custom of value, although funeral directors speak of increasing numbers of people who request immediate disposal with no funeral services of any kind. For the Christian it has a further value as an expression of faith in Jesus' promise of risen life. Although an unfathomable mystery, Christians believe that it is the whole person, spirit and flesh, that God has destined for the fullness of life with him. Whatever, in the language of faith, the mystery of the resurrection of the body will ultimately mean, Christians show their faith in that mystery by special symbolic respect for the bodily remains, both during this interval and after final disposition.

Exaggeration or extremes either through a lack of respect (immediate and disrespectful disposal) or absolute preservation of the corpse (as if natural decomposition has anything to do with the mystery of final resurrection) are as much out of line with the Christian meaning as extravagant scenarios displaying the corpse in the manner described in Evelyn Waugh's *The Loved One*.[32]

Services

The Introduction draws all of this into the understanding and use of the *Rite* by reaffirming that Christians are to respect and honor the bodies of the dead in faith and therefore that either neglect or exaggerated display is unchristian. "Therefore it is good," continues a more explicit rendering of the Latin, "at least at significant times between death and burial, to proclaim faith in eternal life and offer suffrages (prayers) for the dead" (no. 3). The ICEL interpretation of this part of paragraph no. 3 well emphasizes the need to provide sufficient opportunities for prayer and the proclamation of paschal faith. Yet, it misses the emphasis which the Introduction places on the reason for such gatherings. Following consequently upon no. 2 and the beginning of no. 3, the purpose of these opportunities is to enable the specifically Christian expressions of faith and hope to find their place in the funeral. Pastorally speaking this is an important emphasis, for it specifies the guiding principles of faith and liturgy for everything that follows. The *Rite* itself does nothing more than to provide the accepted Catholic form and to suggest scriptural and prayer texts that help to make a funeral Christian. It is the bereaved, with the help of the funeral minister and the support of the faith community in God's grace who make any funeral a truly Christian proclamation of paschal faith and prayer for the deceased. The *Rite* cannot do that for one; it can only show the way.

Significant Moments

Custom governs when those significant times are, and the Introduction follows suit. "Depending on local custom, the significant times during this period would seem to be the following: the vigil in the home of the deceased; the time when the body is laid out; the assembly of the relatives and, if possible, the whole community, to receive hope and consolation in the liturgy of the word, to offer the eucharistic sacrifice, and to bid farewell to the deceased in the final commendation, followed by the carrying of the body to the grave or tomb" (no. 3). There is nothing in the *Rite* itself or in the Directives for the United States that canonizes these times. Family customs, unexpected circumstances (such as travel difficulties), work schedules and the like often need to be considered when discerning these "significant moments."

Vigil in the Home of the Deceased

To the younger American reader this designation of one of these significant moments sounds strangely archaic, like an anachronism from early medieval times, or reminiscent of family stories about how great grandmother had been laid out and "waked" in her own living room or even about the famed Irish wake. Others among us will have experienced such moments of importance in the home, with or without the presence of the body. This practice is still quite common outside the United States. Both younger and older readers will remember that the *Rite* attempts to include principal cultural situations of the world over. Hence one recognizes the importance of the phrase "depending on local custom." What is "local custom" in the United States today?

During the past several decades the American funeral home has almost entirely replaced the family home as the place of the "wake." Yet, despite these changes, the notion of "wake" or spending time with the corpse, remains an essential part of the American funeral. Analysts of changing funeral customs include the "visitation or wake" among those that should continue.[33] This kind of wake provides a temporary context during which the proposed "vigil" might take place. We noted above that the vigil's purpose as a Catholic "wake service"[34] is to provide a timely opportunity for a specifically Christian expression of the meaning of death and, in that context, for prayer on behalf of the deceased. Times for prayer during this interval of the wake are nothing new to the American Catholic funeral. Generally speaking, Americans have inherited from their ethnic churches the practice of praying the Rosary at wakes, and this practice carried over from the home wake to the funeral home. The *Rite*, following the spirit of the liturgical renewal, returns to an earlier liturgical tradition and recommends a scriptural service modeled after the ancient vigil.[35] No mention is made of the Rosary in the *Rite*, but this does not require that implications be drawn that it is thereby not fitting as a popular devotion during the wake. To render the Rosary even more fitting to the occasion, attempts have been made to draw the prayerful attention of the participants to the paschal mystery, e.g., by reading short passages from Scripture between the decades and by explaining the relationship of the mysteries to the mystery of death.[36] The goal of the *Rite* is not to discourage devotional prayer during the wake, but to encourage and shape liturgical prayer that brings the treasure of the faith to the occasion and gives the Catholic faith context within which devotions such as the Rosary take on an even greater meaning. Again, this implies, of course, that both faithful people and clergy will grow to appreciate more deeply the value of ecclesial community and worship as Church in the liturgy.

Prayer When the Body is Laid Out

The other point of time singled out by the Introduction as significant, where customary, is the "time when the body is laid out." The service of washing, preparing and laying out of the body has for some time no longer been a ministry carried out by family and friends in the United States. Throughout this century it has become rather a professional service rendered by the funeral director and paid for as such. Rarely do Americans even see the body of the deceased between the time it is removed by the funeral director and it is laid out in the funeral parlor. (Even when a family member or friend comes to identify the deceased, the body will often already have been embalmed and made up.) Nowadays more and more funeral directors are offering grief counseling as a service for their customers. Although quite new and still the exception, it is encouraging to hear of funeral directors who invite bereaved family members who so desire to assist with certain details of arranging the body, e.g., dressing the deceased, giving instructions about posture or arranging the body in the casket themselves, putting the final touches on dress, "tucking in" the deceased, closing the casket and the like.[37] While all this is a response to the felt need of grieving people, it offers an opportunity to recognize the place of the faith dimension in this for the Christian. Thus the funeral is considered a value insofar as it embraces the sociological, psychological, and philosophical needs of those who mourn.[38] The *Rite of Funerals* calls us to specify the faith needs of the Christian as well and asks that those needs too be recognized by the funeral director.

There are times analogous to that of laying out the body when American Catholics might follow the invitation of the *Rite* to join in prayer. Looking to the American directive inserted at the beginning of Chapter I of the *Rite*, such times might be "when the body has been prepared and placed in the coffin, when the coffin is placed on the bier, when the family first comes together for prayer at the coffin, when the coffin is closed, or . . . before the body is taken to the church." These are times when the intimate family and friends of the deceased confront most graphically the reality of death and loss—times when they feel grief and pain most deeply. It is at such moments that the *Rite* recognizes the need for paschal faith and the consolation of Christian hope. This is part of the call by the *Rite* to a renewed funeral liturgy; it reaches far deeper than white palls and paschal candles, however significant a role they certainly play in the expression of this deeper meaning. This is likewise a call to renewed pastoral ministry. These are times when a parish priest, deacon, or lay minister offers a needed presence in witness to the paschal faith and embodies for the bereaved the value of Christian community, i.e., of Church that unites them and the deceased to Jesus dead and risen. However professional and competent the funeral counselor may be, he or she does not replace the priest or his designated representative in the ministry of the faith to the bereaved. A Catholic lay person can indeed carry out the funeral director's profession as a very worthwhile ministry in service to the Christian community, but that ministry is first of all to be a good funeral director. In addition to a special familiarity with and sensitivity to the funeral needs and desires of Christians, this ministry would include standing by the bereaved in their need for moments of prayer. All the same, the ministry of gathering the believing, praying Church around the bereaved remains the ministerial responsibility of the ordained. Yet, how often it falls to the funeral director to fulfill the roles of priest and Christian friend in addition to caring for the business of the funeral.

Renewed priorities will allow the Christian parish community of the future to be present in the person of its priest or deacon or special minister(s) when a bereaved family first sees the deceased laid out. Such a moment of utter reality is a Christian time for prayer. The priest might arrange to meet the family at the funeral home before they go into the parlor to see the body. He might offer to accompany them, should they wish, or to come in a little later, if they prefer that. The point is that he or another minister is there *for* them. In some agreed upon manner, the priest would then invite the family to join him briefly in prayer. Afterwards, speaking practically, he has a good opportunity—also briefly—to make final choices and arrangements for the eucharistic celebration and burial liturgy. Sometimes, when the family comes to see the body just prior to the first evening visitation hours, it is convenient to celebrate the wake service that same evening. Finally, during intervening moments, the priest will often have an opportunity to confer with the funeral director about specific details, if any, of this funeral. Likewise a brief, to the point conversation between parish priest and funeral director about the *Rite of Funerals* on such occasions would help correct what is surely one of the greatest obstacles to renewal of the Catholic funeral: lack of understanding and communication between these two servants of the people.

The two significant moments for prayer noted in no. 3, the vigil or wake service and prayer when the body is laid out, are taken up in greater detail in Chapter I of the *Rite*. The remainder of no. 3 focuses on the third suggested moment for special prayer. It embraces the remainder of the *Rite*, burial itself preceded by the liturgy in the church.

Liturgy in the Church and Burial
One cannot help notice the importance that the *Rite* places on the liturgy of the word, the eucharist and final commendation. Although the paragraphs to follow and Chapters II to IV of the *Rite* itself treat three different models or plans, the outlines presented here enjoy a

certain preference. The unity between burial (or other disposition) and the celebration of the eucharist which this traditional outline models is a paradigm from which the other practices are encouraged to draw inspiration. The *Rite* recognizes the legitimacy of different cultural patterns and is primarily interested in their ability to be a context for paschal faith and Christian consolation. This, as we have seen, has always been the case with Christian funeral rites. They have enabled many different cultural patterns to be Christian, always drawing ultimate inspiration from the simple truth of the paschal mystery, no matter how unlikely the bearer. While proposing an ideal, the *Rite* allows pastoral priorities to mold the ideal in order to serve different situations. This applies to the local parish as well as to the universal Church. Thus, the *Rite* is normative and descriptive of pastoral practice; it is not obligatory in its detail. It says with authority, "This is the way Catholics bury their dead." Therefore, even the ideal pattern of the American version of the *Rite* in which the liturgy in the church has its special place is a model to serve pastoral practice. Parish priests and other ministers of the funeral are expected to discern together with the bereaved the best way the *Rite* can give form to the funeral in specific circumstances. This does not imply that planning a funeral must become an additional burden to the faithful; nor should the model American *Rite* be regarded as one among an "anything goes" collection of rites. Quite simply put, the *Rite* is for the people, not *vice versa*. This liturgy in the church, and especially the celebration of eucharist remains the principal Catholic proclamation of paschal faith and source of Christian consolation. It deserves primary attention in planning the various services of the funeral. Even if the eucharist be celebrated at a time other than at this point between death and burial, it should take place as closely as possible to burial.

1. *Rituale Romanum* ex decreto sacrosancti oecumenici Concilii Vaticani II instauratum auctoritate Pauli PP VI promulgatum, *Ordo Exsequiarum* (Typis Polyglottis Vaticanis, 1969).

2. *Bishops' Committee on the Liturgy Newsletter* 7/4-5 (1971), s.v. Funeral Rite.

3. Commission on the Sacred Liturgy, *The Rite of Christian Burial* (Chicago: Archdiocese of Chicago, 1968).

4. *The Roman Ritual* revised by decree of the Second Vatican Council and published by authority of Pope Paul VI, *Rite of Funerals*: Study Edition (Washington, D.C.: United States Catholic Conference, 1971). Editions by other publishers are listed in *BCL Newsletter* 7/6 (1971), s.v. Funeral Rite—Official Books.

5. November 1, 1971, was announced as the mandatory effective date for use of the revised *Rite* by John F. Cardinal Dearden, President, National Conference of Catholic Bishops. See *BCL Newsletter* 7 (1971), s.v. Funeral Rite.

6. Frederick R. McManus, "The Reformed Funeral Rite," *American Ecclesiastical Review* 116 (1972), 45-59; 124-139.

7. Centre Nationale de Pastorale Liturgique, *La Célébration des Obsèques* I (Paris: Desclée-Mame, 1972), pp. 7-14; National Office for Liturgy, *Catholic Funeral Rite* (Ottawa: Canadian Catholic Conference, 1973), pp. 7-26; Die kirchliche Begräbnisfeier in den katholischen Bistümern des deutschen Sprachgebietes, hrsg. im Auftrag der Bishofskonferenzen Deutschlands, Österreichs und der Schweiz und des Bischofs von Luxemburg (Einsiedln–Köln–Freiburg–Basel–Regensburg–Wien–Salzburg–Linz, 1973), pp. 11-20.

8. This is not the place to discuss the precise theological meaning of traditional eschatological images such as incorporation into Christ dead and risen, passage through death to life, purification of souls, assumption into heaven with the saints, the parousia or bodily resurrection. We take these as the Introduction itself intends, viz., as an assertion of faith in the paschal mystery and all its consequences for the faithful. A good contemporary summary of such theological reflection is

Michael Schmaus, *Dogma VI: Justification and the Last Things* (Kansas City/London: Sheed and Ward, 1977). For consideration of how this biblical faith serves as a corrective of unrealistic funeral liturgy, see John P. Meier, "Catholic Funerals in the Light of Scripture," *Worship* 48 (1974), pp. 206-216.

9. See the *General Instruction of the Roman Missal (GIRM)* no. 135 where the very same text is used when referring to the Mass only.

10. See *GIRM*, nos. 1-4.

11. Roman Catholic tradition has always preserved it. The revised American Episcopal *Book of Common Prayer* has restored the practice which had not entirely disappeared from the preserve of Anglican tradition despite official *Prayer Book* editions after 1552. For a thorough survey of Reformation and Post-Reformation rites and contemporary Anglican revisions see Rowell, *Christian Burial*, 74-98 and 102-110; Bürki, *Im Herrn entschlafen*, 238-241 and 265-270.

12. The Latin version reads: *offerre*. Although the ICEL rendering of *offerre pro* by "celebrate for" is quite understandable, the distinction ought to be kept in mind as one studies contemporary American attitudes toward Mass and prayers *for the dead*.

13. Cf. *Rite of Penance*, Prayer of Absolution (no. 46).

14. This work on the *Rite of Funerals* presumes, as the *Rite* itself does, a community of faith and does not take up the question, however important, of those who die estranged from God.

15. See the reiteration of this teaching by Pope Paul VI in his apostolic constitution on Indulgences (*Indulgentiarum doctrina*), Jan. 1, 1967 in *The Pope Speaks (TPS)* 12 (1967), 124-135.

16. Background to the following includes Paul VI, *Mysterium Fidei* (Sept. 3, 1965) *TPS* 10 (1965), 309-328; Sacred Congregation of Rites, *Eucharisticum Mysterium* (May 25, 1967) (Washington, D.C.: USCC, 1967); Josef Jungmann, *The Mass* (Collegeville, Minn.: Liturgical Press, 1976), esp. pp. 97-152; Karl Rahner and Angelus Häussling, *The Celebration of the Eucharist* (New York: Herder, 1968); Pierre-Yves Emery, *The Communion of Saints* (London: The Faith Press, 1966). An easily

accessible summary of these views and others is found in Lucien Deiss, *It's the Lord's Supper: Eucharist of Christians* (New York: Paulist, 1976).

17. See, among others, *GIRM*, Introduction, Chapters I and IV and *Notitiae* 3 (1967), 195.

18. See, for example, Rahner–Häussling, *Eucharist*, p. 82: "The conception of grace which is attested by the texts of the Masses for the dead in the Roman liturgy implies awareness of our communion with those who have died in Christ, and the belief that we are able to be close and helpful to them by celebrating Mass *for* the dead. By that Mass, they are drawn afresh into communion with Christ who overcame death in death and whose communion with the dead leads to resurrection; that is the communion which for early Christians was *pax* and *communio* absolutely. The *pro* in the expression *offerre pro defunctis* does not mean directly 'in order to help'; here too (as in fact elsewhere) it primarily expresses the occasion for the celebration of the Mass ('on the occasion of the death of the late —'), then a remembrance (especially when the name is mentioned) and finally a representation: we offer sacrifice to God in place of the deceased."

19. Paul VI, *Indulgentiarum doctrina*, *TPS* 12 (1967), 135.

20. Jungmann, *Mass*, pp. 148-150; see also Nicholas Halligan, *Sacraments of Initiation and Union*, I (New York: Alba House, 1972), pp. 166-169.

21. Rahner–Häussling, *Eucharist*, p. 39.

22. DS 1743; 1751-1754. Cf. Jungmann, *Mass*, p. 143-144.

23. E.g., Halligan, *Sacraments I*, pp. 169-191.

24. On this matter Fr. Jungmann has written that "there is little point in forcing distinctions between fruits of varying value or in arranging the different grades of efficacy in neat categories. For the ultimate success of a prayer does not depend on the one who prays but on the free will of the One who grants, and that One does not need a computer." Jungmann, *Mass*, p. 149.

25. Pierre-Marie Gy, "Le Nouveau Rituel Romain des Funérailles," *La Maison-Dieu* 101 (1970), 20-21. An English

translation of this article is available in *The Way* Supplement 11, Fall 1970: "The Liturgy of Death. The Funeral Rite of the New Roman Ritual," pp. 59-75.

26. See also the Consumer Union book *Funerals: Consumers' Last Rights* (New York: Norton, 1977) and counter arguments by the National Funeral Directors' Association (available from the NFDA national office, Milwaukee, Wis.). In this context the NFDA *Code of Ethics* has been appended for easy reference, Appendix III. Cf. Thomas J. Reese, "The Funeral Industry: Living Off the Dead," *America* 140 (1979), 506-509.

27. Philippe Aries, "Death Inside Out," in *Death Inside Out, The Hastings Center Report,* Peter Steinfels and Robert M. Veatch, eds. (New York: Harper and Row, 1975), pp. 20-24.

28. See Introduction no. 25, 1 and *Rite of Anointing and Pastoral Care of the Sick*, nos. 26-30 as well as full context of ministry to the sick.

29. One successful approach to greater simplicity for funerals generally is that offered by cooperative Memorial Societies. In the last twenty years many such societies have spread widely across the United States and Canada. They are nonprofit corporations dedicated to funeral reform and founded to assist members to obtain desired mortuary services at reasonable cost. Informative publications are available from the Continental Association of Funeral and Memorial Societies (Washington, D.C.) and the Memorial Society Association of Canada (Edmonton, Alberta). For a concise description of their services and a comprehensive list of Societies and Coop Funeral Homes in the United States and Canada, see Barbara K. Harrah and David Harrah, *Funeral Service: A bibliography of literature on its past, present, and future, the various means of disposition and memorialization* (Metuchen, N.J.: Scarecrow, 1976), Appendix 6 and 7, pp. 289-302.

30. See Appendix IV for an initial listing of state embalming requirements.

31. To survey the vast literature in the fields of sociology and psychology is beyond the scope of this book. The reader is referred to two recent bibliographical guides where a representative selection of pertinent works can be found: Albert J. Miller and Michael James Acri, *Death: A Bibliographical Guide*

(Metuchen, N.J./London: Scarecrow, 1977) and Barbara K. Harrah and David F. Harrah, *Funeral Service*.

32. Evelyn Waugh, *The Loved One* (Boston: Little, Brown and Co., 1948). See the same author's nonfictional account of his visit to Forest Lawn in *Life* 23 (1947) 73-83.

33. See, for example, Howard C. Raether, "The Place of the Funeral: the Role of the Funeral Director in Contemporary America," *Omega* 2 (1971), 131-149.

34. Although these two words have the same root meaning from the Latin *vigilia* (watch, wake, vigil), "vigil" is used here in the meaning of a liturgical service, the "celebration of God's word," an application derived from the liturgy that once took place during the long night watches or vigils in the literal sense.

35. See the *Rite*, nos. 26-28.

36. See Alfred C. Rush, "The Rosary and the Christian Wake," *American Ecclesiastical Review* 152 (1965), pp. 289-297. It is curious that so few funeral ministers have followed Fr. Rush's excellent suggestions for the wake Rosary. The time is now ripe to reconsider them seriously, for they will illustrate the place of devotions in relation to the liturgy. One example of the "Scriptural Rosary" at the wake is found in *Holy Cross Funeral Liturgy* (Notre Dame, Ind.: Congregation of Holy Cross, 1976), pp. 31-32.

37. Roy Nichols and Jane Nichols, "Funerals: A Time for Grief and Growth," in *Death: The Final Stage of Growth*, Elisabeth Kübler-Ross, ed. (Englewood Cliffs, N.J.: Prentice-Hall, 1975), pp. 87-96.

38. Nichols, p. 94.

Chapter Four

The Rite in Specific

Three Plans for the Universal Church (nos. 4-9)
International consultation by the subcommittee preparing the *Rite* indicated, as we noted above, that three basic plans or patterns of funeral rites represent Catholic practice across the world. Pierre-Marie Gy, whose work on the revision has been monumental, describes the three plans as follows. "According to the first plan, *viz.* that of the traditional Roman Ritual, as generally employed in countries such as Italy and France, the principal liturgical action of the funeral would take place in the church. According to a second plan, quite widespread in German-speaking countries—at least in the cities—the body of the deceased is not taken to the church but directly to the cemetery where the principal liturgical action is held. Finally, there exists a third plan according to which the principal action takes place in the home of the deceased, either because of the distance from the church or cemetery or because of local traditions, such as is the case in certain regions of Africa."[1] Gy states that the subcommittee was of the opinion that these different plans for the funeral would answer the real needs that derive from legitimate customs and deserve a place in the new *Roman Ritual*.

The First Plan (nos. 5-6)
"The first plan is the one found until now in the Roman Ritual." The typical American Catholic funeral before 1971 was already an adapted version of the Roman *Rite for the Burial of Adults*; it followed basically the same

147

three-stage pattern, with the principal liturgical action centered in the church. Already the station in the home of the deceased had shifted to the funeral home, and the liturgical opening of the funeral there (*in domo*) according to the *Rite of Burial* gradually became telescoped into the liturgy at the church. Thus already the liturgy in the church began with a meeting of the body at the church entrance. Mass, followed by the absolution service, constituted the essential funeral liturgy. The service at the cemetery had its own autonomy and gradually was becoming something for the family and close friends, with the parish priest officiating when possible. The American adaptations had already abandoned the processions between stations because of the problem they posed for modern urban life and traffic.

World-wide consultation by the Commission for the Implementation of the Constitution also revealed similar influences on funeral liturgy. Among other things the process of urbanization favors Plan II, but in the case of Plan I, urbanization contributed not only to the elimination of processions with the body, but also even of the stations in the home of the deceased and at the cemetery. This is an accurate description of the American scene before 1971, as both experience and consultation in the United States confirmed. Taking developments such as these into consideration, the new *Rite* strives to enable a truly Christian celebration of funerals not only where earlier, mostly rural conditions prevail, but also under the changed conditions of urban life and ministry.[2]

Paragraph no. 5 accepts these changes as a cultural given and recognizes the adaptation that the form of the funeral has undergone in various countries. If this is the case, what was so "new" about the new American *Rite*? Was it simply a matter of casting the American funeral in a new liturgical color and flavoring it with happier liturgical music and decorations? Unfortunately, some

148

American Catholic parishes failed to go beyond that level of novelty. It is not these changes but rather renewal itself that is the key to the new *Rite*.

Also of pastoral importance in no. 5 is the advice that in the absence of a priest or deacon the faithful themselves should be urged to recite the customary prayers and psalms.[3] Thus even where circumstances have virtually eliminated stations in the (funeral) home and cemetery, the *Rite* strives to preserve the spiritual value of these moments. Only when this is impossible, would one omit these stations entirely. American practice in this matter varies greatly from region to region. Parishes with active permanent deacons are discovering the great value of ministry to the bereaved at these times during the funeral. Utilizing such opportunities of the renewal to respond to the spiritual needs of the faithful at the time of death has revealed the wisdom of the earlier traditions in Catholic funeral liturgy. Christian people want the ministering care of their Church, and the new *Rite* offers a way to serve those needs. While the responsibility for genuine pastoral liturgy rests with the parish priest and deacon, the exercise of their responsibility in the liturgy itself has been extended more and more by Catholic authority to lay ministers. The potential for serving that "funeral ministries" offer is vast, as we shall see in paragraph no. 19 below.

Paragraph no. 6 takes up some details of the liturgy in the church according to Plan I. Eucharistic liturgy is, as we have seen, the norm. To emphasize that norm the exceptions are immediately cited. It is only "during the Triduum of Holy Week, on solemnities, and on Sundays of Advent, Lent, and the Easter season" that the very nature of these days themselves prohibits the funeral Mass. Whatever confusion may have existed with regard to celebrating a funeral Mass from the morning of Holy Thursday through Easter Sunday has been cleared up by the Congregation for Divine Worship. The second typical edition of the *Roman Missal* (1974) revised the paragraph of the General Instruction that apparently was the source of confusion. It now reads as follows: "The funeral Mass has first place among the Masses for the dead and may be celebrated on any day except solemnities which are holydays of obligation, *Holy Thursday, the Paschal Triduum* and the Sundays of Advent, Lent and the Easter season."[4] The United States Bishops' Committee on the Liturgy published the clarification in its *Newsletter*.[5]

Even on these days, however, the body is brought to the church for the celebration of the liturgy of the word and the rite of final commendation and farewell. Nourishment and consolation are thus offered through the word of God in the very place where the table of God's word is joined in worship with the table of the Lord's Supper.[6] Analogous to the baptism of infants outside Mass, where the worshiping community is invited to move from the baptistry to a position around the altar for the Lord's Prayer (in anticipation of full eucharistic participation), so too the funeral of Plan I when Mass cannot be celebrated still desires to gather the community around the deceased in the place where they ordinarily celebrate the eucharist. In such cases the eucharist itself is to be celebrated on another day insofar as that is possible. Although the parish church remains the symbolic house of the people of God and serves as such especially in Plan I, pastoral reasons may recommend celebrating the funeral Mass in the home of the deceased. This pastoral option, with the approval of the local ordinary, is indicated explicitly in Plans II and III of the *Rite* (nos. 59 and 78). Even following Plan I, situations have arisen pastorally where two sets of circumstances coincide: the funeral falls on a day when the celebration of the funeral Mass is prohibited and, for example, the spouse of the deceased is confined to bed at home. In such cases the liturgy of the word (and final commendation) will have been celebrated in the church as in Plan I, whereas Mass might be celebrated, according to the judgment of the local ordinary, on another day soon afterwards in the home of the spouse. Even when Plan I takes place in its entirety as usual, Mass celebrated for the deceased in the home (where home Mass is permitted) has proven to be a genuine source of paschal faith and consolation for family and friends in special need.

Paragraph no. 6 closes with a reference to the service called final commendation and farewell. This genuinely new peak moment of the *Rite* is treated separately in no. 10 below.

The Second and Third Plans (nos. 7-8)
Plans II and III of the *Rite* are noted briefly. Details of Plan II are left to Chapter III. The Introduction merely states, "The second plan has only two stations, in the cemetery chapel and at the grave." However, the pastoral reader is reminded that the celebration of the eucharist is to take place either before or after the funeral. As was pointed out above, this plan is most common in German-speaking lands where it has long been the custom and, in some places the law, not to bring the corpse into the church. This plan extends into modern times local funeral customs and corresponding liturgical rites whose roots we observed in our survey of the funeral in medieval Europe. In those regions where the practice exists of celebrating eucharist immediately following the liturgy of the word and burial rites at the cemetery, Mass may begin with the liturgy of the eucharist (preparation of the gifts). In this way the unity of the funeral and the funeral Mass is well preserved and untimely duplications avoided. Pastoral concerns may suggest pursuing a similar approach in the United States for those exceptional cases when Plan II is followed.

Even less likely in American practice is Plan III where the principal funeral liturgy is celebrated in the home of the deceased. Nevertheless, it teaches pastoral–liturgical principles of value. It shows, for example, that bringing a Christian faith dimension to death and the disposition of the dead is a living tradition, capable of adapting to many different needs. Plan III merely serves to guide the response to those needs and, where appropriate, to include liturgical "elements common to the others, e.g., in the liturgy of the word and in the rite of final commendation and farewell" (no. 8). The epitome of such adaptation is apparent when no. 78 of Plan III suggests: "For pastoral reasons the local ordinary may permit the funeral Mass to be celebrated in the home of the deceased," as noted above. American Catholics can learn from this that the *Rite of Funerals* both respects legitimate cultural and ritual usage and yet refuses to become mere ritualism. The *Rite* points the way that Catholics today can put the renewal of faith and ecclesial life into practice. It remains a means, as the circumstances of Plan III so well demonstrate; it is not an end in itself, as celebrations of Plan I sometimes tend to be. A typical American danger is that the funeral liturgy becomes just one more thing the bereaved have to go through, or an expected bit of Catholic pageantry, rather than the very heart of the Christian care for the dead—that around which everything else turns.

Pastorally, Plan III alerts the American Church that occasions may arise in the United States too where one could have sufficient reasons to celebrate the principal funeral liturgy, including Mass when authorized, in the home of the deceased. Although out of the ordinary because of the special role the eucharistic, ecclesial community plays in the funeral liturgy, such an exception is a recognized manner of celebrating the *Rite of Funerals*, most frequent in the African Church. Criteria for permitting such an exception to the ordinary American Plan of the *Rite* would, of course, have to be founded on the principle of fostering ecclesial life rather than fragmenting it.[7]

Particular Rituals

Closing these general remarks on the three plans, no. 9 summarizes the procedure whereby particular rituals are prepared in harmony with the Roman typical edition of the *Rite*. Because of the great variety of funeral customs world-wide, national conferences of bishops were accorded extensive freedom to consider their special pastoral needs and to arrange their versions of the *Rite* accordingly. Guidelines for that process are spelled out in nos. 21-22 below.

Some national conferences chose, for example, to set out in their edition of the *Ordo Exsequiarum* one plan that is customary in their regional Church. Such is the case with the Canadian and the French editions, for example. These books reveal a good understanding of ritual behavior—especially of funerary ritual—that is essentially uniform in a given culture and conservative. Respect for this dimension of ritual life cannot be overlooked. Furthermore, the approach is pastorally commendable, for it results in a very usable, unencumbered ritual book. On the other hand, at this stage of liturgical renewal, such a choice tends to limit the openness of the *Rite* itself to adapt to the ever-changing needs of complex society. Even the most conservative of rituals must retain their ability to change in response to changing experiences of people. A single plan may indeed be the ordinary usage, yet familiarity with the other plans and their rationale opens new possibilities of pastoral awareness. Similarly, the tendency for a specific usage to fossilize is greater when it becomes the only model.

At the risk of ritual hardship and some pastoral confusion the Bishops' Conference in the United States opted to publish in English translation the entire typical edition of the *Rite of Funerals*. This choice was made in strict adherence to Roman directives as understood at that time. Proper American adaptations are included in their respective places. In effect the United States Bishops' edition presents the American version of Plan I, including options for prayers, readings, chants and the like, as the usual practice; the other two plans follow as options. That was not an easy book to edit, and the consensus of parish priests interviewed by this author is that it is not an easy book to use pastorally. Nevertheless, this author does not agree with those colleagues who repeatedly insist that the official *Rite of Funerals* for the United States is the worst possible edition of the poorest of the renewed rites. The American editors deserve credit for tackling the problem of presenting *all* the potential of the *Rite* from the beginning, even if experience will show a better way of editing the material. The cultural differences represented by the Catholic Church in the United States are themselves sufficient reason for the decision to publish the American *Rite* in its present form. The Bishops' Committee on the Liturgy was faced with a situation not unlike that faced by the *Consilium* for the universal Roman Church. Its choice was to follow a similar solution: an edition of the *Rite* that establishes a threefold model to serve local pastoral needs. The *Rite* differs from the Roman typical edition, however, in that it *both* establishes Plan I as the *usual* American practice *and* includes some specific optional adaptations that prior experimentation revealed to be acceptable to American Catholics. The editors did all of this in a remarkably clear way for study purposes. For pastoral use, however, a future revised edition must consider different editorial options,[8] as well as review the American adaptations in light of a decade of experience. Much can be learned from an international consultation on pastoral experience with the *Rite*, especially with so many of those different cultural expressions likewise represented in the United States.

Specific Parts of the Rite (nos. 10-14)
Just as the essential faith dimension of the *Rite* remains the same proclamation of paschal faith and the consola-

tion of hope for the bereaved, no matter which plan is celebrated, so too certain elements are the bearers of that constant faith. They too enjoy a constancy in all the plans of the present *Rite*, just as they have throughout the history of the development of the Christian burial liturgy. Besides the eucharist which the *Rite* cites as the primary proclamation of paschal faith and consoling hope, these elements are: the new rite of final commendation and farewell, biblical readings, psalms, prayers, and Office of the Dead.

Final Commendation and Farewell (no. 10)
"After the funeral Mass the rite of final commendation and farewell is celebrated." These words of no. 10 introduce the concluding rite before burial. Taken together with no. 46, they immediately include what the Introduction presents as its usual place in the funeral of Plan I. Although the *Rite* (no. 50) offers the option: "If the priest and the congregation accompany the funeral to the cemetery, the final commendation and farewell may be celebrated at the grave or tomb itself," the position after Mass or the liturgy of the word enjoys a pastoral preference. The reason is to accommodate the community. Nevertheless, where the people do go to the cemetery, it may be pastorally preferable to celebrate the final commendation and farewell there, especially where the cemetery is close to the church.

Next, the Introduction teaches us what is so important about this short rite that all should have the opportunity to participate in it. It tells us first what the rite is not: "This rite is not to be understood as a purification of the dead." This strong negative assertion is meant to counteract remnants from past funeral theology that continue to confuse this rite with an absolution from sin.[9] The Introduction reminds us that any such "purification" is effected rather through the eucharistic sacrifice, although even there sacramental absolution is not implied. This rite is understood rather "as the last farewell

155

with which the Christian community honors one of its members before the body is buried." These words of Cardinal Lercaro, then president of the *Consilium*, were incorporated into the Introduction (no. 10).[10] They articulate the theological reinterpretation which the *Consilium* has given to the former rite of *absolutio* after the funeral Mass. This significant renewal is founded on earlier Byzantine practice that preserved the Christian adaptation of the ancient, cultural gesture of a "farewell kiss" for the deceased. The Introduction cites Simeon of Thessalonica, "The Order of Burial," where he explains that this last farewell is sung for the departure of the dead and for their separation, but also because there is a communion and a reunion. In death Christians are not truly separated from one another, Simeon explains, because all follow the same path to the same destination, *viz.* communion with Christ where all the faithful will be together in Christ.[11] Thus while expressing hope and consolation through paschal communion, this rite also graphically terminates the human relationship severed by death. When this rite serves its proper faith purpose in the Catholic funeral, it can be one more spiritual moment of letting go, of closure, and further outlet for grief. Again, it is not as separated pieces but as integrated realities of life and faith that grief and the rite of farewell blend in mutual service.

It was the intention of the *Consilium* that the rite of final commendation and farewell stand out as a permanent and recognizable faith moment in the *Rite*. It is always to be included. Even when the eucharist cannot be celebrated, the commendation and Christian farewell are never omitted. Not only does this renewed rite differ in spirit and theology from the former absolution after Mass, it is thus also no longer viewed as an appendage to the funeral Mass. According to the normative understanding of the *Rite of Funerals*, the final commendation and farewell are more significant than, for example, the American opening to the *Rite* (always optional) or even the rite accompanying burial at the cemetery. This is not to disparage either of the latter, but to place the rite of commendation in its proper perspective. Observation and pastoral interviews have convinced this author that such an understanding of the rite of final commendation and farewell has not taken hold generally in the United States. By and large the American Catholic funeral has simply transposed the former absolution with the new rite, which in effect is little more than a change of words to accompany the former gestures.[12] Admittedly this is a case where the *Rite* is attempting to introduce something quite new, and that takes time. Coming as it did in 1970, so close to the revised *Order of Mass* and *Rite for the Baptism of Infants*, the *Rite of Funerals* was accorded a remarkable reception. Nevertheless, while it is understandable how this new dimension of the *Rite* failed to attract its deserved attention in the United States at that time, pastoral renewal in the 1980s cannot fail to take account of its potential for further renewal of the American Catholic funeral.

The rite of final commendation and farewell is very simple, yet requires preparation and care if it is to be most effective. It combines two basic elements of the liturgical renewal, active participation and prayerful silence, both difficult to realize in the very mixed congregations that usually gather for a funeral. Sensitivity to the particular group and especially to the bereaved family, and a sense of timing are both crucial. These differ depending on whether the rite immediately follows Mass or is celebrated at the cemetery.

Invitation to Pray: "The priest introduces this rite with an invitation to pray: then follow[s] a period of silence." Taking a place near the closed casket, the priest first invites the community to pray. This alerts all present to the distinctive character of the moment, and the prayerful silence that follows allows them to enter personally into this final commendation and expression of

157

last farewell. Here one sees the principle of active participation and silence at work. This invitation to prayer and the manner of extending it frequently makes all the difference whether or not what follows is truly an opportunity for faith-filled prayer commending the deceased to God and at once a proclamation of paschal faith and consoling hope. *What* the priest says at this time is important. This invitation to prayer deserves to be prepared as delicately as the funeral homily. The texts provided in nos. 46 and 183-186 offer models both of content and form. Sometimes they will serve as they are, but even then, they are to be personalized according to circumstances. Frequently, however, these models will only serve to guide the celebrant to prepare an invitation proper to the occasion, as no. 46 indicates with the directive, "He . . . introduces the rite in these or similar words." In either case those present are invited to pray and at once are guided to prayer during the silence that follows. Such prayer-filled silence during the liturgy is new to Catholic people, but what better time than the closing moments of a funeral to experience the power of such moments in the liturgy! The psychology of prayer again goes hand in hand with the psychology of grief. At this significant moment the silence that allows the bereaved and the assembled community to make their own the faith of Christians committing their dead to the mercy of God through Jesus dead and risen, likewise offers the opportunity of accepting death's human finality. In both faith and life the bereaved thus says "farewell." Only then can any true consolation come from faith in communion and hope in a future reunion in the kingdom.

Holy Water and Incense: Following upon the invitation to prayer and an appropriate period of silence the *Rite* presents the sprinkling with holy water and the incensation. These symbolic actions have been part of the service before burial in the West ever since earlier medieval times, as the history of the funeral has shown. For many they seem anachronistic in the late twentieth century, and their liturgical value remains to be seen. However that may be, the *Rite* has preserved the use of holy water and incense and offers a clear explanation of the symbolism, both in general for the funeral and specifically for the rite of farewell: "The sprinkling with holy water, which recalls the person's entrance into eternal life through baptism, and the incensation, which honors the body of the deceased as a temple of the Holy Spirit, may also be considered signs of farewell" (no. 10). The general explanation which also applies to other moments in the funeral when holy water and incense may be used, is rooted in their natural symbolism and long tradition. Their significance as "signs of farewell" is a further interpretation proposed by the drafters of the Introduction. This author fails to appreciate the liturgical reasoning for the suggestion, except of course that it is an attempt to reinterpret two traditional and recognizable actions of this short rite in accord with the reinterpretation of the rite itself. In the United States the option has been granted to dispense with incense altogether, whereas the use of holy water may not ordinarily be omitted (no. 22 *addendum*). The same paragraph continues, "Neither holy water nor incense should ordinarily be used more than once during the station in the church." Following these directives the sprinkling with holy water in the United States is usually reserved for the opening rite at the entrance of the church. Should the incensation be included in the rite of final commendation, then it might be understood as a "sign of farewell" in that it is a *last* special gesture of honor toward the body of the deceased that looks forward to resurrection as well as a sign of the Church's *final* prayer of commendation rising like the fragrant smoke to God, according to traditional biblical imagery. Although incense enjoys the kind of ritual ambiguity (honor, prayer, purification) that permits this kind of adaptation theoretically, it remains to be seen how contemporary American Catholics in fact interpret the use of incense at the rite of commendation and farewell. For many it is simply the Catholic thing to do—an added bit of solemnity. Even that much acceptance, together with a prayerful manner of incensation by the priest, can help the bereaved and others present to appreciate the special spiritual character of the rite.

Song of Farewell: The least familiar and least understood part of this short rite is the song of farewell. In the United States it remains virtually an unused "option." Yet this song of farewell is intended by the *Rite* to be "experienced as the climax of this entire rite" (no. 10). Few American churches have ever attempted it on a regular basis; yet, "the text and melody of the latter [song] should be such that it may be sung by all present" (no. 10). Why is the American practice not consistent with the rite?

The principal reason is the general failure from the beginning to appreciate the intended reinterpretation of this rite. The song of farewell simply never became its climax, because the theology of commendation and farewell never really came to characterize the rite. Despite excellent initial efforts to the contrary by Frederick McManus, the Liturgy Training Program of Chicago, and others,[13] this service after Mass remains merely final ritualized prayer of intercession for the deceased. In the minds of many, commendation and committal belong together, and both belong at the grave, where "the last farewell" really takes place. Because of this logic the *Rite* includes the option to celebrate the commendation and farewell at the cemetery. Nevertheless, the importance of the commendation and farewell as the liturgy of the ecclesial community requires that it be celebrated where the people are gathered. In the United States the practice continues to grow where virtually only members of the family and close friends accom-

160

pany the body to the cemetery. Thus the anomaly is not resolved by the cemetery option in the *Rite*. That option remains practically unrealistic in America except for rural parishes and churches with the cemetery nearby. Even then, the custom of celebrating this rite in the church is so widespread that few venture to transfer it to the cemetery.

In our opinion, the song of farewell as climax of this rite was never rejected as such, but rather simply never had a chance. As principal expression of the rite's faith dimension, *viz.* commendation and farewell in faith and hope in the resurrection, its absence consequently has an affect on the understanding and appreciation of the entire rite. As time went on, no one missed it. Even before the *Rite* appeared officially in 1969 and in English in 1970, the song of farewell was practically doomed to failure in the United States. Hindsight reveals that the *Roman Rite of Funerals* issued as a guide for official experimentation in 1967[14] does not mention the "song of farewell" by title or indicate its specific importance. The responsory "Saints of God" was already included there, but it seems to serve more as a replacement from the tradition for the responsory *Libera me* than a new climactic song of farewell. By 1968 the so-called Chicago Rite, developing this Roman experimental rite, was published and likewise has no hint of the importance of a song of farewell. In addition to a responsory as proposed by the Roman experiment, the Chicago Rite offered a short litany "expressive of the better sentiments in the *Libera* . . . but better relating our 'deliverance' through the power of Christ's mysteries."[15] This Chicago Rite was accepted widely, even beyond the bounds of the diocesan experiment, and, as we saw above, greatly influenced the final American version of the *Rite* (1970). By that time the experimental rite of commendation and farewell already took roots in American soil and, although included only as a "substitute" in the *Rite* of 1970, it was destined to become the usual practice. Meanwhile, the subcommittee of the *Consilium* collected similar experiments and reactions to experiments from across the world and during 1968 prepared the typical edition of the *Rite* which was presented to the *Consilium* in October of that year and promulgated by Paul VI on August 15, 1969.[16] It was apparently during this final year of revision that the song of farewell emerged as the appropriate climax of the rite of final commendation and farewell. Unfortunately, it came as something quite new to the American experience when it appeared in the *Rite* of 1970. At least one article from 1970, commenting on the *Rite*, doesn't even mention the song of farewell.[17] Not only were other forms already more familiar, but introducing such an important sung piece encountered the already difficult situation that music in the liturgy was experiencing at that time.

Now, however, all this is history, and liturgical renewal in the 1980s cannot any longer claim the prerogatives of a necessary interim. One may look forward to "strong and effective songs of farewell"[18] that will characterize the rite of final commendation and farewell and thus allow it to express more fully the paschal faith and be a greater source of consoling hope through community song.

Limits and Exceptions: The final directive of no. 10 together with its American *addendum* flows also from the true nature of this rite. "The rite of final commendation and farewell is to be held only in the funeral celebration itself, that is, with the body present." In the United States an exception is made for those situations "where it is physically or morally impossible for the body of the deceased person to be present." Obviously a rite of giving the deceased over into God's hands and of leave-taking makes no sense when the liturgy being celebrated is not a funeral, properly speaking. This consequent position eliminates the anomaly of the former *Rite of Burial* where the *absolutio* was permitted after anniversary and memorial Masses for one or many of the faithful departed. That rite, carried out around a token bier or catafalque, was a remnant of medieval memorial services. Because the service was primarily one of intercessory prayer for the dead, the dramatic effect of such a catafalque was apparently believed to elicit greater devotion and prayer. The practice, still familiar not so long ago on All Souls Day, obviously lost all its meaning for twentieth-century Catholics and passed quietly into liturgical folklore with the coming of the liturgical renewal.

Quite a different matter is the situation where it is physically or morally impossible for the body to be present. Because the liturgy celebrated in such circumstances is every bit a "funeral" in the common understanding and sensitivity of the American people, a service of commendation and farewell is appropriate. Although the body cannot be physically present, the paschal faith dimension ritualized by prayer of commendation and a song of farewell deserves nonetheless to be expressed. Both the consoling hope thus celebrated and deepened and the opportunity for "leave-taking" ought not to be minimized, especially when the reality of death is rendered all the more veiled due to the absence of the corpse. Nevertheless, the principle concluding no. 10 in respect to the reality of commendation liturgy must likewise govern the adaptation of this rite to situations where the body is not present. Under no circumstances would holy water or incense, for example, be appropriate. The invitation to prayer and the commendation prayers themselves need to be appropriately adapted to the circumstances, always the responsibility of the priest (no. 24, 6). In such exceptional situations, it is again the song of farewell that clearly is the climax of the liturgy of commendation and of the entire *Rite of Funerals*. A future revision of the *Rite* for use in the United States might well consider the liturgical adaptations necessitated by this American exception and include some pastoral suggestions to facilitate its celebration. Even occasional abuses point up one thing for certain: a sound understanding of the nature of this rite of final commendation and farewell both necessitates and ought to guide these pastoral adaptations.

Finally, by way of evaluation, the rite of final commendation and farewell has not received sufficient attention in the United States. The place to begin is with brief, sensitive liturgical catechesis during preparation sessions with families and above all with the "doing" that is the celebration itself. At the present time few who take part in American Catholic funerals, including the bereaved, experience the commendation liturgy as something really special.

Pastorally the question arises whether "donating one's body to science," as it is stated colloquially, renders it morally impossible for the body to be present for the funeral liturgy. Ordinarily the body will be available as usual, but in each case an appropriate answer and pastoral solution will depend on the specific purpose for which the corpse is to be studied.

Except for those situations where, for example, medical research requires the entire corpse for a study of body tissue in a state as close as possible to the living state, there is generally no haste. Similarly, where certain vital organs have been pledged, they are ordinarily removed as close as possible to death, and the body is available for the funeral liturgy. When the body has been donated for teaching purposes, such as dissection of cadavers, it is ordinarily embalmed thoroughly, and may be delivered by the funeral director sometime after celebration of the liturgy in church. In these cases, authentic Catholic tradition requires, of course, that reasonable effort be made to safeguard the respect due the human body after death and to preserve the memory of the deceased. Occasionally one sees on family cemetery plots a simple plaque bearing the name of the deceased and an indication that his or her body had been donated for the betterment of human life through science, or the like.

The occasion of placing such a plaque on the family plot, where customary, can provide an excellent pastoral alternative to the ordinary ritual experience of terminating the funeral liturgy at the cemetery. Something similar might be considered any time the body of the deceased is not available for interment or cremation. In this way the integrity of the total ritual dynamism of the *Rite of Funerals* is preserved and allowed to serve the faith needs of the faithful.

In conclusion, therefore, "donating one's body to science" does not ordinarily constitute a moral impossibility for funeral liturgy with the body present. On the other hand, however, it does challenge pastoral creativity to provide both appropriate catechesis and a funeral liturgy fully imbued with the faith and principles of the *Rite of Funerals*.

Scriptural Readings (no. 11)
The biblical emphasis guiding the entire liturgical renewal receives special focus in the *Rite of Funerals*. Readings from Holy Scripture play a primary role in the funeral. Paragraph no. 11 tells why: "These [readings] proclaim the paschal mystery, support the hope of reunion in the kingdom of God, teach respect for the dead, and encourage the witness of Christian living." Put in another way, biblical readings are to be emphasized because they open up to those gathered for a funeral the God-given source of the paschal faith and consoling hope that makes the funeral Christian. This paragraph presumes the presence of biblical readings in the funeral liturgy; its purpose is to encourage their proper emphasis.

Another question altogether concerns the appropriateness of other than biblical readings. The Introduction

165

does not address this issue. One should follow the guidelines in the *Lectionary* and the General Instruction on the *Roman Missal*. In brief, it seems that there are sufficient opportunities during the times of visitation or wake as well as at the cemetery or place of disposition for those other-than-biblical pieces to be read by means of which one may wish to honor or pay tribute to the deceased. A reference or very brief piece might also be included in the homily by way of extension into today's world of the biblical faith proclaimed by the readings. In the opinion of this author, to replace Scripture with any other reading, no matter what the masterpiece, is to denude the *Rite* of an essential approach to faith through God's word. The pastoral task required by the *Rite* is to bring this death into touch with *God's word*. Any other "word" that can help do that—within reason, of course—is a welcome aid, but never a substitute. Yet, why is it that a nonbiblical reading, when taken as a substitute, seems to stand out in participants' memories? A pragmatic question, to be sure, and one that ought to help pastoral ministers be even more alert to their charge to preach God's word while seeking ever more effective means.

This paragraph, no. 11, stands in close relation to the later directives on the liturgy of the word (nos. 39-42), and especially no. 41 on the homily. "A brief homily should be given after the gospel, but without any kind of funeral eulogy." The Latin reads *"brevis habeatur homilia,"* which this author interprets as stating a pastoral norm. A funeral without a homily would thus be the exception. In 1968 the Chicago Rite left no doubt about the mind of its drafters: "A homily is obligatory, not optional," and, it elaborates, "it is not to be a eulogy."[19]

A pastoral note is added to no. 41 that reveals practical familiarity with funereal practice and a valuable catechetical sense. It works to encourage the homily from two points of view.

First, it contrasts praise of the deceased (eulogy) with "praise and gratitude to God for his gifts, particularly the gift of a Christian life, to the deceased person." This offers the homilist an opportunity to take the circumstances of the specific funeral into account. Unfortunately, still too many seem to read this directive as an excuse to deliver a secular eulogy with a veneer of Christian virtue. To prohibit this kind of eulogy is nothing new, as diocesan statutes indicate. Thus liturgical renewal in the 1980s must concern itself with this abuse wherever it exists, for too many faithful Catholics who expect and deserve what the *Rite* promises, are frustrated by the canned funeral eulogy that *mutatis mutandis* can apply to anyone[20] or by biographical sketches that hardly reflect Christian faith.

In the second place, the pastoral note to no. 41 gives the direction a homily, as distinct from a eulogy, would take. By summing up the fundamental theology expressed throughout the *Rite*, it requires the homily to take seriously the relation of Christian death to the paschal mystery and to the hope of eternal life. This means that the event of human death that has brought the participants together will be related to the paschal event. As delicately but also as frankly as possible the homily preaches the kerygma that death here and now is being touched by another now event, the effective presence of the risen Savior. Because of the paschal mystery, this particular death—in faith and in Christian community—becomes itself a Christian mystery, a baptismal mystery, a communion with the death and resurrection of Christ. Thus this death points beyond the now to the hope of everlasting life that the paschal mystery proclaims. The funeral homily offers the opportunity to dwell for a moment on this proclamation of faith.

To avoid this is to avoid the message that makes the Christian funeral unique. Why fear to preach this message of hope toward which the deceased person lived? Why deny the consolation of this hope to the bereaved who continue to live the tension between the "now" and the "not yet," who continue to live in a world where life is "being toward death"? With this basic direction the homilist will find in the Christian life of the deceased *and* in the Scripture readings chosen the right word to unfold briefly for these people here and now God's word of future hope and of being toward life.[21]

Psalms (no. 12): The *Rite of Funerals* employs the prayer of the psalms "to express grief and to strengthen genuine hope." With this concise designation the Introduction continues its emphasis on the place of Scripture in the Catholic funeral. The psalms are the inspired prayers of God's people, both individually and collectively. In them God's own word becomes our prayer in dialogue with him. For the Christian the psalms are thus also ecclesial and christological prayers, two important factors for their use in the funeral.[22]

The place of this *Rite* in its long Christian tradition leaves no doubt that psalms are meant to play a primary liturgical role in the contemporary Catholic funeral. The primacy of the psalms among funeral chants is not, however, a matter of quantity. It stems rather from the belief that inspired prayer by its nature is the expression and the nourishment of the faith in the face of grief and death.[23] The psalms open up to the bereaved Christian a means of uttering in prayer every movement of the soul faced with death, from the deepest anger to the most confident trust. Likewise the psalms paint in vivid biblical imagery the meaning of the sacramental actions by means of which the Christian community takes leave of its own. In a unique way the psalms and especially their antiphons in the first person put on the lips of the community the deceased's own prayers of praise and intercession. As such they are the accompaniment *par excellence* of every liturgical action surrounding the funeral: they guide the bereaved community meaningfully step-by-step from the very time death approaches through burial and into future times of commemoration.

These are some of the reasons why the psalms are so essential to funereal liturgy. Hence pastors, those responsible for pastoral liturgy, are urged by the Introduction to take seriously the need for catechesis whereby they try "to lead their communities to understand and appreciate at least the chief psalms of the funeral liturgy." Scriptural scholarship and exegesis do not constitute this catechesis, however much these disciplines undergird the teaching. Rather, such understanding and appreciation should open the faithful to the power, just indicated above, of the psalms "to express grief and to strengthen genuine hope." These phrases of paragraph no. 12 do not limit but summarize the many dispositions of paschal faith that the psalms express in the funeral. Like the song of farewell the funeral psalms remain unearthed treasures for most American Catholic parishes. Reports on the use of the experimental rite in 1968 correctly indicated pastoral difficulty with the psalms. By 1978 some progress has been made, yet this is an area that awaits special attention for any proposed renewal of the funeral liturgy during the 1980s. Time has not reduced the pastoral responsibility to catechize about the meaningful use of these psalms; the past decade has in fact made the task all the more crucial. The psalms are so important to the celebration of the *Rite* that the genuine renewal of Catholic funeral liturgy, up to now only barely initiated, ultimately will succeed or fail depending on the way people make the psalms their own prayers of grief and hope.

Related to this instruction on the psalms (no. 12) is the question of music in the funeral liturgy. The Introduction simply takes for granted that the psalms are by their nature poetic pieces to be sung. This is probably the single most serious factor behind the widespread failure to use the psalms well in the liturgy generally. And music at the funeral poses an even more difficult problem, as observed with the song of farewell above. Nevertheless, great musical progress is presently being made on the American scene. When pastors and musicians are convinced both of the priority of music in the liturgy and of the essential place of the psalms in the *Rite of Funerals*, then it will not be long until the Catholic funeral too will enjoy the fruits of contemporary musical progress. When for whatever reason funeral psalms are not sung, one ought to develop a style of recitation that is appropriate to the poetry and faith dimension expressed in the psalms. With very few exceptions, the psalms are not taken as readings, nor should they be read as such. Even to have a solo cantor chant the psalms or to have them recited against an instrumental background is often possible and preferable to much of what one hears in practice. When songs other than psalms are chosen because of "pastoral considerations," the Introduction (no. 12) directs, "these should reflect a 'warm and living love for sacred scripture' (*Sacrosanctum Concilium*, no. 24) and a liturgical spirit." It would seem that the latter spirit is best discerned through prayerful study of the funeral psalms themselves. Such a study undertaken to search out liturgically sound hymns and songs for use at funerals has led more than one parish ministry team to a new appreciation of the psalms themselves. It is not surprising that they next found ways to allow those psalms their rightful, musical place in the *Rite*.

Prayers (no. 13): The prayers of the *Rite* both declare in faith and petition in hope that the faithful dead enjoy happiness with God. Although these prayers express the same faith that is revealed in the readings and is made one's own in the homily and psalms, they have a special purpose. It is in the prayers that people are to articulate in a contemporary way this heritage of the faith. The drafters of the *Rite* had to face many questions in this regard. Thus it seems best to allow one of their own group to explain the intention with which they composed or restored the prayers in the *Rite of Funerals*. The following is this author's translation of remarks on these prayers by P.-M. Gy.[24] "These [prayers] must express, in a manner accessible to our contemporaries, the significance of the funeral liturgy, that is at once: expression of the faith of the Church regarding man's destiny, human respect due a deceased person and prayer for his salvation. With regard to the faith, it was fitting that the prayers express better and more amply the relation of Christian death to the paschal mystery; this has been done abundantly. It was likewise desirable that prayer asking that the deceased be purified of his sins (prayer in which the substance of Catholic faith about purgatory is implied) be disengaged from a certain number of allusions to a mythical journey by the soul after death. On the other hand, the text of the *Subvenite* did not seem to present any drawback.

"From time to time one hears criticism, in the name of biblical anthropology, that the Roman prayers for the dead pray especially for the soul of the deceased. This criticism is accurate, but only in one area. It holds for the prayers of the rite of burial of infants (*Rituale Romanum*, 1952, VII, 7) which seem to have been composed at the end of the Middle Ages. Those prayers speak only of the soul of these infants who already enjoy the vision of God, but they do not even hint at the existence of their bodies. It is to be sure neither necessary nor desirable that every prayer contain the entirety of Christian eschatology, but it is fitting that funeral prayers, taken as a whole, proclaim clearly that man is called to bodily resurrection and that, except in the case of infants, his soul would first have to be purified in order to enter the happiness of God. The first of these truths is expressed explicitly and with great insistence by the New Testament. The second, concerning which the New Testament offers no clarity at all, is found since antiquity in the prayer of the Church, and it is there she has confessed her faith. Yet, all truths are not of equal import; nor does this exclude research into new ways of expressing the deposit of the faith in the liturgy.[25]

"Up to now funeral liturgy prayed for the deceased, not for the living in their grief. In the sixteenth century the reformers adopted an opposite position in general: the living should pray for themselves, but to pray for the dead does not conform to the gospel. From an examination of the liturgical heritage of the Reformation and of the religious circumstances of the funeral, it seemed good to include (for example, for the station at the home of the deceased) prayer for the bereaved[26] as well as an element of thanksgiving for what the love of God was able to achieve in the life of the deceased. These are welcome additions that in no way detract from the importance of prayer for the deceased that Catholic faith requires. In some cases liturgies of the Anglican tradition[27] provided a source of inspiration or even models for editing texts that conform to the genius of the *Roman Ritual*, always less sober and less austere than the Missal.[28]

"Prayers at the funeral of infants posed two difficulties in particular. First of all, whether because infant mortality has diminished or because of the changed mentality toward family, one often experiences the death of a baby as a greater sorrow than formerly. Thus it was fitting that the prayers, while certainly professing that the baptized infant is enjoying happiness with God, ought not appear to neglect the parents' sorrow. The other difficulty concerned the funerals, not of baptized infants, but of babies who, although their parents wished to have them baptized, died before they could receive the sacrament. For this situation the prayers had to be prayer for both the parents and those around them and yet not ratify by the *lex orandi* and the magisterium of the Church the private opinions of theologians. Those in the *Rite* (nos. 235-237 and 226) pray only indirectly for the deceased baby but implore God's mercy for the parents who confide their child to him with all their faith and their hope.

"It is not expedient to return here to the general euchological pattern of the *Rite*.[29] But this is the place to point out one special difficulty with funeral services. Prescinding from the particular character of the Mass and the rite of farewell, funeral services do not require a thematic progression, and their prayers are very often interchangeable, as the rubric preceding no. 167 explicitly allows. Yet, one will always need to be careful about the choice of prayers at the beginning, especially if the faith of those gathered for the funeral does not seem very vital."

Office of the Dead (no. 14): The Office of the Dead has had a rich history in the devotional life of monastic communities since its introduction over a millenium ago. At different times and places, it likewise enjoyed a certain popularity in cathedral and parish life as well as in other religious communities. In recent times the renewal of the Liturgy of the Hours has incorporated this Office into the restored plan for the sanctification of time. Thus one looks to the principles of the *General Instruction on the Liturgy of the Hours* to guide the pastoral application of paragraph no. 14.

In the United States the growing awareness of the pastoral role the Liturgy of the Hours has in the life of a parish[30] urges pastoral teams not to pass over this paragraph of the *Introduction* as insignificant. Where the revised Liturgy of the Hours or the cathedral form of the hours is becoming the morning and evening prayer of the parish, it is fitting that one of these prayer services be celebrated as vigil for a deceased member of the community. In some places it is already customary to celebrate the wake service on the evening before the funeral in the church (no. 29), whether the body is laid out there or in a funeral home. That is an excellent opportunity to allow the renewal of the hours to guide the prayer of the local Church for the dead and the bereaved. When liturgically appropriate according to the calendar, the Office of the Dead offers a selection of readings, psalms, and prayers that serve well to focus one's prayer on the relationship of this death and its mystery to the paschal mystery of Christ. That Office thus highlights the faith dimension and the ecclesial character that are most indicative of the Christian funeral.

Pastorally, paragraph no. 14 recognizes the "demands of modern life" and other considerations that generally render a form of vigil or celebration of the word more feasible than the Office. Even where particular law, foundation or custom still prevail, such pastoral adjustments for the greater advantage of the people are recommended. Although one reads in this paragraph that the Office of the Dead "may continue to be celebrated," it certainly does not receive very enthusiastic encouragement. One reason for this is surely the fact that (much like Benediction of the Blessed Sacrament) it has simply passed out of pastoral practice, even in those relatively few places where it was recently still customary. Genuine pastoral renewal of the Liturgy of the Hours would still be many years in coming, despite the restoration of the Office already underway when this Introduction was drafted. Nevertheless, the similarity of wake service to the Office of the Dead (frequently quite superior in form and content) together with the favorable signs of the renewal of the hours in the United States leads this author to be more optimistic than the Introduction seems to be. A future pastoral Introduction proper to the United States could well include greater encouragement in this area.

Cremation and the Rite

More and more, Americans are changing from traditional burial or entombment to cremation or the more recent flameless process called calcination. Both processes are included in the term cremation, as used below. Since the Vatican Congregation for the Doctrine of the Faith (then the Holy Office) in 1963 made it permissible for Catholics to request cremation,[31] gradually increasing numbers of American Catholics have opted for this choice. Both the 1963 Instruction and paragraph no. 15 of the *Rite*, however, maintain the traditional preference for burial or entombment "as the Lord himself willed to be buried." Cremation or calcination is permitted to Catholics as long as local ordinaries see to it that the burial tradition is preserved—that no one is pressured to choose cremation—and judge that the request for cremation does not stem "from a denial of Christian dogmas, or from a sectarian spirit, or hate for the Catholic religion and the Church."[32] Similarly, scandal and religious indifferentism are to be avoided. Acceptable reasons for the choice of cremation include hygiene and economics as well as other public or private reasons. These are such that pastoral judgment in this matter rests finally on the presumed good faith of the persons making the request, unless serious evidence to the contrary prevails. Generally, most people who choose cremation do so for reasons of economy. On the average, cremation costs about one-fifth the price of traditional earth burial where casket, vault, cemetery lot, etc., also are required. Some opt for cremation for ecological or hygienic reasons. In addition, Christians often find this form of disposition attractive because of its simplicity. Some are asking whether the simplicity of cremation might not be more Christ-like today than the often arti-

175

ficial and far from simple arrangements of many American funerals with interment.

There are further considerations that pertain to cremation in the liturgical context. Obviously the availability, location, and layout of the crematory will affect the choice of plan and the unfolding of the liturgy.

In the matter of liturgy the *Rite* goes beyond the Instruction of 1963 which did not allow funeral rites to be celebrated in the crematory itself. Paragraph no. 15 envisions the funeral where cremation is to take place as following the full plan of the *Rite* customary in the region. According to the American version of Plan I everything except the station at the grave would take place as usual. "The rites ordinarily performed (*fiunt*) at the cemetery chapel or at the grave or tomb may be used (*peragi possunt*) in the crematory building." This final station or service would differ slightly according to whether it is celebrated in the place of cremation (crematory building) or, when appropriate, in the place of interment of the ashes.[33] Obvious care is necessary to adapt the ritual to the differing situations, and only repeated pastoral practice will indicate the most appropriate way to proceed.

In any case, Plan I in the United States with cremation ordinarily implies movement from the (funeral) home to the church and from the church to the crematory. Final disposition of ashes would take place at some later time, allowing for cremation and cooling (upwards of four hours minimum), as well as respecting family wishes and state law. Plan I becomes awkward and involves returning the body to the funeral director for cremation, postponing a service at the cemetery. The question has already been posed whether the funeral might be held in the church after cremation with the urn containing the ashes present in place of the body itself. Is it not simpler, and more economical, to allow the funeral director to proceed with cremation prior to removal of the remains of the deceased to the church? Practically speaking, one would answer in the affirmative. Liturgically, on the other hand, it is the body and not just remains that is honored during the funeral liturgy in the Church. The Congregation for Sacraments and Divine Worship thus offers a liturgical answer:

"It does not seem suitable to celebrate with the ashes present the rite which is intended to honor the body of the dead. This is . . . to respect the integrity of the signs within the liturgical action. In fact, the ashes which are an expression of the corruptibility of the human body are unable to express the inherent character of one 'sleeping,' awaiting the resurrection. The body, not the ashes, receives liturgical honors since it was made the temple of the Spirit of God in baptism. It is important to respect the verity of the sign in order that the liturgical catechesis and the celebration itself be authentic and fruitful."[34]

What are the pastoral alternatives offered by the *Rite* that respect both liturgy and the practical needs of the bereaved? In the first place, knowledge of the *Rite* and its spirit is all the more imperative in these new pastoral situations, both to guide families in making liturgical cremation arrangements and to preside at the liturgy itself where cremation is involved.

Once the funeral director and crematory have been chosen, the next step is to determine whether Plan I as celebrated in the United States will serve appropriately in view of the above principles. One criterion for the use of Plan I must be whether it is feasible to celebrate the liturgy in the church with the body present. Every attempt should be made to render the full celebration of the American rite possible. Where distance between (funeral) home, church, and separate crematory is the issue, the growing practice of waking the deceased in the church itself has the advantage that the body is already present in the building (often in a space or chapel set aside for wakes) before the station in the church

177

formally begins. Thus the station "in the home," the procession with the body into the church proper, and the funeral Mass, with or without the commendation liturgy, would all take place as usual. Afterwards, depending on distance and arrangements, the funeral liturgy proper would be concluded at the crematory with either the final commendation and farewell, if not previously celebrated in church, or an adapted form of the station at the cemetery. Again, reception and final disposition of the ashes would have to be considered separately, though also liturgically, insofar as possible in the circumstances.

Where the cremation arrangements make it morally impossible to bring the body to church, the funeral Mass can often be celebrated as usual (with or without the final commendation and farewell) before cremation and followed by the closing station (with or without final commendation and farewell) at the crematory. Similarly, where the funeral arrangements conflict with a time for the funeral Mass before cremation, one might choose Plan II, thus celebrating the liturgy of the word and the commendation liturgy in the cemetery mortuary chapel, if this is a (cemetery) chapel properly speaking and not just a chapel-like funeral parlor. In such a case, the final commendation and farewell would be preferred over the alternate third station. As soon as possible afterwards—preferably immediately as part of the whole funeral—the funeral Mass would be celebrated. Here two additional pastoral options for use in the United States deserve recommendation. In the situation just mentioned, where the funeral Mass in the parish church follows cremation immediately, it would be pastorally advisable and liturgically sound to begin the Mass with the liturgy of the eucharist. Not only does this practice, not uncommon elsewhere,[35] keep the funeral liturgy from becoming too long and burdensome, it likewise demonstrates graphically that all the parts constitute one unified funeral liturgy. Secondly, when

178

even such an arrangement would be a severe inconvenience due to distance, illness or the like, the option to celebrate the funeral Mass (with or without the body present) elsewhere than in the parish church, e.g., the family home, a hospital or nursing home chapel, ought to be available to the parish priest. With sound pastoral judgment, founded on knowledge of the *Rite* and committed to the faith the *Rite* proclaims, he and his pastoral team hereby serve their people with greater flexibility and inspiration.

One further liturgical alternative suggests itself: Where the arrangements work out that the cremation will have taken place between a final service of closing the casket and the funeral mass and commendation liturgy in the church, the funeral can be brought to a fitting conclusion by celebrating the third station around the final disposition of the ashes—especially if that is to be an interment or entombment of the ashes. Concretely this plan lends itself best for those funerals where an interval of time, such as a full night, intervenes between the service of closing and the final disposition of ashes. The casket closing can take place as part of a wake service or, if immediately before Mass, as an adapted form of the first station in the (funeral) home.

Although Catholic directives have not taken up the manner of disposing of the ashes after cremation, the role the cemetery plays in the memory of Christians as a pledge of resurrection suggests a certain preference for preserving the ashes in a columbarium,[36] usually available in modern cemeteries. This idea has taken even more explicit form in one Dutch church visited by this author[37] where a space in the vestibule was being converted into such a columbarium for the ashes of the parish dead who request cremation. In doing this the pastoral team is aware, of course, that catechesis accompanying the move must insure that cremation is not thereby shown greater approval than earth burial and also that an elitist attitude does not develop around a twentieth-century version of interment *ad sanctos*. However this may be, the experiment impresses upon us the attention due the kinds of pastoral circumstances that surface when greater numbers of Catholics begin to choose cremation. One of the greatest marks of the new *Rite* is its ability to provide an appropriate faith dimension for Catholic funerals even under these newest of circumstances. Once again the *Rite* itself invites us to be pastorally creative; it is a pastoral responsibility to translate this invitation into living liturgy for an ever-growing number of Catholics who request cremation.

OFFICES AND MINISTRIES TOWARD THE DEAD (NOS. 16-20)

Having introduced the *Rite of Funerals* in its various forms from the most traditional model to the most recent adaptation to local needs, the Introduction now returns in greater detail to the context of Christian community as first mentioned in no. 2, within which Catholic funerals can alone have their full meaning.

Ministry of the Whole Church

Paragraph no. 16 spells out what is the key to a genuine renewal of the Catholic funeral: all who belong to the people of God have a responsibility to the dead according to their relationship within the Christian community. The exercise of offices and ministries flows from Christian community. Thus the community as a whole shares a common concern for the funeral liturgy. Each one must therefore contribute accordingly to its celebration, if it is to proclaim the paschal faith of the community and at once offer hope-filled consolation to the bereaved. All of us are thus required by the *Rite* to discern and exercise our role and welcome all others concerned to do the same. This is a challenge to priest and people alike. Yet, we all must be open to it, if the liturgical renewal is to happen—if funeral liturgy is to have its place in the life of the Church as a truly liturgical action.[38]

Most intimately related to the deceased are, of course, the parents, spouse, close friends and relatives, those we term "the bereaved." They both minister to the dead and are ministered to themselves, by the community. Their ministry consists mostly in preparing a last farewell, in calling family and friends together for leave-taking. Here the funeral liturgy plays a principal role for Catholics. One anomaly of contemporary American Catholics (and other Christians, as well, to be sure) is that most time and effort devoted to the funeral has hardly anything to do with the spiritual. Most bereaved come to the liturgy in the church almost totally unprepared spiritually and with a deep sigh of relief that it is almost over. They desire most simply to sit back and rest peacefully, enjoying the consolation of their faith, while the priest does what the Church requires for Christian burial. Of course their participation in the liturgy is above all an active silence, an active listening, a being touched. Whatever their grief allows them to sing or say or hear is sufficient; others of us perform those ministries both for them and the deceased. Yet, their ministry of preparing the funeral for themselves and their families and friends cannot rightfully overlook the climactic moment of the Catholic funeral—the liturgical moments in the interval between death and burial. It is the ministry of the priest and those who care for funerals (parish lay ministers as well as the funeral directors, especially when they are themselves members of the Catholic community) to stand by the bereaved in their service of preparation. What parish priest has time to spend more than several brief visits with the family struck by death? Yet, at what other time in the life of that family is his ministry more crucial? While certain shifts in priorities are imperative to provide time rightly due to parish liturgical life—including the funeral—even then priests will need to engage the help of others in the funeral ministry of the Church. His responsibility is not only to minister to the dead and bereaved himself but to animate others in their responsibility. The ministry of "those who take care of funerals" in the United States falls primarily to funeral directors, but it is the priest who is responsible for their liturgical formation. We saw by way of example above how Catholic funeral directors have a special ministerial role in the Catholic community—a ministry of their own profession and a shared ministry with the priest. In addition to the funeral director, "those who take care of funerals" could include parish lay ministers who offer time and energy to help with immediate family needs but also to stimulate, through discussion groups, home visits and the like, an on-going awareness of the Catholic funeral as something very special in Catholic Church life. Part of this helping ministry—by funeral directors and others—is to aid the bereaved to see the priority and importance of liturgical preparation. Enough has been said above about the interrelationship between liturgy and the psychology of grief also to appreciate such an emphasis. In other words, the *Rite of Funerals* is inviting us to work toward a goal with very radical consequences for parish funeral ministry. Despite the chaos surrounding death everything in the *Rite* implies that sufficient time must be spent with bereaved Catholics to help them prepare spiritually and liturgically. Meeting with the funeral director, choosing a casket, looking over a cemetery lot or tomb, following up on insurance policies, etc., cannot be allowed to continue to devour all of their time and energy at such a crucial moment of faith. The more Catholic people can be encouraged to pre-plan much of the details of their funeral and the more lay funeral ministers can begin to serve the parish community assisting bereaved families with crisis details (buying extra groceries, lodging, children, etc.) and adult funeral education, the more will spiritual and liturgical preparation for the funeral begin to characterize Catholic pastoral care for the dead and the bereaved. The "busy therapy" that occupies mind and heart with details of death's trappings can then give way to occupying oneself with the liturgy of death's mystery that is caught up in the mystery of Jesus' death and resurrection—the mystery of life through death. Is the color of the casket's lining or the wording on the family wreath really more important—even humanly speaking—than the family's choice of gospel reading or the opportunity to talk prayerfully about the baptismal symbolism relating this death to the paschal mystery, or even the opportunity to approach the sacrament of reconciliation (especially at such a time when the need for healing memories and for family reconciliation is often so great)?

This attitude toward funerals will not happen without years of parish catechesis. Also, seeing it happen little by little but over and over again cannot but convince all of its value. The era of the pornography of death is past. People are now willing to talk about death and dying. With the right counsel many would act on the value of pre-planning much of their funeral, including much of its liturgy. Both spiritually and psychologically such an approach is good, human grief therapy. It is obvious, therefore, that the *Rite of Funerals*—the funeral liturgy—belongs in the full life context of death and care for the dead and the bereaved.

This is the ministerial context of Christian community, therefore, in which the priest exercises his office and ministry as teacher of the faith and minister of consolation. Rather than being an isolated figure who performs church rituals, he serves a real Christian need of the bereaved and the community. As teacher of the faith he will have wrestled himself prayerfully with the mystery of death and the paschal mystery, so that he may better open the Scriptures and Catholic tradition to those he touches personally and to those who listen to his homily and interventions in the liturgy. As minister of consolation nothing will have a greater effect than his own faith in Jesus dead and risen and his hope in the fullness of baptismal life in God's "time" beyond death. Few consoling words are needed; mostly just his priestly presence and that of the helping Church may well be enough. Thus, as celebrant of the funeral liturgy and above all the eucharist, he relates the deceased person, all the bereaved, the local parish community and all the communion of saints with Christ who offers eternally his saving sacrifice of love to his Father.

The Responsibility for Funeral Ministry (nos. 17-20)
The *Rite* impresses upon us that the Catholic funeral is especially a liturgy of paschal faith. Having introduced the need for a sense of funeral ministry, the Introduction reminds priests and all concerned of certain specific duties (offices) proper to this ministry.

One of these duties concerns the faith dimension of the Catholic funeral. Beyond the spiritual preparation of the bereaved leading into the funeral liturgy, it is the duty of priest and ministers "to strengthen the hope of those present and to foster their faith in the paschal mystery and the resurrection of the dead" (no. 17). This implies a good sense of pastoral balance. The liturgy that directly focuses attention on commendation of the deceased at once includes the living and does so in a way that supports their faith and hope while taking care not to be insensitive to their grief. The specific blend of celebrating paschal faith and offering the consolation of hope in the resurrection while being sensitive to grief and mourning was touched on above.[39] What deserves attention here is above all the pastoral sensitivity to grief that is asserted again in paragraph no. 18. Far too often celebrants of funeral liturgy fall into the subtle trap of

184

confusing paschal faith with superficial glee—of allowing the secular mood of death denial to influence liturgical expression of a faith that takes death so seriously. Christian happiness for the deceased who are entering into a new form of union with God is very subtle, and is itself part of the mystery of death. Accepting death, Christian joy in faith cannot deny grief. It is an injustice to the bereaved when the *Rite* that offers so much by way of Christian support and hope is misused as an attempt, however unconsciously, to cover up grief and the reality of death with saccharine eulogies, music, and rhetoric. A harsh statement, admittedly, but perhaps shock therapy will convince all of us once and for all of the need to devote time to prayerful and faith-filled study of the Christian eschatology implicit in the *Rite*.[40] Such a deepening of one's paschal faith together with coming to grips with one's own mortality—no small thing—cannot help but make the celebrant of the *Rite* more aware of the pastoral sensitivity called for by his duty to lighten the burden of the faithful while respecting their grief.

The *Rite* asks the homilist to avoid banal remarks that could apply to any death, but rather to take into account the authenticity of faith that marked the life and death of the deceased. Relating the death of a given deceased person to the saving death and resurrection of Jesus cannot fail to take his or her life into account. It is reconciliation and salvation through the paschal mystery that the Christian funeral proclaims—not primarily the sanctity of the deceased. Although one's sins remain a matter between the deceased and God, sinfulness is acknowledged implicitly by the *Rite*, and God's universal will to forgive is proclaimed. While the celebrant (generally) would have no reason to dwell on one's sinfulness or, for example, situations of "public sin," he certainly ought to be aware of such circumstances every bit as much as he is of the outstanding virtues of the deceased.[41]

There is another set of circumstances to which the Introduction wisely calls the celebrant's attention, namely, the almost universal fact that people of all kinds gather for funerals. Besides the Catholic and other Christian faithful there are persons, Catholic or non-Catholic, who seldom or never participate in the eucharist or who seem to have lost their faith, as well as those who are not Christian and those who are atheist. The priest is reminded that he is a minister of Christ's gospel to all people; a fact that is nowhere so evident as at the funeral. Pastorally the celebrant will of course be respectful of opinions and faith convictions different from those manifest in the *Rite*. Nevertheless, his faith in that which marks the Catholic funeral as Catholic is always his guide to celebrating the *Rite*. In fact, times when a large percentage of those present represents such a varied background provide a good challenge. They test the celebrant's ability to preside in such an authentic way that the inherent meaning of Catholic funeral symbolism finds its proper expression—a good test of both celebrant and *Rite*. A further degree of sensitivity is needed when members of the immediate family itself are not of the Catholic faith or are separated from the Church. The French edition of this pastoral instruction advises concisely that one should be sensitive to their way of thinking and welcome their legitimate desires, but at the same time help them understand the meaning of what the Church does.[42]

This is an appropriate context in which to note the 1976 Decree by the Congregation for the Doctrine of the Faith on "public celebrations of Mass in the Catholic Church for other deceased Christians."[43] Although these are not funeral Masses properly speaking, they are memorial Masses, and people often think of them in the same context as a funeral. This is especially true when such a Mass is celebrated for a person of national renown. When a very diverse group gathers for the occasion, the celebrant and those responsible would want to be attentive to the same kind of pastoral needs. In both contexts one of the most sensitive issues is the matter of intercommunion among Christians of different traditions. Catholic directives governing occasions when other Christians may be admitted to eucharistic communion[44] exclude in principle intercommunion at funeral or memorial Masses. It is simply irresponsible to pretend this directive does not exist. However painful this experience of separation in faith, it is not considered sufficient reason to deviate from the Roman Catholic theological principle that in practice, eucharistic communion is a sacrament of unity and ecclesial communion is its manifestation. Exceptions are permitted under specified conditions only because eucharistic nourishment is held to be a source of divine grace that one ought not to be deprived of when it is otherwise unavailable. The Secretariat for Christian Unity interprets this decree of the Vatican Council strictly. Pastorally, that official interpretation is not universally observed. As a result not a little confusion exists among Catholics and other Christians alike. Such a state of confusion only aggravates the pain of separation, especially at moments of intensity such as death. Some pastors believe, however, that the Christian unity between the bereaved and the deceased, together with the hardship of ecclesial separation at the time of death, is sufficient pastoral reason to invite non-Catholic members of the funeral—especially family and close friends—to receive communion, should they wish to do so according to their own consciences. There are those who do this delicately and with sufficient explanation, during the funeral liturgy, stating, for example, why the Christian family of the deceased has been invited to receive together if they wish, while other non-Catholics are asked to refrain. Still others indiscriminately offer invitations to all present just prior to holy communion. Although neither approach is presently acceptable according to the ecumenical Secretariat, the former shows pastoral respect for the principles of the Vatican II Decree on Ecumenism but interprets them differently. The latter is inexcusable pastoral carelessness that ultimately fosters nothing but an empty sacramentalism and ecclesial indifferentism. Unfortunately it is questionable, however, whether either unauthorized approach is fostering true ecumenism; the Secretariat for Unity clearly believes they are not. Meanwhile a certain common-law practice seems to be developing. For the present, however, sound pastoral practice must take seriously its responsibility both to the Catholic *magisterium* and to the local church. While recognizing that there are exceptions to the current law on intercommunion, this author advocates following the pastoral directives and interpretation of the Secretariat for Christian Unity but with two action-oriented recommendations. First of all, whether for funerals or other situations, pastoral care demands that the faithful and others involved be advised delicately but clearly how Catholic Church law regards intercommunion. Serious parish-wide catechesis, including especially the reasons of Catholic faith underlying the present directives, is undoubtedly the best way to disperse the present confusion. One ought to include also some emphasis on the sensitivity involved in dealing with ecumenical pastoral needs and the need to discern whether the exceptional nature of the Christian funeral might not constitute sufficient gravity of reason to warrant a further relaxation of the general rule. (In this context it is good to explain also the canonical tradition that any person approaching communion in good faith will ordinarily not be refused without grave reason. Thus Catholics will be better prepared for those occasions—not so infrequent anymore—when other Christians who share the Catholic faith in the eucharist approach and are given holy communion.)

The second recommendation concerns the nature of the Christian funeral and its consequences in ecumenical pastoral perspective. The very nature of the Christian funeral offers an invitation to parishes, diocesan liturgical commissions, the Federation of Diocesan Liturgical Commissions, and the United States Bishops' Committee on the Liturgy to study the whole problem of sacramental intercommunion. For intercommunion at a Catholic funeral to be acceptable according to the Vatican II decree, there must exist a theologically valid reason for granting a further exception to the Catholic principle that governs eucharistic communion and ecclesial communion. Eucharistic communion at the funeral Mass explicitly manifests belief in the communion of saints of which all the faithful are members and in which the deceased now participates in a new way. That unity of believers extends beyond the boundaries of the Church on earth and beyond the theological differences that divide the one Body of Christ. Eucharistic communion at the funeral Mass (according to the *Rite of Funerals*) sacramentalizes the unity of the full Christian community in the mystery of the communion of saints, and thus expresses explicitly the belief that the deceased is still one with the faithful on earth and enjoys the fruit of their intercession on his behalf at the eucharistic commemoration of the Lord's Passover.

On the occasion of a funeral Mass, therefore, it seems that those other Christians among the bereaved who share eucharistic faith with Catholics who wish to receive eucharistic communion as sacrament of the full Christian unity now enjoyed by the faithful deceased deserve special pastoral attention. The verity of sacramental communion at the funeral, where it is a manifestation of faith in everlasting life, specifically relating the death of this Christian to the paschal mystery of Christ, seems to demand the fullest possible participation by all who believe in eucharistic communion with Jesus dead and risen. Thus adherence to the Catholic sacramental theology that establishes the ecclesial principle would determine this ex-

189

ception. Exceptions to the principle are presently allowed because of physical and moral impossibility to share eucharistic communion and the spiritual nourishment it offers the individual Christian in genuine need. In the case of intercommunion at the funeral the exception would flow from Christian faith that life after death and the communion of saints transcend the failures of all our earthly churches to embody perfectly the Body of Christ. All the other conditions required by the Secretariat for Unity for use of such exceptions would, of course, apply. Sacramental intercommunion at the funeral Mass would thus be explicitly the sacrament of that everlasting communion with Christ into which the faithful deceased has been received and at once by exception, the sacrament of longed-for ecclesial communion.

These few concise lines which the Introduction devotes to the responsibilities of the priest leave no doubt about how awesome is his ministry toward the dead and the bereaved. Taking the funeral in its fullest context, extending even from before death in most contemporary cases through follow-up pastoral visits to those left behind, there is no other pastoral opportunity its equal. In order to exercise this ministry to its fullest possible extent, local bishops and parish priests are urged by the *Rite* itself to involve deaconal and lay ministers in their work. The importance of lay leadership at funeral prayer in the absence of an ordained minister has already been established in no. 5 above. Paragraph no. 19 takes up two specific situations of shared funeral ministry. A prior question deserves attention, however: What is the ecclesial rationale for this variety of office and ministries in face of death?

Death itself, we must remember, holds such an important place in the mystery of Christian life that the death of any one Christian is a community—an ecclesial—affair. It places demands on the entire community; it creates immediate needs involving the dead person and the living which the Church knows are hers to meet. The responsibility to meet those pastoral needs, both spiritual and broadly human, belongs to the office of the ordained minister. By virtue of his relationship to the Catholic community—his pastoral office—the parish priest (or presbyter) has the primary responsibility to see to it that Christian deceased and bereaved enjoy the ministry of the Church which has its climax in the liturgy of Christian burial. The parish priest is thus the first responsible minister of that liturgy. Current law as well as the *Rite of Funerals* extends to the deacon the "ordinary" ministry of presiding at the funeral, except at the funeral Mass.[45] The principle is, of course, a pastoral one, responding to the spiritual needs of the faithful as fully as possible. It is the same principle that extends liturgical funeral ministry to the laity in the absence of a priest or deacon—one more graphic witness to its importance in ecclesial life. Because the Christian funeral is considered an ecclesial duty as well as of special spiritual benefit to the deceased and bereaved, pastoral necessity calls forth lay ministers to exercise the liturgical ministry in place of priest or deacon. This is an "extraordinary" or special funeral ministry flowing from the authority of the local ordinary or, in some cases, from liturgical law, the *Rite* itself. In paragraph no. 19, as the redactors assure us, the Introduction provides directives for *two* distinct situations of this shared funeral ministry.

The first section deals with situations where no priest is available at all. Where the parish enjoys the ministry of a deacon, the care for the funeral falls first to him. Where no ordained ministers serve the Catholic community the local ordinary may designate lay persons (men and women) to provide the funeral liturgy of the Church, and implicitly, therefore, the attendant pastoral care as well. Section three, appended to no. 19 in the United States edition, directs local ordinaries that the National

191

Conference of Bishops has authorized them to depute lay persons for this special ministry, in the total absence of priest or deacon. The curial language makes this sound very exceptional. It is rather this pastoral situation that ought to be exceptional, especially in the United States where permanent deacons cover so many pastoral needs of service. Yet, where such situations do not exist—not infrequently in remote rural American missions—the *Rite*, confirmed by the American bishops, offers the local ordinary the next best solution to an exceptional pastoral situation. How many ordinaries have actually appointed lay funeral ministers? Some are not aware that the opportunity exists; others believe it is not opportune. "The people are not ready," some insist. Unfortunately little or nothing is being done to help them to be ready. Meanwhile, at the time of death the pastoral needs of the faithful in these remote areas are barely met, if at all. Yet, here is the exact situation where the instituted lay acolyte or lector, because of their official service to word and sacrament, or even male or female readers and special eucharistic ministers of the parish, could well serve these exceptional needs. As a reminder to all in pastoral authority, the *Rite of Funerals* insists by means of this directive that no Catholic should face the death of a loved one without the prayer of the Church for the deceased and, for the living, the funeral celebration of paschal faith and the consolation of Christian hope.

The second section of no. 19 leaves this extreme situation—presently still relatively rare in the United States—and turns to the increasingly more frequent one where the priest can only be available for the funeral Mass and not the other parts of the Christian funeral. Where there is also no deacon (or, we would add, other special minister), the laity themselves are urged to lead the liturgy at the wake and cemetery. Obviously, this is but one final effort to insure the faith content of these special moments surrounding death and burial. Here the *lex orandi* is impressing upon us again the importance for the faith (*lex credendi*) of the full Catholic funeral. Nevertheless, in practice the bereaved and other mourners are ordinarily not sufficiently grounded in leading others in prayer or, when they are (such as certain members of prayer groups), the situation is frequently too emotionally loaded to take advantage of this option. Much pastoral catechesis remains to be done in this entire area, but where lay group prayer at wake and cemetery is concerned, the charismatic renewal has special gifts to offer Catholics generally.

Here as in so many ways, the *Rite of Funerals* again invites us "to be somewhere we have never been before." Consider for example the following scenario: The parish priest or deacon, accompanied by a well-trained, responsible and spiritual lay minister, man or woman, visits the family (hopefully not the first visit, if the deceased has been seriously ill for any length of time). As arrangements for the funeral liturgy in all its dimensions are being made, the ordained minister asks the family if the lay minister can be of any help with prayer at special moments in the funeral home and cemetery. The priest and deacon, and possibly the lay minister, will often not be strangers to the family; sometimes the deacon, in his ministry of service, will have been even more directly involved with the family than the priest. Where possible, these same ministers would also assist the priest at the liturgy in the church, especially at the eucharist and the rite of farewell. Their presence mirrors the thread of unity present throughout the full liturgy of the funeral. This kind of shared funeral ministry is the best preparation of both parish and deacon or lay ministers for those situations where the deacon or laity alone care for the entire funeral. Obviously such a scenario is unrealistic—unless, of course, Catholics today continue to pursue the priorities of renewal. Sharing the ministry of funerals, especially with deacons and special lay ministers, is not merely a patch on an old wineskin. It is

193

already proving to be the new wineskin whereby the liturgy of paschal faith and hopeful consolation can be celebrated fully by American Catholics as they look forward to the twenty-first century.

Closing this overview of shared responsibility for funeral ministry the Introduction cites *verbatim* no. 32 of the *Constitution on the Sacred Liturgy*. In the liturgy—and certainly in death—all persons are equal before God. Those responsible for the liturgy of funerals are directed by the Council itself that the days when funerals were ranked according to prestige and stipends are past history. Any hint of distinctions other than those of service within the life of the Church are inappropriate, and even some of those deserve monitoring. Pomp and circumstance, even the verbal variety not untypical of the eulogy, is no more welcome here than exaggeration at the funeral home. Once again, gospel simplicity lends the Christian funeral its most noble beauty, and gospel simplicity is the same for all.

National Adaptations (nos. 21-22)

Paragraph nos. 21-22 treat adaptations by the Conferences of Bishops. There remains little to add to our earlier remarks on the preparation of the American study edition of the *Rite*. Suffice it to emphasize here further directives that may come from the bishops.

Paragraph no. 21, 4-6 reminds all that future pastoral adaptations of the study edition can be expected. The Bishops' Committee on the Liturgy has before it the task, awaited by a majority of the American clergy, of publishing an edition that is "best suited to pastoral purposes" (no. 21, 6).

The pattern chosen for the Canadian *Rite* offers a clear model. Following the option to print only the plan in general use as their point of departure, the editors managed to maintain a simple flow of "three services" from the home (in this case, the wake) to the church and

194

finally to the cemetery. All variations on this central plan are printed as options separately elsewhere in the book. For example, on those occasions when the final commendation might take place at the cemetery, the full third service is printed separately. The same is done when cremation is part of the third service. And so on. Similarly, in each position where optional prayers, chants and the like are to be chosen, they print two; the others, including some proper to the Canadian church, are collected in an appendix. A glance at the book's Table of Contents[46] reveals this pastoral clarity:

PASTORAL NOTES

FUNERAL OF ADULTS
I. Wake service: first form
                    alternative form

II. Service in the church
    Reception at the church
    Funeral Mass
    Final commendation and farewell

III. Prayers at the cemetery

FUNERALS OF CHILDREN
I. Wake service: for a baptized child
                    for an unbaptized child

II. Service in the church
    Reception at the church
    Funeral Mass
    Final commendation and farewell

III. Prayers at the cemetery

APPENDIX OF PRAYERS
1. General prayers for the dead
2. Prayers in special circumstances
3. Prayers outside Mass

4. Third penitential rite
5. General intercessions
6. Song of farewell
7. Cremation
8. Commendation and farewell at the cemetery
9. Delayed funeral liturgy
10. Antiphons

We have already pointed out in this chapter the need for a revision of the present American version of the Introduction as well. The task there is "to adapt and supplement the introductory material . . . so that the ministers will fully *understand* the significance of the rites and *celebrate* them effectively" (no. 21, 5; emphasis added). We saw above that failure to celebrate funeral liturgy effectively results generally from a faulty understanding and practice of liturgical renewal. Structurally very little about the funeral has changed; liturgically everything has a new emphasis. A revised American edition of the *Rite* will be in a better position to teach this change of emphasis than the 1971 edition. Our own American experience through a decade of pastoral use of the *Rite* and other national editions, such as the Canadian, French, Irish and German ones noted above, offer rich pastoral resources from which to prepare a revised Introduction.

At the same time the options of no. 21, 4 would be given renewed attention. The translations can now be evaluated against considerable experience, and appropriate hymns and music added. The greatest single weakness of the present American *Rite* is the lack of music in the book. Again, the last decade in the United States has seen the composition and use of excellent hymns, psalm settings, and specific funerary chants. Again, other more recent national *Rituals* have shown the way to implement the task of adding American music to the Roman typical edition. Pastoral experience suggests that certain pieces be included in their proper place in the *Rite*, e.g., music for the song of farewell. A music supplement could also be appended to the book. Although not every parish will use the music in the same way, its very presence in the printed *Ritual* demonstrates the principle that music is normative for the fullness of liturgical celebration. Another advantage of including music in the national *Rite* is the fostering of a national musical tradition for funeral liturgy. Mobility in the United States is such that people come from all parts of the country to "attend" funerals. A national repertoire—however small—of funerary compositions could help translate "attending" funerals into liturgical participation. In the same way a regional or diocesan music supplement could make local and ethnic favorites readily accessible to every parish. Here again fullness of celebration through sung participation must be understood and accepted as a priority before faithful people and priests will undertake the time and effort necessary to reach such a goal—surely the intention of no. 24, 4 where the Introduction recommends that singing be made available "as often as opportune."[47]

In paragraph 22 there remain two points that the experience of the last decade highlights. First, a revised edition should take into account special American situations where proper prayers not in the Latin *editio typica* may be needed (22, 6). Some examples include prayers when the body of the deceased cannot be present, prayers for the death of a teenager, prayers in the case of a sudden, tragic death, prayers for the rural funeral. And so on. In this context one becomes very aware of the need for model prayers that the pastoral minister might adapt as needed. Model prayers could be given to guide the celebrant just as in the case of invitations to prayer the rubric "these or similar words" guides the content of his interventions. Good models, both in the *Ritual* and in practice, would serve to moderate persisting tendencies toward verbosity. Here again, a common-law practice is already current. Thus, teaching good liturgical prayer by example would be a far better solution than pretending that only the prayers of the *Rite* are being used. The revised *Rite* can offer a fresh solution to these pastoral needs.

In the second place no. 22, 4 reminds the Bishops' Conference of its policy, appended to no. 19, that a lay person may be deputed to lead the station in the church. A review of this practice and a look at the even greater needs than a decade ago might lead the Bishops' Committee on the Liturgy to consider the proposal noted above regarding lay funeral ministers who could assist the priest or deacon in the broader funeral ministry rather than only substitute in their absence at liturgy. Such a ministry would render their service in the liturgy itself far more meaningful.

Paragraph no. 22, 6 states the principle guiding the choice of liturgical color for the funeral liturgy. The American *Rite* specifies that white, violet, or black vestments may be worn at funeral services. The color black has almost entirely fallen into disuse. American Catholic sensibilities no longer seem able to express "Christian hope enlightened by the paschal mystery" in black vestments. We are still too close to the identification of funerary black with dread, dirge, and near despair. On the other hand, there are some funerals when white vestments might be "offensive to human sorrow." In such cases violet, especially a springtime violet that expresses both the harsh reality of winter and the spring's hope for new life, or a blend of violet and white might serve best. Only pastoral sensitivity can discern the right decision, but it is well for funeral ministers to consider these options for the genuine good of the bereaved. Some commentators recommend violet for the wake and white for the funeral liturgy in the church, intending to ritualize thereby a movement from grief to acceptance and joyful hope. That is a helpful guide, but pastorally one would not want to force such distinctions. Grief does not obey liturgical structures. Sometimes just the reverse will occur, where the hope and support experienced during the wake give way to agonizing sorrow at the utter finality of the funeral Mass, that last Mass when the body is in the parish church, and ultimately interment. In the same way one ought not to presume that white vestments are always to be preferred. The American *Rite* is pastorally wise to preserve all three colors, expecially white and violet, even though the white of Easter hope remains the predominant choice in practice.

The Role of the Priest: Preparation, Planning, Celebration (nos. 23-25)
The Introduction closes with summary remarks about the priest's duties of preparing and planning the celebration. Most of these items have been treated earlier in this chapter. His responsibilities and freedom are emphasized (no. 23) and general guidelines specify peculiarities of the *Rite* to which he should be alert (no. 24). Paragraph no. 25 appropriately places his funeral ministry in a total pastoral context. As it sets the stage in the *Rite* for the funeral liturgy to follow, no. 25 both draws together all that went before and looks beyond to the *Rite of Funerals* come alive in pastoral usage. It is precisely this fourfold mandate that serves as the context for our final chapter on funeral ministry today.

"25. The celebration of the funeral liturgy with meaning and dignity and the priest's ministry to the dead presuppose an integral understanding of the Christian mystery and the pastoral office.

"Among other things, the priest should:
1) Visit the sick and the dying, as indicated in the relevant section of the Roman Ritual.
2) Teach the significance of Christian death.
3) Show loving concern for the family of the deceased person, support them in the time of sorrow, and as much as possible involve them in planning the funeral

199

celebration and the choice of the options made available in the rite.

4) Integrate the liturgy for the dead with the whole parish liturgical life and the pastoral ministry."

NOTES

1. Pierre-Marie Gy, "Le Nouveau Rituel Romain des Funérailles," *La Maison-Dieu* 101 (1970), 20-21. An English translation of this article is available in *The Way* Supplement 11, Fall 1970: "The Liturgy of Death. The Funeral Rite of the New Roman Ritual," pp. 59-75.

2. Gy, "Funérailles," p. 21.

3. This author prefers "customary" as the translation of *consuetus*; to speak of appointed prayers and psalms connotes a ritualistic formalism not intended by the *Rite*.

4. *Missale Romanum*, Editio typica altera 1974, no. 336. This edition contains the third official revision of the *GIRM*. The italics indicate parts of the text added to the first edition.

5. *BCL Newsletter* 12 (1976), 56. Note the misprint of "now" for "not" in the reference to the revised Roman Missal: "days on which funeral masses are now [corr: not] to be celebrated."

6. Cf. *GIRM*, no. 8.

7. Cf. criteria for permitting the sacraments of initiation, especially baptism, and matrimony outside the parish church.

8. Generally speaking the most frequent complaint about the American edition of the *Rite* on the part of parish priests has been its unhandy format. In the English-speaking world the Canadian edition offers, in the opinion of this author, the most practical pastoral model. Future North American revisions leading to a better American "typical edition" will be based on the fruit of these ten years of mutual experience, as well as that of other national churches belonging to ICEL. Pastors will be pleased to hear that their critique has not gone unheard, according to members of the ICEL committee for the preparation of texts.

9. See our historical treatment above and Gy, "Funérailles," p. 25; Frederick McManus, "Liturgy of Final Commendation," *American Ecclesiastic Review* 162 (1970), 405-408.

10. Gy, Funérailles," p. 26.

11. Simeon of Thessalonica, *De ordine sepulturae* in PG 155, 685B.

12. See our remarks below on the song of farewell, pp. 160-162.

13. McManus, "Funeral Rite," pp. 45-59; 124-139. *Rite of Funerals*: Celebrant's Manual for the Church Service, With Pastoral Directives for use in the Archdiocese of Chicago (Chicago: Liturgy Training Program, 1971), pp. 49-55. Cf. also *Liturgy for Christian Funerals* (Green Bay, Wis: Commission on the Liturgy, 1968).

14. *The Order of Funerals for Adults*. Experimental Rite for use by permission of the Holy See (Washington, D.C.: National Conference of Catholic Bishops, 1967), pp. 29-30 (nos. 30-34).

15. *The Rite of Christian Burial*. Adapted for use in the Archdiocese of Chicago by the Commission on the Sacred Liturgy. (Chicago: Archdiocese of Chicago, 1968), pp. 31 and 33-35.

16. *Notitiae* 2 (1966), 353-363; 3 (1967), 155-164. See also Gy, "Funérailles," pp. 21-22.

17. A.G. Leystan, "The Revised Funeral Rite," *The Priest* 26 (1970), 55.

18. McManus, "Funeral Rite," p. 133.

19. *Rite of Funerals*, ed. 1968, p. 25.

20. This is a criticism that funeral directors frequently direct against the clergy.

21. These ideas are well developed in A.-M. Roguet, "La prédication de la mort," *La Maison-Dieu* 44 (1955), 104-110; Marcel Tissier, "L'Homélie aux Funérailles," *La Maison-Dieu* 101 (1970), 117-126.

22. See John A. Lamb, *The Psalms in Christian Worship* (London: The Faith Press, 1962) *passim* and esp. pp. 73-75; 124-125.

23. Gy, "Funérailles," p. 28.

24. Gy, "Funérailles," pp. 28-30. Translation approved and printed with permission of the author.

25. Cf. *Unitatis Redintegratio* (Ecumenism), 6; *Gaudium et Spes* (Church in the Modern World), 62.

26. Cf. nos. 34 and 36, as well as the invitations to prayer for the farewell, the litanies and, for infants, nos. 225-226 and 235-237.

27. *Book of Common Prayer, Scottish Book of Common Order, The Liturgy of South India.*

28. Cf. nos. 48, 168, 198, 199.

29. Cf. Gy, "Funérailles," p. 30, notes 35-37.

30. Thanks to Dr. William G. Storey and his many students of the Notre Dame programs in Liturgical Studies a growing number of Catholic parishes are beginning once again to appreciate the place of morning and evening prayer in American church life. See, e.g., Storey *et al.*, eds., *Morning Praise and Evensong* (Notre Dame, Ind.: Fides, 1973). This revival of the cathedral hours has received international attention through ICEL, the *Societas Liturgica* and a Münster dissertation, Thaddäus A. Schnitker, *Publica Oratio: Laudes matutinae und Vesper als Gemeindegottesdienste in diesem Jahrhundert*, (Münster: privately printed, 1977). An adaptation of evensong for Sunday has been included in *Holy Cross Funeral Liturgy*, pp. 4-15, as one of the options for the vigil. The Irish edition of the *Rite* includes the option of celebrating the hours of morning, midday, or evening prayer either together with the eucharist or as "A Celebration with the People." Liturgical Secretariat, Irish Episcopal Conference, *Christian Burial* (Portarlington: Mount St. Anne's Liturgy Centre, 1976), pp. 26-30; 65-84.

31. *Acta Apostolicae Sedis* 56 (1964) 822-823.

32. *Acta Apostolicae Sedis* 56 (1964), p. 823, no. 2.

33. See the Canadian *Catholic Funeral Rite*, pastoral note 14 and pp. 130-133.

34. *BCL Newsletter* 13 (1977), 59: English translation of the response of the Congregation for the Sacraments and Divine Worship, "De celebratione exsequiarum pro iis, qui proprii cadaveris cremationem elegerit," *Notitiae* 126 (1977), 45.

35. E.g., in some German-speaking lands.

36. Columbarium is defined as a "vault or similar structure with recessed niches in the walls for storing the ashes of the dead. In modern facilities, the niches are faced with protective glass, bronze or marble." Harrah, *Funeral Service*, p. 263.

37. The Dominican Church, Leeuwarden, the Netherlands. Interview with Rev. Eric Osendarp, O.P., August 16, 1977.

38. Cf. Romano Guardini, Letter to the Mainz Liturgical Congress, April 1, 1964, in: Herder Correspondence, August 1964, pp. 237-239.

39. See above, pp. 115-135.

40. See the bibliographical references above, pp. 142-143, note 8.

41. The reason is obvious, and a favorite anecdote reinforces the value of its emphasis in the Introduction (no. 18). A priest acquaintance was called upon to preside at a funeral of a certain parishoner's relative who had been killed in a motorcycle accident. The deceased was laid out in his riding gear, and some three hundred members of West Coast motorcycle gangs constituted most of the congregation. For pastoral reasons the funeral was celebrated without Mass and held in a mortuary chapel. The priest—a total stranger to the scene—consulted with the family; he learned about the deceased's military service in Vietnam and the circumstances of his death. It happened when his motorcycle struck a wall while he was trying to avoid hitting several children at play. Concluding his remarks the priest referred to the dead man's self-sacrifice both in the military and on the occasion of his deadly accident as "Christ-like." At this, one of the gang members uttered an audible protest. Next, according to the agreed-upon plan of the service, the priest invited those present to express any

sentiments they might wish. One spokesman, seated with the deceased's girlfriend, brought the service to an effective close with the farewell, "Adios, you son of a bitch."

42. *La Célébration des Obsèques*, p. 9.

43. *BCL Newsletter* 12 (1976), 91. See Appendix V. See also pastoral note 15 of the Canadian *Rite*, below p. 271.

44. *Acta Apostolicae Sedis* 64 (1972), pp. 518-525. In this matter of intercommunion several documents of the Roman Catholic *magisterium* are essential to the discussion: the Decree of Vatican II *Unitatis redintegratio* (Nov. 21, 1974) in Flannery, *Vatican Council II*, pp. 452-470, esp. no. 8; the Instruction *In Quibus Rerum Circumstantiis* (June 1, 1972) in Flannery, pp. 554-559; the interpretation of this latter instruction *Dopo le publicazione* (Oct. 17, 1973) in Flannery, pp. 560-563.

45. *Lumen Gentium*, no. 29 in Flannery, p. 387; Motu proprio *Sacrum diaconatus ordinem* no. 22, 5 in *The Pope Speaks* 12 (1967), pp. 237-243. See also Reiner Kaczynski, *Enchiridion Documentorum Instaurationis Liturgicae I* (Rome: Marietti, 1976), pp. 352-353. For the deacon with diocesan appointment this is "ordinary" ministry in the traditional Catholic sense of the term. Neither the absence of a priest or designation by the local ordinary for specific funerals are necessary to validly exercise this ministry. The deacon exercises it by virtue of his ordination to service (*ad ministerium*) and his pastoral appointment. It is understood, however, that he is replacing the parish priest who carries the primary responsibility but who, for legitimate reasons, is hindered from being present.

46. *Catholic Funeral Rite*, pp. 3-4.

47. The Latin reads: *additis, quotiescumque opportunum fuerit, melodiis cantui aptis.*

Present and Future

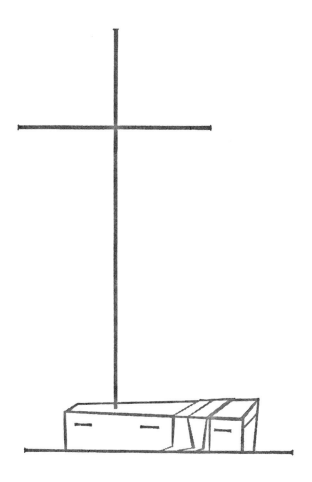

Chapter Five

The Present: Reform and Renewal

This chapter is not the result of a systematic and controlled survey but the fruit of conversations and observation by the author during the past several years. Its purpose is to share pastoral experiences with the funeral more broadly than most 'funeral ministers and bereaved Christians ever have a chance to do. Its one obvious prejudice is to favor the best experiences with the *Rite*. There is little value in mentioning bad ones; they are all too familiar to us.

PASTORAL PREPARATION

Parishes where the *Rite of Funerals* enjoys the reputation of being genuine community liturgy are, generally speaking, parishes where considerable effort has been devoted to remote preparation.

This has included parish-wide catechesis, especially about death itself in the twentieth century, Catholic faith and contemporary teaching in face of death and about the liturgy of death and burial. More than one parish priest has insisted that the best vehicle for such effective funerary catechesis is the funeral liturgy itself, realizing that recurring good example demonstrates in practice—not in long, tedious commentaries—what is taught in homily, school or parish education classes.

A plan of action has also been part of successful education programs. Although they differ in details and approach, most include means to attain the following goals: a parish guide to funerals, explicit channels of communication with funeral directors who serve the parish, a parish cantor and funeral choir, and appropriate participation aids for all liturgical services.

207

The Parish Handbook for Funerals

One of the best ways to insure the continuance of the fruit of education about funerals is to provide every family with a simple handbook or guide to funeral practice in the parish.[1] The handbook is a companion to a more comprehensive diocesan manual. It offers the family a brief theology of death in the Catholic community, gives explicit directives about what to do when someone dies in the family, and provides information about the funeral liturgy as celebrated in that parish.

The handbook urges parishoners to inform the pastor about the death as soon as possible *and* to plan a meeting with a parish priest before making arrangements with the funeral director. Reasons for such an emphasis include establishing priorities for a funeral that is founded on Christian values and facilitating the choice of options offered by the *Rite* and parish custom, both of which could affect arrangements with the funeral home. Furthermore, experience has shown that groundless fears about denial of Christian burial can often be alleviated and due pastoral care rendered when people approach the parish priest first. This is especially true when the mortuary in question is not Catholic. Similarly, Catholic funeral directors exercise a needed service when they familiarize themselves with current canonical legislation and assist Catholics through accurate information to seek the consolation of their faith in face of death. Such information is generally available to the parish pastoral team and funeral director alike in regional or diocesan guidelines for funerals.[2]

Through its information about the liturgical customs of the parish funeral the handbook serves as background for planning the funeral with the parish priest or other minister. Frequently it facilitates family discussions about planning ahead, especially in the case of terminally ill patients or, equally often, on the part of elderly Christians who are realistically in touch with death's imminence. Also important is the emphasis which the handbook places on music as an ordinary accompaniment of funeral liturgy in the parish. Here again the matter of music does not come as a surprise to the bereaved, and the question is no longer whether to have music but which pieces are most appropriate to this funeral.

Communication with Funeral Directors
Successful celebration of the *Rite of Funerals* may well depend on the understanding and cooperation of funeral directors and other mortuary personnel. Where this does not yet exist it is seldom due to ill will on the part of either party, but it is frequently the result of poor communication and misunderstanding. This is especially the case in large cities where many different funeral directors serve the same parish. Both parish priests and morticians have spoken of their frustrations about their obvious failure to cooperate in liturgy. In other cases, both parties are satisfied with the *status quo* of routine funerals. The *Rite of Funerals* is a common guide to relieve the former frustrations, as the 1970 film on the new Rite, *Of Life & Death*, by the National Association of Funeral Directors indicated. No *Rite of Funerals* can succeed, however, where liturgical renewal is thwarted by ministerial carelessness or professional commercialism. Both groups would appreciate greater communication but are unclear about areas of mutual responsibility and uneasy about where to begin a dialogue. Funeral directors are in business to bury the dead. Because that business involves grieving persons, the funeral industry extends its service to "grief counseling" in conjunction with the funeral. Thus, funeral directors give where appropriate a "religious" dimension to the services they provide. The funeral industry is concerned with the *end* of life; the mortician's art leaves no doubt that *this life* is its object.

The concern of the parish priest and the *Rite of Funerals* is broader. It embraces the genuine service rendered by the funeral director in a pastoral context that begins with life and continues long after death. Thus many parish priests have taken the responsibility to approach funeral directors with a knowledge of and appreciation for their professional service, offering to assist them with the peculiarities of funerals in Catholic parishes. Few funeral directors care to "take over" the liturgy of funerals, but most appreciate information about its celebration so that they can do their job efficiently and effectively. Where efficiency or professionalism interferes with Catholic funerary values, it is again the Catholic client who has the responsibility to demand appropriate service. Catholic people and clergy, who do not expect that their faith values are the primary concern of the funeral industry and who have learned to do business with funeral homes accordingly, find channels of mutual communication remarkably clear. The result can be the kind of collaboration that enables the funeral liturgy to be a memorable ecclesial event in the life of the bereaved and a worthy commemoration of the deceased by all participants.

Parish Cantor and Funeral Choir
Music at the American Catholic funeral is a long and established tradition. Equally long and established is the practice of listening passively to a choir or solo organist. The invitation issued by the liturgical renewal, however, is to translate this into participation, whereby music comes to enjoy its place as an integral part of funeral liturgy. Our research reveals several ways this is happening in the United States today.

A way that one hears about more and more frequently is the formation of a special funeral choir or *schola*. Frequently made up of older, often retired men and women who continue to enjoy singing, as well as younger homemakers whose children are in school, such choirs

210

exercise a valuable music ministry. The very mixed groups that assemble for funerals render congregational singing nearly impossible without the choir's musical support. Yet the choir alone, without a cantor to direct and lead congregational participation, runs the risk of being seen as a performing group rather than a liturgical choir. Likewise, the cantor alone is not as successful without choir support. The solution that is working best employs both choir and cantor. This is the approach of parishes where music is a liturgical priority, to be sure, yet no more so than Catholic liturgical renewal since Vatican II requires. The odds against congregational participation during funeral liturgy are great. Some parish teams have given up after a decade of failure; others are seeking still further answers for the failure—such as the need for choir and cantor, or a familiar (perhaps regional) repertoire of funeral hymnody, or clearer participation aids, or education itself. In this context one choir director writes, "I have experienced very few times where congregations during the grief process were able to participate with the hymns and acclamations." Yet, among those few, very remarkable things happen. "On one occasion I remember, at the death of a teenager, the church was filled with his peers. I asked them to render their full support to the members of the family with their hymns of Christian hope. The response was a fully Christian one."[3]

Another way some parishes are using to make music a more integral part of the funeral liturgy is to work systematically toward a familiar repertoire of singable, good hymns. Many hymns appropriate for funerals can be taught and sung equally well at Sunday liturgy. By keeping the funerary repertoire small and simple, certain pieces will become familiar enough that people will overcome their long-time hesitation to sing at funerals. One pastor who demonstrated the success of this approach in an active rural parish, where many of the same people tend to come to funerals, is testing it currently in a larger urban parish, with initial signs of success. Perhaps the most encouraging fact about music at funerals is the experience that "the paschal character of Christian death" (SC, no. 81) means far more than exuberant Alleluia's and other Easter hymns. A widespread use of joyful but sensitive psalmody, sung responsorially, as well as recent compositions specifically for the funeral are giving greater balance to the enthusiasm of the early renewal. This is apparent in certain diocesan and local participation books for use at funerals where a balanced selection of music is included for use at appropriate points in the *Rite*. Many parish musicians look forward to a revised American edition of the *Rite of Funerals* that will offer a model for music at the funeral, following the example of the French, Irish, and to a certain extent, the Canadian national editions, among others.

Participation Aids
There are two opposing positions among American funeral ministers regarding participation aids for wake and funeral services. One position insists that ministers ought not to confuse the bereaved with service sheets, because they are not necessary.[4] The other holds that appropriate participation aids—not grubby ditto sheets, of course—are necessary if one desires participation that is more than the intermittent recitation of familiar prayers.

In unfamiliar situations and surroundings, like wake or funeral, people appreciate knowing what is going to take place. The first service provided by a good participation aid, therefore, is a clearly recognizable *order of service*. Secondly, people want to know what, if anything, they are expected to do. If this is not clear, the natural reaction is to do nothing. Thus the service sheet indicates in clear type both nonverbal and verbal participation in the *liturgical action*: stand, be seated, kneel, respond, silent prayer, sing and the like. These are conveniently printed in the margin of the page where they stand out but do not distract from the order of service itself. This basic format also allows for personalization. The name of the deceased can be printed in the title. The names of those who take part in the liturgy, such as readers, pallbearers, etc., along with specific references to the readings chosen, and the words, music and/or hymnal references of familiar hymns are usually inserted in their appropriate places. In this way the service sheet also becomes a *memento* of the liturgy for the participants. This implies printing work for each funeral, but when a basic master layout is used and only the specific references are inserted, this is no more complicated than printing personal holy cards.

Both positions agree on the principle of "noble simplicity." Unfortunately many participation aids are unnecessarily complex and frequently verbose. The above sketch indicates the plan for a very simple aid. Sometimes it is no more than a single page (5½ by 8½ inches) that guides the assembly in meaningful participation while serving as a page marker for the parish hymnal. At other times it can be a self-contained booklet of several pages. The greatest pastoral difficulty is finding a suitable simple format that allows personalization as well as fosters participation. In its simplest form personalization involves choice of readings, interventions and prayers by the celebrant and hymns and responses by the people. The most successful wake booklets, for example, provide the order of service, indicate by title the variable parts and print out in full *only* the congregation's parts. Two options for the latter, separated by "or," offer variety within the order of service and a music section at the end provides readily accessible hymns. [5]

A decade or more of experience is now available against which to evaluate the many different model service sheets being used at wakes in the United States as well as the manner in which they are used.[6] The comments of one Virginia pastor, drawing on twelve years' experience with a specific wake service aid, are not untypical and highlight concerns for fresh pastoral evaluation. His original compilation grew out of specific needs and desires: to replace outdated participation cards; to provide a dignified aid for people of all faiths to participate in the Catholic wake (a request of funeral directors as well); to establish a standard service sheet and eliminate separate handouts for each occasion; to have a format that allows free choice of Scripture, homily and music; to give the priest more time to work on the funeral itself. After twelve years this pastor can assert that the funeral directors, who paid for the printing and include their logo on the back page, are pleased; people, including those of other faiths, are impressed; the priest celebrant has sufficient freedom to adapt to specific needs within the service, such as short personal interventions, a decade of the Rosary at the casket when requested, or a final sprinkling of the body with holy water at the closing.[7]

The Funeral Workshop

An approach that integrates all of the above concerns about remote preparation is the parish funeral workshop. Only one such workshop has emerged in this research, and a participating priest described it as follows:

"Last spring a funeral workshop was sponsored by the liturgy commission of our parish. Three speakers offered presentations, a funeral director, a lawyer and a parish priest. The funeral director gave a careful explanation of the services provided by the funeral home, including the many options available. He spoke about the costs involved and some legal aspects pertaining to the funeral. In this latter section he outlined state requirements and tried to dispel mistaken notions about needing caskets and especially about presumed obligatory embalming. The lawyer discussed what is involved in preparing a last will and testament, pointing out who

214

handles it, how it is handled, and what must be in it. The third part of the workshop took up the role of the priest at the time of death. The pastor explained what we do when we hear that a parishioner has died. (He said that we immediately drop whatever we are doing and go to the home of the family, remaining with them as long as necessary. At that time we do not begin to plan the funeral liturgy. Rather, we extend the invitation to the bereaved to help plan the liturgy and indicate that we will come back another time to do that. We close that visit mentioning the custom in our parish of having a home Mass with the family and their relatives on the evening before the actual funeral.) Following these presentations a question and answer session closed the evening. A wide range of about forty persons participated in this first funeral workshop in our parish; some were very young, some with families, and some without, some who were concerned about a terminally ill relative, and even a few people in very bad health themselves who might likely die in the year ahead. This first workshop was considered such a success that our liturgy commission plans to offer it again, possibly once each fall and spring. It was very timely in our parish. In less than one year we had eleven deaths, and most of them were rather tragic. The workshop had helped all of us to care for the deceased and their bereaved families."[8]

The best of participation aids, the most talented funeral choir and cantor, fluid communication between parish priests and funeral directors, and the most helpful parish funeral handbook and workshop—aspects of parish education and complementary plans of action—are all but context within which funeral liturgy happens. They constitute the backdrop on the stage of parish life that suddenly becomes crucial when death occurs. They are remote preparation for the priest's pastoral visit to begin preparation for the funeral liturgy itself.

PASTORAL VISIT

The priest's first visit with the bereaved after a death has been announced is a pastoral challenge second to none. His genuine pastoral presence, the presence of the Church, is primary. Ministers with years of experience describe this visit as more a time of listening than speaking. Listening is part of liturgical planning for the funeral. Much is said about the deceased that can enable the minister to ask the right questions, at the opportune time, in order to firm up specific details for the liturgy. Special and favorite scriptural themes surface; particular names emerge. Listening helps the priest or other minister begin to prepare a mental outline. At an opportune moment he or she requests time to concretize, as much as possible, liturgical plans for both wake and funeral. Many ministers use a simple planning sheet for this.[9] On it one finds the order of service with blanks provided to fill in appropriate personal choices. Most pastors find it helpful to assist the bereaved to complete as many choices as they can at the time of this visit; the wake especially needs to be determined immediately. Frequently people will want to think about the Scripture readings and choice of readers for Mass. The priest then sets a time when they will give him those choices. In the experience of the author, the principle that guides most ministers during the pastoral visit is delicate attention to the desires of the family while preserving the integrity of the liturgical life of the Church.

This visit is crucial for good funeral liturgy. Together with the background sketched above, it determines the creative dimension of the new *Rite of Funerals*. It provides the principal opportunity for rendering Catholic funeral liturgy the funeral of *this* specific deceased Catholic. As noted above also, a successful pastoral planning visit, prior to firming up arrangements with a funeral director, enables Catholics to specify their peculiar values and needs for the kind of mortuary care they

216

prefer. Of all the revised liturgical rites the funeral enjoys the greatest openness to creative liturgy; of all the related elements constituting that liturgy, a successful pastoral visit is considered by many faithful people and clergy to be the key to that creativity.

THE WAKE

Chapter One of the *Rite of Funerals* in the United States bears the title *Vigil for the Deceased and Prayer when the Body Is Placed on the Bier*.[10] An introductory note to the American usage explains,

"This chapter includes the kinds of service of prayer which may be followed at appropriate times during the period from death to the funeral itself. . . . These are: 1) A *wake service* or *vigil* in the form of a celebration of the word of God. . . . (nos. 26-29). 2) *Prayer at other times* before the funeral rite (nos. 30-31)."

In pastoral practice generally, however, the wake service or Rosary are the only services one encounters. These take place most frequently in a funeral parlor, sometimes in the parish church, but almost always with the corpse present.

The Church Wake

Celebrating the wake in the church (or parish hall adjacent to the church) is becoming more and more common. Ordinarily this entails bringing the body to the church on the evening before the funeral liturgy and making provision for its security. Specific details for this arrangement need to be worked out with the funeral director. Among other things, for example, it entails an extra round trip for vehicles and personnel to the parish church: once to deliver the body and once to remove it to the cemetery. The funeral directors interviewed by this author indicate a willingness to contract for this service, presently an "extra" to the ordinary Catholic package.

217

Among the many excellent church wakes that one hears about today, the following example from rural Oregon is described most vividly by the pastor who prepared it and presided at its celebration. After setting out the details of things to be dealt with in view of the tragic death of a young father of three and reviewing the pastoral planning visit, the priest describes the vigil as follows.

"We brought the body to the church Tuesday evening, where we celebrated the formal entrance into the church, usually had before the funeral Mass. The casket was taken to its usual place for the funeral liturgy; it was positioned facing the congregation and opened for the wake. Hymns were sung at appropriate times during the service.

"Because there were many non-Catholics present, I gave the homily as part of the entrance rite. I explained the water, white pall, and paschal candle as primary symbols of baptism, when the deceased was plunged into the whole mystery of Christ's death and resurrection, which now in death were no longer symbols.

"Since the deceased had just recently harvested his grain, his wife got the idea of making a wreath of unharvested wheat that would be set next to his casket. Draped down from the wreath was a scroll, and on it the principal text of the vigil and funeral Mass, written in calligraphy by the wife: 1 Cor. 15.35-44. The deceased's wife read this passage at both the vigil and funeral. The Gospel selection for the vigil was John 12.23-26. Both these readings involve wheat as a basic symbol. There were long pauses after each reading, as well as after the intervening psalm. The church was stone-quiet during the long pauses. (I had mentioned in the introduction that the vigil was a time for the community to renew its own faith in the death and resurrection of the Lord and in their meaning for all of us.)

"The vigil ended with everyone passing by the coffin into the wing of the church for refreshments and a chance to meet the deceased's family. The many children at play during the refreshments really added in their own way to the overall point of the funeral."[11]

The Home Wake
Another pastoral shift from the ordinary American experience of the funeral parlor wake is the home wake *without* the body present. This approach to the wake is believed to be unique. It began with the experience of the pastor-chairman of the diocesan liturgical commission who took his inspiration for the change from a careful study of the *Rite of Funerals*.

One notices in Chapter One of the Rite (both in the American Introductory Note and no. 26) that the home is listed first among locations for celebrating the vigil. Surely this was done in light of the tradition, and local custom where the tradition still lives on, of laying out and waking the deceased in the family home. The presumption of the American note favors the custom of a wake with the body present, now usually in the funeral home. Nevertheless, the *Rite* recognizes that it must be adapted to new conditions as they arise, just as it adjusts to existing custom.[12] Moreover, the ordinary American version of the wake is a combination of the prayer vigil (nos. 26-29) and times when the bereaved and others assemble at the coffin (nos. 30-31). The home wake designates the vigil as a service of prayer in support of the family and other bereaved persons and separates it from the opportunity for condolences and last respects at the funeral home where the deceased is left. The author of this proposed change, drawing on his experience with it, describes the home wake as follows.

"Most commonly now in our parish, families choose to have the vigil prayer [wake] service at home the night before the funeral without the body present. . . . Why in the home? The vigil is really the family's own prayer of hope and strength for each other, more so than the prayer of the community for the deceased. The chief prayer of the community is the Mass and the Mass should be the service that all are encouraged to attend. . . . Planned by the family and carried out in the home, with close friends invited and family members taking the different psalms and prayers, it becomes a really personal thing. . . . Most homes can hold far more people than we imagine. . . . One thing avoided by family wakes is the obligation of all to view the body which many people prefer to skip. All those so desiring can easily visit the funeral parlor the day or evening before, or in the morning before the funeral Mass."[13]

This family vigil at home suggests another creative alternative to the stereotypical American Catholic wake service at the funeral home. Because that service frequently loses its effect due to the mixed beliefs and motives of those present, the general atmosphere of the space itself, traffic during the service, and so on, pastoral alternatives such as the church wake with the body present, and home or church prayer vigil without the body present, provide different ways to meet the particular spiritual needs of Catholic families in face of death.

Other Services

Neither of these alternatives implies that a prayer service at the funeral home would therefore be eliminated. The *Rite* provides for such services "at other times before the funeral rite" (nos. 30-31). They are characteristically brief enough to fit the funeral home situation and appropriately prayerful to maintain a Christian attitude toward death. Even though the parish priest or other minister may not be present at the funeral home for all such short prayer services, the American *Rite* reminds us: "It is appropriate that the priest make a selec-

220

tion of such prayers available for use by the family of the deceased." Funeral directors too might see to it that they have such spiritual aids on hand for the Catholic funeral and mention them during their counseling sessions with the bereaved. Such a brief prayer service at the casket might frequently be omitted where services by special groups or fraternities are planned. One would not ordinarily omit the vigil or wake service (wherever celebrated) on their account, however. The reason for this distinction rests in the fact that the wake is more specifically part of the funeral liturgy and, in the United States, effectively takes the place of the station in the home of Plan I (nos. 26; 32-34). In any case, these observations again point up the creative potential of the revised *Rite of Funerals*.

The Canadian edition of the *Rite*, drawing on a study of pastoral experience with the funeral, combines such alternatives clearly in what is termed the *First Service*. This *Service* results from an interpretation based on pastoral practice that reveals that the wake and a station in the home before the funeral Mass are usually experienced as a single liturgical moment among Canadian Catholics who use the English-language *Ritual*. This clear pastoral position is grounded in the *Rite* itself (nos. 26; 21-22) and eliminates much confusion in the use of the published ritual.[14]

The Home Mass

One other special liturgical service prior to the funeral liturgy in the church has recently come to our attention: the home Mass on the evening before the funeral. Once again those who exercise this special funeral ministry can best describe their experience.

"We offer the home Mass on the evening before the funeral as a way for the family to gather its thoughts and memories in the prayerful context of the eucharist. We see it as an opportunity to begin, in prayer and together with the relatives, to deal with the loss they have just experienced. This is a very simple Mass that we ourselves prepare, unless the family requests something specific; one of the parish sisters offers guitar accompaniment for music during the Mass. This too is kept very simple, perhaps an opening hymn, an *alleluia* and an *amen* concluding the Eucharistic Prayer. After reading the Gospel the presiding priest reminds the family that the eucharist is a special time of remembering, of commemorating the great works of God and above all Jesus the Lord, dead and risen. In this context he offers them the opportunity to remember in their own way the deceased one who has left them. At this time the family begins to recall for each other memories, happy and sad, which they had shared with the deceased. Funny incidents are recounted and some very serious ones, things said to the deceased and words spoken by the deceased to them. This is likewise a controlled situation in which they can say some of the things they wish they would have said or done—in short a very healing time for the family. It helps them to take their hurt, their sorrow, their loss, their hopes, their joys, their questions to the Lord and ask him to bless them and their lives together. This period of remembering can go on for a long time. I have seen it continue for as long as an hour and fifteen minutes. On the average, it lasts about forty-five minutes. The time allows the whole family to participate, and it is seldom that someone has nothing to say. Recently, a few days after such a home Mass, one of the relatives related what a tremendous healing experience it had been—how much hope it gave the family, how much closer it drew them together in prayer. Some have questioned the interruption of the flow of the liturgy with such a long interval of "remembering," and have proposed placing it after reception of communion. I don't believe that this would serve as well, for there is something remarkable about the way this period of remembering prepares the family for the liturgy of the

222

eucharist that follows. It would not be the same following upon the eucharist. Finally, this home Mass usually takes place in the home following the Office for the Dead celebrated in the church."[15]

The People Speak
Above one notes how these active pastors view the wake and other services before the funeral Mass. In Chapter Three we have commented on the wake as presented in the *Rite*.[16] All of this must, however, take into consideration how the people themselves experience the wake. From the many opinions collected, this author believes that the majority of Catholics view the wake service, whether scriptural vigil or Rosary, as an opportunity to pray *with* the bereaved *for* the deceased. The context for this prayer is a visit to the funeral home that is intended to be a sign of "last respects" to the deceased (whether viewed in an open casket or not) *and* thereby a sign of condolence to the bereaved. Frequently people who never knew the deceased will go to the funeral home to offer sympathy and support to the spouse or members of the family whom they do know. Or, one will pay respects to a deceased friend without knowing any of the bereaved and offer his or her support all the same. Within this varied existential context, more and more Catholics seem to be planning their condolence visit around the wake service. Without much explanation as to reasons, they indicate that attending the wake service seems to be the appropriate Catholic way of showing sympathy and paying their last respects. Those who cannot conveniently take time off from work to attend a morning funeral appreciate this liturgical opportunity to pray with the family rather than "merely" viewing the deceased, saying a personal prayer at the casket and offering condolences.

Some have pointed out that they feel more positive about the liturgical wake service than about the Rosary, which many regard as the prayer service of a special group, such as the Altar and Rosary Society and Knights of Columbus. They are comfortable with it because it is familiar, but prefer the vigil service as the more universal prayer of the Church. Others insist that a wake without the Rosary is just not a wake for them. Although some parish teams have observed that they do have the Rosary far more often than the scriptural wake, increasing numbers of Catholics under the age of thirty and of non-Roman Catholic participants at wake services no longer understand the Rosary devotion. While they do not oppose it for others, some almost resent being asked to take part in its traditional form as the community's prayer at a wake. Many tolerate reciting the Rosary at wakes because "that's what the deceased would have wanted." For these and other serious reasons noted above,[17] this author does not agree with the pastoral position that presents the Rosary to the bereaved as an equal option with the vigil service proposed by the *Rite of Funerals*.[18] Obviously, the pastoral art requires delicacy toward the wishes of the deceased and of the family, but it also requires delicately educating people of faith to the values of the funeral liturgy and to the faith of the broader Catholic and Christian community. There are sufficient moments during the hours spent in the funeral home for group devotion.

Finally, one notes in these interviews how much people relate the wake service to the funeral home and to the presence of the body. This is a deeply rooted tradition that moved with the earlier wake by the body from the family home to the mortuary. Alternative solutions, that seek to render the vigil more fruitful spiritually than one frequently experiences in the funeral home, will need to take this religious sensibility of the faithful into careful account. Both the home wake and the vigil in the church cannot overlook those whose Christian manner of ritualizing their response to the death of a brother or sister centers on their visit with the family and the deceased in the funeral home.

224

THE FUNERAL LITURGY AT CHURCH

If there is any place in liturgical life today where the Church's prayer (*lex orandi*) explicitly proclaims Catholic faith (*lex credendi*), it is surely in the funeral liturgy at church. No Catholic would hesitate to specify the funeral Mass with its special opening and closing as that which makes a Catholic funeral Catholic. This has certainly been the impression of this author, gained through interviews with young and old, clergy and lay persons. Moreover, despite details of interest reviewed below, there is an overall acceptance and appreciation of the funeral liturgy at church according to the new *Rite* (Chapter Two).

Rite at the Entrance of the Church
Because the station in the home of the deceased had already been replaced in the earlier American version of the Roman Ritual by a rite of reception at the church entrance, the revised opening rite in the church fell on good soil. One can affirm without hesitation that its use in the United States is almost universal and well liked by the faithful. Few parish priests think of it as optional and few vary the form or content presented in the American insert to the *Rite* (between nos. 38 and 39). After the funeral of Pope Paul VI, however, some have been heard to express an interest in the other symbols suggested in no. 38, especially placing the gospel book or Bible on a plain (wooden) coffin. All the same, the use of water, paschal candle, and white pall to relate this death to life through initiation into the paschal mystery is an ingenious part of the American *Rite*. Some commentators find it contrived, however, and a far too explicit use of baptismal symbolism, especially with the cumbersome and difficult text from Romans 6 incorporated into the liturgical action. Others do not discredit the use of these symbols, but are critical of the manner in which the rite is "executed." Unfortunately, far too many celebrants feel obliged both to use all of the en-

225

trance rite as printed despite the rubric "these or similar words" *and* to add further lengthy commentary to explain the symbols. Others avoid liturgical verbosity by giving a concise account of what is about to happen before the liturgy begins, especially helpful for those of other faiths. Simply sprinkling the body with holy water, placing the white pall on the coffin, and performing the other ritual actions *in silence* has also been known to speak more meaningfully than explanations, especially when the celebrant refers to them in his homily. One priest in particular pointed out that the more Catholic communities experience the symbolism of full Christian initiation and live what is symbolized there, the more they will be able to appreciate the impact of water, paschal candle, and white robe/pall at the funeral.

Although all the American parish priests interviewed use this entrance rite, most have developed their own way of celebrating it effectively. Their adaptations have to do with space, audibility, and visibility. Relatively few parish churches are equipped with audio connections in the vestibule; even where sound is no problem, space and visibility frequently are. Thus the "rite at the entrance of the church" has moved inside. Positions range from inside the church at the back door to halfway down the main aisle to down front at the place where the casket usually rests. All of these adjustments are pastorally understandable. Yet, in effect, the "rite at the entrance" is becoming an "opening rite" for a funeral liturgy in church, and that is not its liturgical function. It is designed as a solemn greeting and reception of the deceased and bereaved, analogous to the reception of candidates for Christian initiation, followed by a solemn final entrance into the church, reminiscent of that first sacramental entrance.

Rather than move the rite into the church, some pastors have instructed the people who gather before the funeral party arrives to take places in the rear of the church where they may turn and observe all clearly. Where there is insufficient room even for the funeral party to stand around the casket (or for reasons of convenience for the bereaved), the last pews are reserved for them. After the rite of entrance, the celebrant leads the casket (preferably carried by the pallbearers rather than rolled). The funeral party follows first, and the rest of the congregation complete the entrance procession. In this way the community-forming symbolism of the opening processional hymn also takes on greater meaning. Pastors who have taken this option likewise insist that such a procession, with all participating, relieves the uncomfortable feeling of the bereaved as they otherwise walk through a forest of eyes focused on them. It eliminates as well the gap in the seating that usually forms between the funeral party and the rest of the congregation.

Still others do not believe that it is necessary for all the participants to see and hear everything that takes place at the entrance. In their opinion, the simple rite at the entrance is primarily meaningful for those attending the deceased; the others experience the special symbols sufficiently throughout the liturgy.

This last opinion is similar to that embraced by the Canadian *Rite*. There the reception of the deceased and bereaved and the covering of the casket with a white pall is handled very simply. Only a short prayer marks the liturgical moment, and the entrance procession follows immediately. To explain this difference in approach, it has been pointed out that the Canadian editions of the *Rite* believe that a rite at the entrance comes too early in the liturgy to allow the symbols to enjoy their rightful power. People are said to be too distracted with other things at that moment to be concerned with serious symbolism. Thus the Canadian *Rite* opens the liturgy of the Mass in the ordinary way, including the penitential rite that can be especially effective in such circumstances. It delays focusing on the symbols of the paschal mystery until the homily, by which point all will have taken notice of them.

All this points to the creative potential of the popular American rite at the entrance to the church. The pastoral efforts to involve all present in its celebration are praiseworthy. Our research reveals many different levels of participation and demonstrates the pastoral sensitivity required to direct such participation at the outset of the funeral liturgy in the church.

The Funeral Mass
The liturgical center of Catholic funeral liturgy is, of course, the funeral Mass. Here the liturgy of the word and the liturgy of the eucharist "are so closely connected as to form one act of worship. The table of God's word and of Christ's body is prepared and from it the faithful are instructed and nourished."[19] At funerals, perhaps more than any other occasion, both laity and clergy emphasize the impact on them of instruction and communion—word and eucharist—of the funeral Mass. People remember "what Father said" or at least "how nice he spoke" and "how beautiful it was to see so many receive holy communion." Many older Catholics comment favorably on the difference from the past when there was neither a homily nor the opportunity for the faithful to receive communion at funerals. This change alone relegated "the eighteen-minute funeral" to the annals of history, for it takes time to celebrate word and sacrament in a manner that nourishes the faith of those present. Our inquiries revealed that great attention was paid to the homily and communion at the funeral Mass.

The Homily
Priests wrestle with the homily–eulogy tension. People expect to hear something about the deceased, many in-

sist. Yet, they know that nourishment at the table of God's word is essential to true Christian consolation. Furthermore the faithful repeatedly confirm the personal benefits of a good funeral homily.

Working in the belief that in the funeral liturgy the death of an individual Christian is related to the saving death and resurrection of Jesus Christ, some homilists draw on the Christian life of the deceased to confirm the hope founded on such an act of faith. Christian death happens in the context of Christian life. Emphasis is placed not on the spectacular but on the daily witness (martyrdom) of an active faith. It is always unique, and can never be generalized. This approach is hardly convincing, however, unless the homilist has followed the deceased through life for some time—increasingly a pastoral luxury in mobile American society—or assisted him or her during a significant phase of faith life, such as conversion or a terminal illness. Circumstances such as these are considered by some priests as the only legitimate ones should a homilist dare incorporate details about the deceased's faith life in the funeral homily. All are concerned about the need to duly recognize the Christian whose funeral Mass is being celebrated. This should not be a eulogy in praise of the deceased, and it is something different from a preached biography, frequently contrived and lacking details that are more familiar to the assembly than to the homilist, not to mention inevitable errors. One associate pastor collected many of the various homily aids that have been published and formed a funeral homily kit for the use of his parish team.[20] Others discuss and evaluate specific funeral homilies given in the parish. One pastor prints the text of his funeral homily as a memento for the participants and especially as a continued source of prayerful consolation for the bereaved. And, finally, another adds the suggestion that the homilist should be honest with the assembly.

229

At this point it is appropriate to take up the thread of the pastoral account above, relating the funeral of a young father. The celebrant's description continues as follows.

"At the funeral next morning, the deceased's wife (dressed completely in white) and the children met everyone at the door of the church. They then went forward to close the casket. The children had made a little bouquet to put in the father's hands. His wife pulled some of the wheat stalks from the wreath and placed them in his hands. The three children kissed their daddy goodbye, and the casket was closed.

"I introduced the Mass by calling attention again to the wheat near the coffin and briefly summarized the service of the previous evening. The dead man's wife again read the passage from 1 Corinthians; for the Gospel we selected Matthew 25.31-40. The homily contrasted funerals of the past with the present (black vestments/white vestments; black pall/white baptismal pall; six orange candles around the casket/white paschal candle dedicated on Easter at the head of the casket; dirgelike music/hope-filled lyrics; no flowers/flowers, etc.) and then went on to explain why this is the case: not a morbid preoccupation with death, but because it's all linked with, and almost overwhelmed by references to the resurrection. It's hard to summarize what I said, but apparently it hit hard and made a point." (The thread of this account will be taken up again later.)

Holy Communion
The other special moment in the funeral Mass for many people is the reception of holy communion. Neither priests nor lay persons offered much commentary on this, except to insist that it is a very appropriate manifestation of shared faith in resurrection life. One non-Roman Catholic person likened holy communion in the liturgy of the Christian community to the family potluck meal after burial services. This author could not help

230

recall the origin in ancient Christian tradition of the funeral eucharist.[21] Attitudes concerning the matter of intercommunion at the funeral Mass have been cited in Chapter Four.[22]

Other Concerns Noted

Among other points of interest concerning the funeral Mass, the essential place of music and difficulties with participation have been noted above.[23] One additional note about participation, however, points up the concern that the faithful no longer know what to expect at the liturgy. In addition to the special circumstances of the funeral (grief, infrequency, people from different parishes, ecumenical mix and the like), the *Rite* allows great freedom and variety in its manner of celebration. The variety and lack of familiarity with the responsory parts of the funeral rite seem to disorientate the people so that they will often not give even the most ordinary responses. This is not surprising when one recalls that their experience of the earlier Roman rite of burial did not include participation by the people. Another observation cites an apparent need for anonymity in such situations where emotions and intimacy are so prevalent. Moreover, one must remember, people are very uncomfortable with death. Anonymity frequently translates itself into being passive spectators, and any voiced or bodily participation threatens that natural coping mechanism.

One must remember that this is the first time since the early Middle Ages that active participation in the funeral liturgy is expected of the faithful. It is believed, however, that a certain sense of ritual pattern and continuity is beginning to assert itself. That this process will take time, especially given the specific context of death and burial, is to be expected. Consequently, from a pastoral point of view one cannot *force* participation at funerals—one can only educate people and stimulate practice. Pastors, however, should not become defeatists about this matter. Participation in the funeral liturgy will not come about of itself; that it is happening at all is a sign that patient effort at liturgical renewal is beginning to have an effect.

The pastor whose description of a rural parish funeral we have been following writes apropos the people's involvement and its consequences:

"The whole thing hit a lot of people hard. I believe the initial reaction was one of shock. People here are not used to seeing the family during their period of mourning. To have the widow reading at the funeral and meeting everyone at the door made several wonder just what was going on. But by the time the vigil service was over, and for sure by the end of the funeral, it had all come together for a lot of people. The whole thing made it very clear exactly what it is we believe in. Several people have talked to me since, asking how they can insure that this kind of service will celebrate their passage. One rather elderly parishioner told her husband that she was going to include detailed instructions with the things in their safety deposit box. The entire two days were days that made people think again about the real meaning of death and how it should be celebrated. It certainly helped one friend of the deceased overcome his initial bitterness, and two 'former' parishioners told me they were coming back to the church."

The use of incense during the funeral Mass is another matter of mixed feelings among clergy and laity alike. As we saw above an American annotation to no. 22, 5 of the Introduction to the *Rite* states that its use is optional in the United States. Also, as in the case of holy water, it is not to be multiplied. In practice this refers to the use of incense at the preparation of the gifts, during the final commendation and farewell and at the cemetery. The last use is almost extinct, and the other practice of honoring the Book of Gospels with incense falls outside the guidelines of the *Rite*. Of the remaining two uses, our

232

research indicates about an equal representation of both. The American version of no. 43 of the *Rite* continues the practice of including an incensation of the body during the rite of preparation of the gifts, followed by an incensing of the celebrant and congregation. Some parishes where this practice is customary, reflecting on what is being symbolized by these different incensations and how the people experience them, discovered quite a confusion among parish personnel and faithful. Not many are willing to consider incensation at this time to be a symbolic purification, a further gesture of preparation of gifts and people, including the deceased, to enter into eucharist. Yet, that seems to be its primary intention. Moreover, the practice of going to incense the casket (purification and honor) while making the round of incensing the altar (a blend of sanctifying space and honoring Christ and the martyrs whose relics rest in the altar) confuses the meaning of the gesture. A careful reading of no. 43 reveals, first, that incensing the body is always a further option when incense is used at the preparation of the gifts and, secondly, that it follows incensation of the gifts and altar: "In the United States, if incense is used, the priest, after incensing the gifts and the altar, may incense the body. The deacon or other minister then incenses the priest and the people." A minor point, to be sure, but if incense is going to be used, one ought to use it in accord with the sign being expressed. Nevertheless, from this author's inquiries, very few of the laity regard incense as having any meaning beyond "pomp" and solemnity. Not a few parish priests were at a loss to say what their people understood the use of incense to be or whether they have any appreciation for it. Others refer to it as "indoor sport for liturgists." Because of the general level of confusion in American parishes surrounding incense for the deceased during the preparation rite, many parishes seem to have reserved its use for the commendation liturgy or eliminated it altogether. At the farewell, as we noted in Chapter Four, a specific designation of the symbol is more readily acceptable.[24]

Taking all this into consideration, one cannot miss the distinct overall impression that American Catholic people and their priests are satisfied with the liturgy of the funeral Mass. Despite an occasional reasoned plea for the return of the sequence *Dies irae*, the balance found in the new prayers for Mass in the *Sacramentary*[25] and the wide choice of readings in the *Lectionary* are termed welcome changes. Some have indicated a desire for greater recognition for the use of contemporary literature, especially poetry, as an extension of the scriptural word. And finally, there is the recommendation, with which this author concurs fully, to request one or more proper Eucharistic Prayers for the funeral Mass. In practice the third Eucharistic Prayer, with its proper commemoration, is the one most frequently prayed—for many Catholics the only one they ever hear even on Sundays. New Eucharistic Prayers would render the funeral Mass something special. One already hears how attentively people listen during the special commemorations. There is a more important reason still, however. Analogous to the Canons for Masses with Children and the Reconciliation Canons, proper Eucharistic Prayers for funerals would further enrich the paschal mystery theme and, potentially at least, encourage a more attentive personal participation in the celebration of eucharist on behalf of the deceased. Preference has been indicated also for a structure that invites acclamatory prayer by the people throughout the canon, similar to Eucharistic Prayer II and III for Masses with Children. Such proper Eucharistic Prayers with special acclamations, some argue, would only take the people further away from the expected and confuse them with more variety. Although our inquiries indicate that participation during the Eucharistic Prayer might indeed be slow in coming, experience gives good reason to assume that actively practicing Catholics would pay special attention to a proper canon at the funeral Mass.

Final Commendation and Farewell
Although the new title for this short service at the casket after the funeral Mass is awkward, it well represents both the intention of the service and the way people experience it. In the American edition, perhaps *Final Commendation* would be sufficient title, for the cemetery or other place of final disposition remains the site of last farewell in the ordinary experience of people. Nevertheless, it has been argued by not a few priests and people, this is the "farewell" of the full worshiping community. The cemetery service, frequently celebrated by only a few and under less than ideal conditions for worship, is rather the explicit close of the funeral following the eucharist and farewell.

Except for one highly publicized commentary[26] these responses no longer note any sense of this service as a rite of purification. Indeed, people do understand "commendation" according to the image of commiting the deceased into God's hands and to his infinite mercy. Yet, rather than ritually doing something more to enhance the deceased's cause before God, as it were, people seem to conceive the rite as a final, explicit articulation of what has been celebrated in the eucharist. In terms of the rhythm of the funeral liturgy—as experienced—this is not a climactic moment; the funeral Mass remains climax. Despite the insistence of the *Rite* itself (no. 10), the commendation rite is not even thought of as separate from the funeral Mass, but rather as its special conclusion. American Catholics generally feel that the commendation liturgy does what seems liturgically appropriate and ritually necessary. That is, it brings the celebration of the paschal mystery, as it touches the life of this dead Christian, to an explicit close and provides a transition to the final moment of

235

disposition, wherever that takes place and with whatever community present.

The option to celebrate the final commendation and farewell at the cemetery or crematorium hall (before cremation) is considered unrealistic by most parish priests. (For the laity, the question is almost purely academic.) Implied in the option, of course, is the close proximity of the place of burial or cremation. Rural parishes that maintain a churchyard and cemetery have used the option quite meaningfully—in good weather—as have religious communities whose cemeteries are near the church or chapel where the funeral Mass is celebrated. Similarly, in cities where a chapel at the cemetery is customarily used for the entire funeral service (mostly without eucharist), celebrating the commendation rite at the graveside has also been described as liturgically effective. In all these situations, however, one must be attentive to the rhythm of the funeral liturgy. Because the final commendation and farewell completely replaces the cemetery service, it has a different liturgical dimension. It not only seals, as it were, the climactic funeral Mass but it encompasses ritually the very power-laden final moment itself of leave-taking at the grave. Celebrants have commented on the need to approach the rite differently in these two different settings; they insist that there is far more than a mere change of physical location to consider. Furthermore, where the commendation and farewell are celebrated at the graveside, the procession with the body from the church or chapel to the grave becomes an important transitional moment. Whenever possible, processional psalms and hymns give meaning to the action, adapted but not too terribly different from the funeral procession mentioned in Chapter One. Where singing is not possible, a prayerful, reflective silence should characterize the movement to the grave. Several religious, who are familiar with this experience, have remarked how important it is that the liturgical intensity, carrying

236

over from the eucharist to commendation and burial, not be lost through nervous, often idle talk during the walk to the grave. There is plenty of opportunity to give expression to the normal release of tension after the liturgy.

Although this option is ordinarily not possible and, where possible, not always practical, it is worthy of attention. Among other things it points up how the Catholic funeral can be concluded in different ways, depending on differing pastoral circumstances and needs. The emphasis here is on *difference*, not mere preference. The commendation rite functions differently according to its place in the liturgical rhythm of the *Rite of Funerals*; either use is equally good. Where it concludes the funeral liturgy in the church, an appropriate cemetery service (not a duplication) follows; where it takes place at the cemetery, it replaces the ritual function of a burial rite. The criterion for a choice (where possible at all) is a pastoral one. It answers the question: Under the circumstances which manner of conclusion is pastorally better for this funeral?

Liturgical expression at the final commendation and farewell differs too, depending on place, although only because of circumstances. Our responses show that incense is frequently used at the commendation in the church and rarely outside the church. The difficulties of transporting a lighted censer or relighting it at the cemetery are cited as reasons for the latter situation. Holy water, on the other hand, is often used in both situations, although less frequently at the commendation in church, especially if holy water was sprinkled during the opening rite at the church entrance. As indicated above, there is little explicit appreciation of anything more than "ceremony" for these liturgical actions at the final commendation. Most responses pertaining to this point suggest simply that water and incense are remnants from the former absolution service. Some priests have dropped both as too identified with purification and only contrived gestures of commendation or farewell. They strive to give new meaning to the commendation rite by taking a position close to the casket, by resting one's right hand on it during prayer, by preparing the transitional invitation to prayer, like the homily at the liturgy of the word, specifically, for this deceased person,[27] by incorporating in the commendation and farewell the gesture of removing and giving the traditional casket cross (or the deceased's Bible, if that was on the casket) to a member of the family, by allowing one of the bereaved to speak a word of thanks to the assembly and to invite all to the funeral reception after burial, and the like.

In this context some have also introduced the new climactic song of farewell with reasonable success. Outside such creative situations, however, only very few responses even hint at an awareness of the climactic position that the *Rite* gives this "song" in the commendation liturgy. Similarly little has been noted in practice about the recessional closing the final commendation (no. 50), except that the traditional antiphon *In paradisum* (in Latin or English) is apparently still well liked and meaningful. Favorite alternatives abound as well, however, one being mentioned in the funeral account above: "After Mass and the final commendation we all gathered around the casket and, while we sang the oft-repeated refrain 'And I will raise him up,' we carried the young father's body out of the church to the waiting hearse."

BURIAL LITURGY AT THE CEMETERY
The third station of the *Rite* according to the usual American plan (I) is celebrated at the cemetery or crematorium before cremation. The most general impression from our responses notes how the great freedom provided by the *Rite* is indeed exercised—not so much within parishes but from parish to parish. This phe-

nomenon, together with the suppleness required of the liturgy at the cemetery by outside circumstances, frame our observations. Think only of the differences in liturgical practice that climate implies, that urban, suburban or rural residence implies, that differing cemetery regulations, laws and the like imply, to mention but a few. We note here, therefore, only those of most general interest.

Cremation

Parish priests and Catholic people frequently ask what is liturgically appropriate for the disposition of ashes (sometimes referred to as cremains). Because the ashes deserve the same respect as buried remains after decomposition, many pastors urge their people, who request cremation, to make arrangements to preserve their ashes in a cemetery rather than having them scattered over countryside or ocean, especially if there is a family plot that members of the family will remember and visit. In Chapter Four we noted the actual establishment of a parish columbarium to insure such respect. In any case, where interment or entombment of ashes follows cremation, the same third station, with proper adjustment of liturgical texts, is quite appropriate. Using the same liturgy for the burial of the ashes also takes away any special attention to cremation. When Catholics thus wish to introduce cremation as part of their funeral plan, some pastors take an attitude of neutrality. Liturgically, the final disposition of ashes is a simple family cemetery service, usually the day after the funeral director has cooled and prepared the ashes for delivery to the family. Where families, at their own insistence or at the prior request of the deceased, choose to dispose of the ashes in some other way, parish priests involved have reacted differently. Some have celebrated a special service at the site of disposition, whereas others conclude their participation at the crematorium. The practice of cremation in the United States is still too recent among Catholics for there to be a pastoral consensus in this matter. In the opinion of this author, sound pastoral judgment will have to guide priests as to the appropriateness of specific requests for a liturgical disposition of the ashes. In general, however, responses suggest that such a liturgy outside a cemetery or the like would be the exception.[28] A felicitous compromise was once noted in the case of a California youth who, during a terminal illness, requested that his ashes be mixed with good soil in which a giant sequoia would be planted as a sign of "eternal life" for future generations. The ashes were buried in the boy's parish cemetery, and his tree was planted on the spot as he requested.

Duplication

One question that recurs very frequently about the liturgy in the cemetery is whether the cemetery service is a duplication of the final commendation and farewell. Our research shows that two opposite opinions dominate the discussion among parish teams.

One position experiences the service at the cemetery to be a duplication of the commendation, but necessary because of the time lapse during the transfer to the cemetery. Once there, according to this view, pastoral sensitivity recommends making the service worthwhile. Thus, for example, the American edition of the *Rite* includes the option of a short reading from Scripture at the cemetery (no. 55, supplement).

The opposite pastoral opinion insists that the liturgy at the cemetery serves a completely independent purpose, separate from the commendation. This position admits, with the *Rite*, that the commendation may replace the cemetery service if it is celebrated at the grave. But if it is not, then a liturgy at the grave serves the distinct purpose of placing the final, most emotional moment of leave-taking in a context of the liturgy of paschal faith. The model service set out in the *Rite* (nos. 55-57) is an explicit profession of the consolation of Christian faith and hope in face of burial—once termed the harshest of human realities and one of the greatest challenges to resurrection faith.[29]

The pastoral issue here is clear. Although the final commendation and farewell, when celebrated at the cemetery, can carry this final moment ritually, nevertheless the liturgy of the cemetery service in the *Rite* is specifically prepared for that moment. This author agrees that the cemetery service is not a mere repetition of the earlier service in church.

Real Earth

Finally, all our research points to a concern about the cemetery industry and its apparent control of liturgy at the cemetery. Just as dialogue with funeral directors has proven helpful to clarify Catholic funeral values, so too there is an urgent need for parish priests and cemetery personnel to discuss the spiritual and liturgical needs of the people they serve. Modern management of cemeteries is essential, and the legitimate demands of those served are part of such management. A legitimate and minimal demand of the Catholic *Rite of Funerals* is to celebrate the cemetery service "at the grave or tomb" of the deceased. More and more this minimum expectation is becoming an exception. Often one must request it explicitly and pay extra for the service. Certainly in large city cemeteries it is less expensive to wait until several bodies are ready for burial and then inter all of them at one time, efficiently and without bereaved spectators present. But are the consequences worth the cost benefit to the bereaved? Certainly all-weather cemetery chapels are being provided for the comfort and convenience of mourners, but what if comfort and convenience are not the most important values to the bereaved? Certainly efficient handling of services, crowd control and easy parking are priorities for which people are grateful and

241

for which they are paying, but does that make them into a "parking lot civilization"?

The Catholic *Rite of Funerals* goes beyond justifying cemeteries because of their potential as parks and bird sanctuaries. Catholics are often shocked at the sight of shelves of unclaimed remains awaiting burial in a common grave. The Catholic bereaved are persons for whom time to say goodbye and the reality of real earth next to an open grave are part of the human ritual of leave-taking. These things are very much part of the Catholic cemetery ritual, and both laity and clergy alike reveal much dissatisfaction at their calculated removal for the sake of efficiency in modern cemetery management.[30] A measure of how far from the grave contemporary cemetery services have shifted is their proximity to real earth. Real earth itself is not the issue; the reality of death and burial is. This concern for reality urges greater effort on the part of Catholic funeral ministers and professional cemetery personnel to gain mutual information and appreciation about the needs of the cemetery industry on the one hand, and the *Rite of Funerals* and Catholic values on the other. In this context one is reminded of the practice in eastern Canada where the priest who accompanies the bereaved to the cemetery remains behind, standing next to the grave until the last person is out of sight. People comment that they cherish this custom very much. It is a sign of the Church's presence to them, a source of great comfort to the family.

Apropos this discussion, our continuing account of one rural funeral closes on the note of real earth:

"The young family's farm is adjacent to the local cemetery. Thoughtfully the widow bought a plot overlooking their home and land—with the site of the fatal accident looming in the distance. Everyone was invited to the home for lunch after the burial, and most people actually came out. It was a festive afternoon, even though I

242

noticed several people watch from the living room windows to see the dead man's grave being filled in."[31]

Throughout this study and especially this chapter, the temptation has been great to project the "rite of funerals" of the twenty-first century. It is our conviction, however, that such a projection would violate all that has been discovered here. Research may indeed herald the future, but only because it represents the real situation in which today's funeral liturgy brings the death of an individual Christian into touch with the paschal mystery of Christ. Tomorrow's funeral must do the same in tomorrow's world, and renewal will remain the key to a continuity of paschal faith.

The United States Bishops' booklet *Environment and Art in Catholic Worship* and the widespread attention it is receiving herald, in our opinion, the most immediate future of funerary renewal. Pastoral concern for the role that art and environment play in the total funeral liturgy is only implicit in our gleanings as well as in the *Rite* itself. Yet, a growing awareness of its importance is apparent. Frequent questions about the appropriateness of certain funeral parlor settings, artistic appointments for the funeral liturgy and liturgical space in church design for wakes and funerals, for example, are already preparing the soil for new seed. The psychological and sociological answers that have guided much of funerary practice during the past two decades will in the 1980s be complemented by new poetic questions. "Like the covenant itself, the liturgical celebrations of the faith community [Church] involve the whole person. They are not purely religious or merely rational and intellectual exercises, but also human experiences calling on all human faculties: body, mind, senses, imagination, emotions, memory. Attention to these is one of the urgent needs of contemporary liturgical renewal."[32]

Where the Catholic funeral today is but a vernacular rendering of the late medieval Tridentine liturgy of

243

burial, it is but a mirror of the past longing toward the future. There the present must yet be made ready to receive the fertile seed of renewal. Where the spirit of renewal has gone hand-in-hand with liturgical reform in word and rite, there the seed has found good soil and reveals in embryo the form of future experience with funeral liturgy. Although rite and word will change, they will be recognizable from their roots in present faith and liturgy. We cannot project ritual detail. We do believe, however, that in the twenty-first century word and sacrament will continue to express an ever new Christian faith in paschal life where only death is visible.

NOTES

1. The author is indebted to Rev. Martin Senko, past Chairman, Liturgy Commission, Archdiocese of Portland, Oregon, for his example of this parish handbook. His experience with this pastoral approach was presented in a diocesan liturgical workshop in 1975.

2. Recent diocesan examples that combine the results of efforts in this direction over the years since 1970 include: *The Rite of Christian Burial in the Diocese of Albany*, New York (Albany: The Liturgy Center, 1976) and *Christian Death and Burial* (New York: The Liturgical Commission, Archdiocese of New York, 1978).

3. Personal correspondence with Sr. Cabrini Bartolo, S.L., July 9, 1977.

4. For example, Walter Schmitz and Terence Tierney, *Liturgikon: Pastoral Ministrations* (Huntington, Ind.: Our Sunday Visitor, Inc., 1977), p. 159.

5. See, for example, a national model, *Rite for a Catholic Wake* (Ottawa, Canada: Canadian Catholic Conference, 1973) and the very popular local *Wake Service* booklets published by the Liturgy Training Program, Archdiocese of Chicago.

6. Think only of the manner of distribution! An usher offering one to each participant upon entering, or passing through the

assembly to do so in a dignified manner is a good example of the noble simplicity explicit in good liturgical renewal.

7. Notes on *The Consolation of God: A Christian Wake Service* by Rev. Carl J. Naro, Charlottesville, Va., 1977. Similar experiences and examples from successful pastoral practice confirm his experience. The author expresses gratitude explicitly in this context for the special hospitality and resources illustrating pros and cons of celebration aids shared by Rev. William J. Neidhart, C.S.C. and his staff at Holy Cross Parish, South Bend, Ind., and Rev. Stephen A. McCarren and colleague priests of the Uniontown Deanery, Diocese of Greensburg, Pa.

8. See below, note 15.

9. A frequently cited aid has been *The Lord is My Shepherd: A Book of Wake Services* and *Toward a New Life* (complete with Funeral Rite Selection Sheet) both by Ave Maria Press, Notre Dame, Ind., 1971.

10. This title follows the Latin text literally.

11. Personal correspondence by Rev. James G. Brady, C.S.C., St. Patrick's Parish, Independence, Ore., September 1978. The description of this funeral will be continued at appropriate points throughout the rest of the chapter.

12. See above, pp. 126-132; *Rite* no. 2.

13. Martin Senko, Workshop Notes, *The Christian Celebration of Death*, Portland, Ore., 1975. Interview, May 13, 1977.

14. See Appendix II, Canadian ed. nos. 4-6.

15. We are grateful to Rev. Emmet Harrington, Pastor, and to Rev. Philip J. Steigerwald, Associate Pastor, for their description of the parish funeral workshop and home Mass developed by St. Paul Catholic Church, Eugene, Ore.

16. See above, pp. 136-140 and Appendix II, Canadian ed. no. 6.

17. See above, pp. 135-137.

18. See for example, Schmitz–Tierney, *Liturgikon,* p. 159. Despite our difference of opinion regarding the Rosary (and regarding participation aids above), the authors are to be con-

gratulated for their proposed wake service (pp. 159-170) and especially for its sensitivity toward the grieving. However, greater concern for music and the liturgical action of the entire assembly would, in this author's opinion, have enhanced the model even more.

19. *General Instruction on the Roman Missal*, no. 8.

20. Today many "sample homilies" are available as models. The homilist is strongly urged to use the directives and theology of the *Rite of Funerals* as principal guides to the use of such models. A careful study to discern why some ought not be models might be the best preparation for truly model preaching.

One wonders why sample homilies that demonstrate sound psychology and pastoral sensitivity to grieving people seem to have difficulty being explicit about faith in the paschal mystery as that which is special to the Christian funeral. See for example Schmitz–Tierney, *Liturgikon*, pp. 176-187, where of the seven sample homilies/sermons, only one (Homily for Funerals 2) is even indirectly explicit about the reason for what is preached, viz., the death and resurrection of Jesus Christ.

21. See above, pp. 8, 55-59.

22. See above, pp. 187-190.

23. See above, pp. 210-214.

24. See above, pp. 158-160.

25. Henry Ashworth, "The Prayers for the Dead in the Missal of Pope Paul VI," *Ephemerides Liturgicae* 85 (1971) 3-15.

26. Commentary during the American Broadcasting Company's coverage of the final commendation and farewell of the funeral of Pope Paul VI, August 12, 1978.

27. Here is another place where due attention can be given the individual's life, again without becoming a eulogy.

28. See, for example, the clear pastoral suggestions on cremation by Schmitz–Tierney, *Liturgikon*, pp. 207-209, and the Canadian liturgy at cremation in *Catholic Funeral Liturgy*, pp. 130-133.

29. B. J. Collopy, "Theology and the Darkness of Death," *Theological Studies* 39 (1978), 22-54.

30. See, for example, "The Demise of Christian Burial," *Liturgy*, Archdiocese of Seattle, May 1978.

31. See note 11 above and the continuation of this account on pp. 230, 232, 238, and 242-243.

32. Bishops' Committee on the Liturgy, *Environment and Art in Catholic Worship,* no. 5.

Foreword

This edition of the *Rite for Funerals*, for use in the dioceses of the United States, is for the most part an English translation of the *Ordo Exsequiarum*, in the version prepared by the International Committee on English in the Liturgy, approved by the National Conference of Catholic Bishops, and confirmed by the Apostolic See.

To this have been added adaptations for the United States, in accord with nos. 21 and 22 of the Introduction, made by the episcopal conference and approved by the Apostolic See. Such adaptations have been clearly indicated by inclusion in brackets or boxes or by a phrase referring to their use in this country (see Introduction, no. 21, 6).

For the convenience of the minister, the optional alternative texts—found in Chapter VI—have also been printed in Chapter II, which is the rite ordinarily followed in the United States. For completeness, rites or variants never or rarely used in this country (funeral processions, funeral in the home, etc.) have been included in this edition.

The principal rearrangement of the text occurs at the end of Chapter II. Since the final commendation may take place either after the funeral Mass ("First Station") or at the grave or tomb ("Third Station"), it has been printed in its entirety in both places. If the rite of commendation is celebrated in the church after Mass, the first form (A) of the Third Station is followed at the grave or tomb. If the rite of commendation is postponed, the alternative form (B) of the Third Station is followed at the grave or tomb.

In the case of optional alternative texts, the choice has been indicated by the use of the letters A, B, C, etc. The number of prayers and rubrics in the *Ordo Exsequiarum* has been retained for purposes of simpler cross reference.

In addition, an introductory note has been place at the head of some chapters. These notes are intended to suggest the principal alternatives available in the planning of the service by the priest together with the family of the deceased person and others (see Introduction, no. 23-25).

Pastoral Notes

1. THEOLOGICAL CONSIDERATIONS

In the funeral rites the Church celebrates the paschal mystery of Christ. Those who in baptism have become one with the dead and risen Christ will pass with him from death to life, to be purified in soul and welcomed into the fellowship of the saints in heaven. They look forward in blessed hope to his second coming and the bodily resurrection of the dead.

The Church therefore celebrates the eucharistic sacrifice of Christ's passover for the dead, and offers prayers and petitions for them. In the communion of all Christ's members, the prayers which bring spiritual help to some may bring to others a consoling hope. (1)

In celebrating the funeral rites of their brothers and sisters, Christians should certainly affirm their hope in eternal life, but in such a way that they do not seem to neglect the feeling and practice of their own time and place. Family traditions, local customs, groups established to take care of funerals, anything that is good may be used freely, but anything alien to the Gospel should be changed so that funeral rites for Christians may proclaim the paschal faith and the spirit of the Gospel. (2)

The bodies of the faithful, which were temples of the Holy Spirit, should be shown honor and respect, but any kind of pomp or display should be avoided. Between the time of death and burial there should be sufficient opportunities for the people to pray for the dead and profess their faith in eternal life. (3)

2. MINISTER OF CONSOLATION

a) In funeral celebrations all who belong to the people of God should keep in mind their office and ministry: the parents or relatives, those who take care of funerals, the Christian community as a whole, and finally the priest. As teacher of the faith and minister of consolation, the priest presides over the liturgical service and celebrates the eucharist. (4)

b) Priests and all others should remember that, when they commend the dead to God in the funeral liturgy, it is their duty to strengthen the hope of those present and to foster their faith in the paschal mystery and the resurrection of the dead. In this way the compassionate kindness of Mother Church and the consolation of the faith may lighten the burden of believers without offending those who mourn. (5)

c) In preparing and arranging funeral celebrations priests should consider the deceased and the circumstances of his life and death and be concerned also for the sorrow of the relatives and their Christian needs. Priests should be especially aware of persons, Catholic or non-Catholic, who seldom or never participate in the eucharist or who seem to have lost their faith, but who assist at liturgical celebrations and hear the Gospel on the occasion of funerals. Priests must remember that they are ministers of Christ's Gospel to all men. (6)

d) *Role of celebrant*: As a prophet for the Church of God, the celebrant proclaims the faith of the Church in the face of this mystery of death. He brings the consolation of faith to the suffering family, he is their friend and spiritual comforter.

Blue Cross Blue Shield of Oregon

PO Box 1271
Portland, Oregon 97207-1271

100 SW Market Street
503 / 225-5221

P 135
141
153
155
156 - use
for ashes at Mass

173
179 - 80
184 .
185 - homily

194
197 music

213

funeral of this specific
deceased Catholic

The priest is a man of reconciliation. The Church does not wish to settle accounts with anyone but to be as merciful as God is and to offer opportunities to the living for reconciliation.

e) The funeral rites, except Mass, may be celebrated by a deacon. If pastoral necessity demands, the conference of bishops may, with the permission of the Holy See, permit a lay person to celebrate the service. (7)

When no priest or deacon is available, the service in the home and in the cemetery should be led by a lay person. (8)

3. DEVELOPING A CANADIAN FUNERAL RITE

It has been the Church's custom in the funeral rites not only to commend the dead to God but also to support the Christian hope of the people and give witness to its faith in the future resurrection of the baptized with Christ.

For this reason the Second Vatican Council in its Constitution on the Liturgy directed that the funeral services be revised to express more clearly the paschal character of Christian death. (9)

Canada was one of the first countries to use the experimental funeral rite developed by the Consilium for the Implementation of the Constitution on the Liturgy. (10) By these rites, a new appreciation of Christian death was gained: death was seen as a final surrender to the Father's will, a hoped-for sharing in the Son's resurrection; now people are beginning to appreciate the role of the Spirit in raising us to a new life. (See Rom. 8:11)

During the past few years, the Easter theme has been proclaimed as the Christian enters into final rest. At the center of the faith of the Christian community is death and resurrection: the core of our faith and hope is the paschal mystery of the Lord Jesus, and our share in it. This faith is being proclaimed in the funeral rites of the Canadian church.

After some years of the experimental rite, the Congregation for Divine Worship issued the Rite of Funerals, and encouraged conferences of bishops to adapt it to the needs of their region. (11)

The Canadian ritual is the result of advice, suggestions and guidance from bishops, diocesan liturgy commissions, pastors, liturgists, musicians and people from all parts of Canada. It is now offered to the Canadian Church in order that from east to west, we will make a perfect offering to God's glory.

4. OUTLINE OF CANADIAN RITE
a) *Three services:* The rite of funerals in Canada corresponds to the first Roman plan, which "provides for three stations: in the home of the deceased, in the church, and at the cemetery." This is based on the former Roman Ritual.

When one or two parts of the funeral rite cannot be celebrated, the remaining service(s) will take place as usual.

˙b) *Complete rite:* In this ritual, the Roman "stations" are called services.

First service: in the home—prayers are offered in the home or funeral home by the assembled community. This service is presented in the form of a bible vigil, and four models are given: two for adults, one for baptized children, one for unbaptized children. In some cases this celebration will take place in the church.

Second service: in the church—this consists of the reception of the body; the liturgy of the word; usually the liturgy of the eucharist; and the final commendation and farewell.

Third service: in the cemetery—during the committal service, prayers are offered by those who come to bury the deceased.

c) *Options:* Wherever possible, a second choice of prayers is added, giving the celebrant a greater opportunity to adapt the prayers to the specific celebration. Most prayers are interchangeable with similar ones through the ritual, and a generous selection of prayers is given in the appendix.

d) *An adapted rite:* The Canadian ritual contains the basic plan of the Roman Ritual, enriched with many options, some traditional prayers, and a few prayers and rites adapted with permission from the *Nouveau Rituel des Funérailles* of the French-speaking nations. (12) Last of all, our ritual adds much pastoral guidance for developing bible services, and for understanding and celebrating the entire funeral rite.

5. INVOLVING THE FAMILY IN THE CELEBRATION

As far as possible, the celebrant should seek to involve the family and the community in planning and celebrating the funeral rites. The nature of the involvement will vary with the emotional stresses of the situation, with the degree to which the family has taken an active part in the community worship in the past, and with the liturgical maturity of the parish.

The texts should be chosen to reflect the wishes of the family and the community. (13) The prayers for special circumstances are quite useful in planning services. (See nos. 141-168)

Even when the family is not able to be involved in planning the services, the celebrant should make a serious effort to avoid routine sameness by preparing each celebration according to the persons and circumstances involved.

The suggestions given here present some of the areas of involvement. From these possibilities, the elements of each particular celebration will be chosen.

a) *Planning the bible vigil:* The family may be consulted about the possiblity of holding the service in the church; about the choice of theme, readings, responsorial psalm, other psalms and hymns. They may also wish to choose the reader. In some cases, the family or community may wish to design a special bible vigil in cooperation with the celebrant.

As the years go on, it is hoped that parishes, communities and even individual families will wish to work with their priest in developing their own bible vigils.

b) *Planning the funeral Mass:* If possible, the celebrant should talk with the family about the choice of readings, responsorial psalms, eucharistic prayer, song of farewell, other hymns and psalms. They may also be involved in choosing the reader(s) and ministers.

6. FIRST SERVICE: BIBLE VIGIL OR WAKE SERVICE
a) *Purpose and benefit:* The reformed liturgy seeks to convey more clearly the paschal character of Christian death. Rather than viewing death with hopeless gloom, Christians should celebrate it as a sharing in the death and rising of Christ, and as our entrance into his eternal life. The ritual expresses the faith which should be ours. (14)

It has been a long-standing custom of the faithful in Canada to gather on the evening before a funeral at the home, funeral home or church, in order to pray for the dead and for those who mourn, and to offer assistance in the spirit of Christian faith. Since the Second Vatican Council, this vigil for the deceased often takes the form of a bible service. (15)

The bible service can be helpful in leading people to a warm and living love for scripture by bringing them into contact with the lavish treasures of the bible in their prayer life. (16) A celebration of God's word provides great flexibility in meeting the spiritual needs of a particular group, and may be designed according to their circumstances. Moreover, all Christians will feel at home with this form of service, since it is common to all Christian churches.

b) *Community prayer:* The believing community joins the family and close friends in reflecting on God's word and praying for the deceased, the bereaved family, and for themselves.

c) *Place:* This service takes place in the home or funeral home where the body is laid out. On occasion it may be celebrated in a community hall or even in the church. Parishes should discuss the possibilities and spiritual advantages of holding this service in the church or in a chapel.

d) *Time:* This service often takes place the evening before the funeral. When held in the church, it is not celebrated immediately before the funeral, so that the funeral service will not be burdensome and the liturgy of the word duplicated. (17)

c) *Developing a bible vigil*
Local initiative—The service may follow one of the outlines presented in the first part of this ritual, but liturgical committees are encouraged to develop these to meet the needs of the local community of the faithful. In parishes where funerals are frequent, it may be desirable to develop other vigil services. The ones given in this ritual are models and guides, not the final word or only form.

Congregational booklet—A people's booklet has been prepared by the National Liturgical Office. It contains the wake services from this ritual, and is enriched with music selected from *Catholic Book of Worship*.

Theme—A suitable theme should be chosen, based on the scripture readings used. This theme should run through the psalms and prayers, and be explained and developed in the introductions and homily.

Examples of themes that may be developed for a celebration:
God rewards the good we do
God will judge our lives
God is merciful, ready to forgive
God is with us in our sorrow
God promises and gives eternal life
God is a Father of mercy
Father, may your will be done
Resurrection into glory
Suffering with Christ, rising with him
Baptism into death and resurrection

Music and singing—The possibilities in the first service are outlined in no. 12 of these Pastoral Notes.

f) *Celebration outlines*: The service of the word may be developed in a number of ways. As well as the order followed in daily or Sunday Mass, and the outlines given in the first service of the ritual, other possible forms are:

brief service
Greeting
Prayer
Reading
Psalm
Homily
Silent prayer
General intercessions
Lord's prayer or another concluding prayer

two readings from God's word
Greeting
Prayer
First reading

Psalm or hymn
Gospel reading
Homily
General intercessions
Lord's prayer or another prayer

two readings—another format
Sign of cross
Hymn
Greeting
Prayer
First reading
Silent prayer or psalm
Gospel
Homily
General intercessions
Closing prayers

g) *Invitation to Mass and sacraments:* A funeral is often an occasion for God's grace for persons who have drifted away from active membership in the Christian community. As the minister of reconciliation with Christ and his Church, the priest should invite the family and others to return to full participation in the sacramental life of the Church.

During the bible vigil, the celebrant should invite all present to take a full part in the funeral Mass, especially by receiving communion. For their convenience, he should make it possible for people to receive the sacrament of penance after the bible service. According to local needs and circumstances the sacrament may be celebrated in the place where the vigil service is held.

h) *Other devotions:* Where another form of devotion is used at the wake, it must follow the guidelines of the Second Vatican Council:

"These devotions should be so drawn up that they harmonize with the liturgical seasons, accord with the sacred liturgy, are in some fashion derived from it, and

259

lead the people to it, since the liturgy by its very nature far surpasses any of them." (18)

7. SECOND SERVICE: LITURGY IN THE CHURCH

a) *Second service:* This normally consists of the reception of the funeral procession at the church entrance, the liturgy of the word, the liturgy of the eucharist, and the final commendation and farewell.

b) *Service without eucharist:* There may be occasions when the eucharist is not celebrated: during the Easter triduum (from the Mass of the Lord's supper on Holy Thursday to Easter Sunday), for example, the eucharist is not celebrated at a funeral, but the rest of the service is as usual. The Mass will be offered on another day, if possible. (19)

When no eucharist is celebrated, the service consists of the reception of the funeral at the church entrance, the liturgy of the word, and the final commendation. The celebrant wears alb or surplice and stole; he may also wear a cope.

c) *Pastoral judgment:* Some people question the anomaly of having the community celebrate the eucharist for the funeral of a person who in life refused to celebrate with the community. Wise pastoral judgment must continue to be used in each case, keeping in mind that the eucharist is celebrated for the community's salvation as well as for the deceased.

d) *Final commendation and farewell:* By this rite, the Christian community honors one of its members with a last farewell. While death separates us for a time, we are members of Jesus Christ and are united to one another in him.

The song of farewell should be experienced by all as the climax of the rite. Ideally, it is sung by all present. Learning to sing it should be one of the objectives of each parish and religious community.

In Canada, this rite is usually celebrated at the end of the funeral Mass (or, when there is no eucharist, after the liturgy of the word). The priest retains Mass vestments for this part of the service, which begins immediately after the prayer after communion, or he may wear a white cope.

The rite is held only when the body is present. (20)

8. THIRD SERVICE: PRAYERS IN THE CEMETERY
a) The service usually follows the outline given in nos. 68-77.

b) If it should happen that the final commendation and farewell is celebrated in the cemetery, the rite given in nos. 189-195 takes the place of the third service.

c) *Cremation:* An adaptation of the third service is provided in nos. 184-188. (See Pastoral Notes, no. 14.)

9. CHILDREN'S FUNERALS
a) *Baptized children:* When a baptized child dies before the age of reason, his parents will find consolation in our belief he is sharing everlasting happiness with God. During the funeral rites, the Christian community prays not for the child but for his parents and relatives, asking the Lord to console them and strengthen their faith in this time of sorrow.

b) *Unbaptized children:* Our faith does not reveal God's plan for the child of Christian parents who dies without baptism. We leave the child in God's merciful care, and pray that his parents may accept God's will with faith and courage.

c) *Outlines of rites:* Special prayers are provided for children who die before the age of reason; their funeral rites are arranged in this way:

First service—bible vigil: Two model services are given, one for a baptized child (nos. 78-93), and one for an unbaptized child (nos 94-109).

Second service—in the church: This is similar to the adult service, but uses special prayers for children.

Third service—in the cemetery: This is similar to the adult service, but has special prayers for children.

The liturgical color for these funerals is white.

d) *Older children:* For children who have reached the age of reason, the adult funeral rite is used, with adaptations as required by the age and maturity of the child, and other circumstances.

10. LITURGY OF THE WORD OF GOD
a) Both in the Mass and in the bible vigil, scripture readings with a sung response, especially from the psalms, form the principle part of the liturgy of the word. The readings and responses are developed and completed by the homily and the general intercessions. (21)

b) *Division of roles:* Good liturgy requires that everyone does *all and only* what he should do. (22) *Readings* should be read by lectors; a deacon or priest proclaims the gospel. The *responsorial psalm* is sung by the cantor or choir, with the people singing the refrain. The *gospel acclamation* is sung by the cantor or choir, and the people respond with the alleluia. In the *general intercessions*, priest, lector and people combine for a public prayer of concern.

c) *Homily:* In the homily, the priest leads God's people to reflect on the meaning of the scripture readings they have just heard. He should expound the mysteries of our faith and the guiding principles of the Christian life. (23)

262

The homily is based on the readings of the bible. When they have been chosen because they have a common theme suitable for the particular circumstances, the priest is able to help his people understand a little more fully the truths God is teaching us in his word.

In the homily, the priest helps his listeners to see their sorrow and grief from God's point of view. The readings show how God acted in the life of his people in the past; the homily helps this assembly of his people to understand that God wishes to act in their lives now in a similar, though perhaps more spiritual way.

A Christian understanding of death as a sharing in the death and rising of Christ, and a gospel attitude toward death as the invitation to enter into the joy of the Lord are gradually deepened by the funeral rites, including the homily.

The celebrant's aim is to lead this group of people to a response of faith, a willingness to accept God's will and to live according to his plan for us, both through a fuller sharing in this liturgical celebration and through our daily living. In this way, God wants to lead us to eternal life.

The homily should be concerned with the word of God as it applies to the listeners. It is important to help believers and non-believers alike to realize that God's word is being spoken to them, in order that they might respond in faith and live according to the word of the Lord Jesus.

d) *General intercessions* (prayer of the faithful): The celebrant directs this prayer. He invites the faithful by a brief introduction to pray with him.

When possible, it is better to have the intentions announced by someone other than the celebrant, such as a deacon, cantor or reader. In the ritual, this other person is called the *Leader*.

263

The whole gathering expresses its prayer either by singing or saying a common invocation after each intention, or by silent prayer.

The celebrant concludes the general intercessions with a prayer asking the Father to hear these petitions of his people.

In this ritual, suggested forms of the general intercessions are provided for each service, and other examples are contained in the appendix, nos. 171-179.

11. NOT ONE BOOK BUT MANY
In leading the Church toward liturgical renewal, the Vatican Council pointed out that each member of an assembly, whether as a minister or part of the congregation, is to carry out his role by doing all his part and only his part. (24)

To help bring this about, liturgical books no longer attempt to carry all texts, and are returning to the long-standing tradition of a separate book for each purpose. Thus, lectors proclaim their readings from the *lectionary*, the celebrant proclaims his texts from the *sacramentary* or *ritual*, the people respond with acclamations, psalms and hymns from their *hymnal*.

Far from being a weakness, this system brings strength and stability to the liturgy. When each member carries out his role fully, the celebrant is able to lead the assembly in a liturgy giving greater honor to God and bringing the fruits of salvation to his people on earth.

12. MUSIC
a) *Music in the liturgy:* A liturgical action gives greater honor to God and sanctifies his people when it is solemnized in song, with the active participation of the people. (25) In order that the celebration may have due solemnity, it is most desirable that the community should participate by song in the funeral services.

b) *Funeral choir:* The presence of a choir is extremely helpful in attaining this ideal. Even five or six people can form such a choir, adding beauty and spirit to the celebration, and giving strong leadership to the congregation.

c) *Cantor:* The celebration is enhanced by the presence of a cantor. Often this role may be filled by one of the choir members. The cantor sings the verses of the psalm, and the gospel acclamation.

d) *Catholic Book of Worship:* The liturgical index of the complete edition offers a good selection of music for funerals. To these hymns may be added general hymns of praise and other hymns considered suitable for specific celebrations.

The family of the deceased person may wish to be involved in choosing the hymns and psalms for the bible vigil and funeral service. (See Pastoral Notes, no. 5)

e) *Planning:* When planning a celebration, celebrants and musicians should take into account the needs of the community, and plan the music for those who will be present. Each occasion demands individual attention and pastoral judgment.

f) *Singing at the wake:* This is an ideal toward which a worshipping community should aim. Though there may be pastoral difficulties, every parish should work to develop the tradition of singing at the bible service for the dead. A selection of hymns from *Catholic Book of Worship* is included in *Rite for a Catholic Wake*.

A cantor may lead the people in singing a psalm, for example. The bible services in this ritual have a number of elements that may be sung, and others may be added.

Especially when celebrated in church, the wake should include singing.

g) *Music at Mass:* The times at which music may contribute to the celebration are described below.

Prelude: An organ prelude before the service begins will help set the tone for the celebration. It may continue until the priest arrives at the church entrance to greet the funeral procession.

Entrance song: There should be no liturgical procession without music. The entrance hymn, or psalm and refrain, may be sung by the choir or the choir and the people as the celebrant leads the funeral procession into the church.

The entrance song opens the celebration, and draws the people into one liturgical assembly.

Since there is only one song at the entrance and beginning of Mass, (26) the "Lord, have mercy" is not sung.

Responsorial psalm: The psalm is sung as a response in faith after the assembly has listened to the first reading from God's word. It will normally reflect the reading.

The psalm should be sung. The verses are sung by the cantor or choir, and the refrain is sung by the congregation.

The psalms express human grief and our prayer for strength and hope. Pastors are encouraged to teach their people to become familiar with the principal psalms used in funeral rites. (27)

Gospel acclamation: A song of welcome is sung to Christ, who will speak to this assembly in the gospel. The acclamation is sung as the gospel book is carried with solemnity to the place of proclamation.

The acclamation is shared between the people and the choir or cantor. The choir or cantor sings the first alleluia, and the people respond; the choir or cantor sings the verse, and the congregation sings the alleluia once more.

Suitable phrases replace the alleluia during Lent. (See *CBW*, no. 208)

When the gospel acclamation is not sung, it may be omitted. (28)

Procession and presentation of gifts: a song by the people or choir may accompany this, or the organ may play briefly during this rite.

Holy, holy: At the end of the preface, the congregation joins the priest and choir in singing the angelic song of praise.

Memorial acclamation: The acclamation after the narrative of institution may be sung by all.

Great amen: Music for the final doxology is included in the Canadian sacramentary. This doxology, sung by the priest alone, expresses praise to God. By singing the amen, the people confirm and conclude the praise of the eucharistic prayer. (29)

Lord's prayer: The priest invites the assembly to join him in singing this prayer. The congregation may also join in singing the doxology ("for the kingdom").

Lamb of God: This chant is sung by the people or the choir during the breaking of bread. *There is no special form of this chant in Masses for the dead.* (30)

Communion song: The communion procession should not take place in silence. It should be accompanied by song, in order that it may become an act of brotherhood. The unity of the communicants with Christ and one another is best expressed by joining in song.

The cantor or choir may sing a psalm, with the people singing its refrain, or a hymn may be sung by the congregation or choir. Organ music may also be used during the procession. A hymn or psalm may be sung after communion. (31)

h) *Music during the final commendation:* The song of farewell is an important moment in the funeral liturgy; the choir or cantor sings the verse, and the people sing the refrain. (32)

During the recessional a hymn is sung by the congregation or choir. If no hymn is sung, the organ should play, so that the procession through the church is more solemn.

13. SYMBOLISM

A number of traditional symbols are used in the funeral services. When they are understood by the celebrant and the people, they have a greater impact.

a) *Easter candle:* The most important symbol used in the funeral rites is the Easter candle. Symbol of the risen Lord Jesus, ever present among his people, it is a reminder of the paschal significance of the death of a Christian. By death, he completes his entrance into the paschal mystery of Christ; now he lives completely and for ever in Christ. The intimate bond between the sacraments of baptism and eucharist, and their relationship with the death and resurrection of Jesus Christ and the individual Christian, need to be explored in each believing community.

The Easter candle—placed in the sanctuary from Easter to Pentecost, and in the baptistry during the rest of the year—is used in each funeral in the church. It is placed in the sanctuary in its usual place, or near the casket. The candle may replace the six candles which were formerly used, even during Lent.

When a wake is held in the church, the Easter candle is used as at the funeral.

b) *Holy water* is a reminder of baptism. Its use in the funeral rite recalls that the deceased person entered into eternal life through this sacrament. This person became a son or daughter of the Father; a brother or sister of

268

Jesus and of all his people, a member of the body of Christ, the family or people of God; a temple of the Holy Spirit, who dwells in his heart. By baptism, Christ has plunged this person into his death, and raised him into life; with Christ, he has died to sin and been raised to life for God.

The use of holy water should also remind all that baptism is the bond which unites this congregation and the deceased person in the communion of saints.

The significance of holy water is brought out and emphasized in the final commendation and farewell. It is desirable that less emphasis be given to its use at other parts of the funeral liturgy.

c) *Incense:* The use of incense is optional. It is a mark of respect for the body of a Christian, a temple of the Holy Spirit, a body marked with the seal of the Trinity. For an unbaptized child, its symbolism is seen in reference to Rev. 8:4 as a sign of prayer.

d) *Sprinkling with earth:* This traditional practice, prevalent in parts of Canada, is a reminder of the stark reality of death. While society today tends to gloss over death, to hush it up and hide it, Christians need to face it in faith as the call of God which all will some day hear.

The rite of sprinkling the casket with earth is included among the optional rites in the cemetery service.

c) *White vestments:* To emphasize the Christian belief and hope in the resurrection of the body and to bring home to all present that death is the beginning of life, white vestments are recommended in all funeral services. The Easter spirit should permeate every aspect of our funeral customs, helping each person in the community to believe more firmly that this deceased person will rise again, as will every believer.

f) *White pall:* The use of a white pall to cover the casket throughout the church service has a twofold benefit. In color, it is a reminder of our faith in resurrection, and by covering the casket from view, it is a vivid symbol that all men are equal in God's sight. The lesson of James (2:1-9) is brought out clearly.

In this way the requirements of the Roman Ritual are met: apart from distinctions based on liturgical function and sacred orders and the honors due to civil authorities according to liturgical law, no special honors are to be paid to any private persons or classes of persons, whether in the ceremonies or by external display. (33)

The pall should be placed on the casket when the funeral procession reaches the church entrance, and be removed just before the procession goes out of the church.

g) *Cross and book:* The Roman Ritual suggests that the gospel book, the bible or a cross may be placed on the casket. In Canada, the custom of attaching a crucifix to the casket is firmly established; while this crucifix is covered in church by the pall, there seems to be no need for duplication of symbolism.

The use of a bible or book of the gospels, however, has merit, and should be seriously considered in each community. As the scriptures return to a more central place in the lives of Catholics, the *effect* of this symbol will become more evident. Where possible, the bible should be one used by the deceased rather than a showy book purchased for the funeral. After the services, it should be returned to the family for continued use in prayer and meditation.

14. CREMATION

Christian funeral rites may be celebrated for persons who choose to have their bodies cremated, unless it is evident that they have acted for reasons which are contrary to the Christian way of life.

The funeral rites in the home and church are celebrated as usual. If desired, the rite given in nos. 184-188 may also be used at the crematorium or when burying the ashes in the cemetery.

The rites should not obscure the preference of the Church for the custom of burying the dead in a grave or tomb, as Jesus was buried. When cremation takes place, any danger of scandal or confusion should be removed. (34)

15. FUNERAL SERVICE FOR MEMBERS OF OTHER CHURCHES

Occasionally a priest is asked to conduct the prayers at the wake or funeral of a person who is not a Catholic. This may occur in an area where there is no clergyman of the deceased person's faith, or because of friendship and respect between the priest and the deceased person or his family.

In preparing these services, the priest should see his role as one of gathering the friends and relatives of the deceased person to *lead them in prayer* at this time of sorrow, and to *bring them God's consolation* in their need. He will exemplify the concern of God and his Church for all.

The service might be twofold: one part in the home or funeral home, the other in the cemetery. The corresponding services in this ritual may be used, either as they are or as a model. The priest should encourage the family to work with him in choosing readings and prayers for this service.

The question of vestments should be discussed with the family and friends while preparing the service. Some may prefer the priest to wear a suit, others may wish him to wear stole and surplice or alb.

16. PASTORAL MINISTRY

The celebration of the funeral liturgy with meaning and dignity and the priest's ministry to the dead presuppose an integral understanding of the Christian mystery and the pastoral office.

Among other things, the priest should:
a) Visit the sick and the dying, as indicated in the relevant section of the Roman Ritual.

b) Teach the significance of Christian death.

c) Show loving concern for the family of the deceased person, support them in the time of sorrow, and as much as possible involve them in planning the funeral celebration and the choice of the options made available in the rite.

d) Integrate the liturgy for the dead with the whole parish liturgical life and the pastoral ministry. (35)

NOTES

1. Roman Ritual, Rite of Funerals, no. 1.

2. Rite, no. 2.

3. Rite, no. 3.

4. Rite, no. 16.

5. Rite, no. 17.

6. Rite, no. 18.

7. Rite, no. 19.

8. Rite, nos. 5, 19.

9. Constitution on the Liturgy, no. 81.

10. National Bulletin on Liturgy, no. 14.

11. Decree, August 15, 1969.

12. Nouveau Rituel des Funérailles, © CCC.

13. Rite, no. 18.

14. Rite, nos. 1-2; Constitution on the Liturgy, no. 81.

15. Constitution on the Liturgy, no. 35:4.

16. Constitution on the Liturgy, nos. 24, 51.

17. Rite, no. 29.

18. Constitution on the Liturgy, no. 13.

19. Rite, no. 6.

20. Rite, no. 10.

21. The Roman Missal, General Instruction, nos. 33, 9.

22. Constitution on the Liturgy, no. 28.

23. Constitution on the Liturgy, nos. 52, 35:2.

24. Constitution on the Liturgy, no. 28.

25. Constitution on the Liturgy, no. 113.

26. Rite, no. 37.

27. Rite, no. 12.

28. General Instruction, nos. 36-39.

29. General Instruction, no. 55h.

30. General Instruction, no. 56e; Order of Mass, no. 102.

31. General Instruction, no. 56i.

32. Rite, no. 10.

33. Rite, no. 20; Constitution on the Liturgy, no. 32.

34. Rite, no. 15.

35. Rite, no. 25.

Industry Codes of Ethics and Practices

CODE OF ETHICS
National Funeral Directors' Association of the United States, Inc.

I
As funeral directors, we herewith fully acknowledge our individual and collective obligations to the public, especially to those we serve, and our mutual responsibilities for the proper welfare of the funeral service profession.

II
To the public we pledge: vigilant support of public health laws; proper legal regulations for the members of our profession; devotion to high moral service standards; conduct befitting good citizens; honesty in all offerings of service and merchandise, and in all business transactions.

III
To those we serve we pledge: confidential business and professional relationships; cooperation with the customs of all religions and creeds; observance of all respect due the deceased; high standards of competence and dignity in the conduct of all services; truthful representation of all services and merchandise.

IV

To our profession we pledge: support of high educational standards and proper licensing laws; encouragement of scientific research; adherence to sound business practices; adoption of improved techniques; observance of all rules of fair competition; maintenance of favorable personnel relations.

CODE OF PROFESSIONAL PRACTICES FOR FUNERAL DIRECTORS
NFDA (originally adopted Nov. 1965; revised 1969 and 1972)

When a death occurs a survivor in the immediate family or the person or persons who will be responsible for the funeral of the deceased should be advised to contact their family funeral director or should direct that said funeral director be notified. This should be done regardless of where or when death takes place. The funeral director then becomes the representative of the family for the purpose of the funeral arrangements.

When once a funeral director is called by the family or their representative and as a result of such call removes the body, he shall provide the necessary services and merchandise in keeping with the wishes and finances of the family or their representatives.

Before any funeral arrangements are made the funeral director should determine, if he does not know, who is the minister, priest or rabbi of the deceased and/or of the family. The funeral director should ascertain if such clergyman has been notified of the death. If this has not been done the funeral director should suggest it be done and should offer to do so for the family.

Before the specifics as to any and all aspects of the religious part of the funeral are decided, they should be discussed and cleared with the clergyman. This can be done either by the family or the funeral director as their representative or by both.

Before the family selects the funeral service, the funeral director should explain the various aspects of the funeral and the costs thereof as to the services and the merchandise he provides and as to that obtained from others such as cemeteries, florists and so forth. This should be done before the family goes into the casket selection room. In such an explanation the funeral director should make clear the range of prices of funerals he has available. Also the funeral director should welcome any questions or discussions as to that which is or is not required by laws and/or regulations to such laws.

The funeral director should review for the family the various death benefits and/or burial allowances that may be available to them such as those involving Social Security, the Veterans Administration, labor unions, fraternal and other organizations. He will assist in the preparation and filing of the necessary forms to secure these benefits and allowances for the family. Where further professional assistance is required he should suggest that the families seek the advice of other professionals.

Because the price of the funeral as to the funeral director is related to the casket selection, there should be a card or brochure in each casket in the selection room. Such card or brochure should outline the services offered by the funeral home. Services and merchandise not included where a unit price method is used should be listed on the card or brochure as separate items.

Representations of the funeral director with respect to caskets should be as to material, construction, design, hardware, mattressing and interior. The use of an outside receptacle in which the casketed body is placed should be fully explained. Facts should be given regarding the requirements of cemeteries as to such receptacles where they exist. The various kinds of receptacles and their materials, construction and design should be reviewed.

276

When a family decides on the kind of service desired the funeral director should provide a memorandum or agreement for the family to approve or sign showing (1) the price of the service that the family has selected and what is included therein; (2) the price of each of the supplemental items of service and/or merchandise requested; (3) the amount involved for each of the items for which the funeral director will advance monies as an accommodation to the family; and (4) the method of payment agreed upon by the family and the funeral director.

When death occurs in a place other than where the funeral and/or burial are to take place, most times the services of two funeral directors are necessary. Under such circumstances the family should not pay for a complete service both where death occurred and also where the burial or cremation is held.

The forwarding funeral director should make an allowance or adjustment for those of his services not required and should notify the receiving funeral director thereof. Likewise the receiving funeral director should not charge the family for the services already provided by the forwarding funeral director unless there is a duplication thereof desired by the family.

The family should pay for only one complete service plus any additional charges incurred because the place of death and the place of final disposition require the services of two funeral firms.

As soon as the details and schedule in the transporting of remains are known to the forwarding funeral director, he shall immediately notify the receiving funeral director thereof.

It is suggested that when a body is transported a report made out by the person who did the embalming should accompany the remains. Such a report could be of assistance to the receiving funeral director in the event additional profession work is required on the body.

Where burial is at a point distant from where the funeral service is to be conducted and a concrete or metal burial vault is to be used, the funeral director called for the service should suggest the funeral director who will be responsible for the interment provide said vault for a number of reasons including the saving to the family of the added cost of handling and transporting the vault to the place of burial.

When a funeral service is conducted in a place other than the church of the clergyman, his wishes and desires should be considered to whatever extent possible.

In the matter of the honorarium or the stipend the personal wishes of the clergyman should be respected. If the family is a member of the clergyman's church or parish it is a personal matter between the family and the clergyman. When the funeral director assumes the responsibility for the honorarium at the direction of the family, it is desirable to use a check for the transaction for record keeping purposes. If the clergyman does not accept honoraria, the family should be so informed in order that they may express their appreciation in other ways. When the family has no choice of a clergyman and the funeral director makes arrangements for one, the matter of the honorarium becomes the responsibility of the funeral director and a cash advance for the family.

When conducting a funeral in a church the polity, rules and regulations of that church must serve as the guide to the conduct of the service. Any exceptions to such procedures requested by the family should be cleared with the clergyman or proper authority well in advance of the time of their actual performance.

The funeral director should remain alert to the needs of the families he serves and when the need for religious or pastoral counseling is indicated he should make proper referrals whenever possible.

Funerals directors should be available to discuss with anyone all matters relative to the conduct of a funeral. Whenever possible the funeral director should assume active leadership in seminars or discussions which will bring a deeper understanding to all concerned about death, the funeral and bereavement.

THE CODE OF GOOD FUNERAL PRACTICE
National Selected Morticians

As funeral directors, our calling imposes upon us special responsibilities to those we serve and to the public at large. Chief among them is the obligation to inform the public so that everyone can make knowledgeable decisions about funerals and funeral directors.

In acceptance of our responsibilities, and as a condition of our membership in National Selected Morticians, we affirm the following standards of good funeral practice and hereby pledge:

1. To provide the public with information about funerals, including prices, and about the functions, services and responsibilities of funeral directors.

2. To afford a continuing opportunity to all persons to discuss or arrange funerals in advance.

3. To make funerals available in as wide a range of price categories as necessary to meet the need of all segments of the community, and affirmatively to extend to everyone the right of inspecting and freely considering all of them.

4. To quote conspicuously in writing the charges for every funeral offered; to identify clearly the services, facilities, equipment and merchandise included in such quotations; and to follow a policy of reasonable adjustment when less than the quoted offering is utilized.

279

5. To furnish to each family at the time funeral arrangements are made, a written memorandum of charges and to make no additional charge without the approval of the purchaser.

6. To make no representation, written or oral, which may be misleading, and to apply a standard of total honesty in all dealings.

7. To respect all faiths, creeds and customs, and to give full effect to the role of the clergy.

8. To maintain a qualified and competent staff, complete facilities and suitable equipment required for comprehensive funeral service.

9. To assure those we serve the right of personal choice and decision in making funeral arrangements.

10. To be responsive to the needs of the poor, serving them within their means.

We pledge to conduct ourselves in every way and at all times in such a manner as to deserve the public trust, and to place a copy of this Code of Good Funeral Practice in the possession of a representative of all parties with whom we arrange funerals.

Appendix IV

State Embalming Requirements (Dec. 1975)

Alabama	Not required if destination reached within 30 hours, if decomposition precludes it, or if shipment is not by common carrier.
Alaska	Not required.
Arizona	Required if body will cross state lines.
Arkansas	Not required.
California	Required if shipped by common carrier.
Colorado	Required if shipped by common carrier; if body deterioration precludes it, case receptacle must be hermetically sealed.
Connecticut	Required if shipped by common carrier.
Delaware	Not required; if shipped, must be in metal or metal-lined permanently sealed receptacle.
District of Columbia	Requirements of common carriers and state to which the body is shipped prevail.

Reprinted by permission from *Funeral Service: A Bibliography of Literature on Its Past, Present, and Future, the Various Means of Disposition, and Memorialization*, by Barbara K. and David F. Harrah. Metuchen, N.J.: Scarecrow Press, 1976. Copyright © 1976 by Barbara K. and David F. Harrah.

Florida	Required if shipped by common carrier unless condition prohibits; then in sealed or metal-lined containers.
Georgia	Not required.
Hawaii	Not required.
Idaho	Required if shipped by common carrier.
Illinois	Not required if destination reached within 24 hours.
Indiana	Not required unless death caused by plague, smallpox, leprosy or other specified diseases.
Iowa	Required for shipment unless destination is the anatomical department of school or hospital.
Kansas	Required if shipped by common carrier; not required for private transit within specified distances.
Kentucky	Required if shipped by common carrier unless condition precludes it, then in tightly sealed receptacle.
Louisiana	Not required; hermetically sealed receptacle if death by typhus, plague, smallpox, Asiatic cholera, or yellow fever.
Maine	Required if condition permits; if not, in hermetically sealed container.
Maryland	As per regulations of the State Board of Health and Hygiene.

Massachusetts	Required if death by virulent disease; otherwise air-tight, sealed container.
Michigan	Required if death by virulent disease; not required if destination reached within 48 hours or if addressed to a medical college.
Minnesota	Required if death by virulent disease; not required if destination reached within 18 hours.
Mississippi	Required if death by virulent disease, shipped out of state, or if disposition is not within 24 hours.
Missouri	Not required if death by non-virulent, non-contagious disease and destination reached within 24 hours.
Montana	Not required if death from non-virulent disease and destination is reached within 24 hours.
Nebraska	Required if death by communicable disease; if condition prohibits, must be sealed in proper container.
Nevada	Not required; hermetically sealed container required if death by dangerous disease.
New Hampshire	Not specified in regulations.
New Jersey	Not required if destination reached within 24 hours.
New Mexico	Required if shipped out of state or if death by specified diseases.
New York	Not specified in regulations.

North Carolina	Required unless condition prohibits; then in sealed outer container.
North Dakota	Not required if destination reached within 24 hours, unless death by virulent disease.
Ohio	Not required if destination is a medical college and is reached within 60 hours; if death is not by virulent disease; and destination is reached within 24 hours.
Oklahoma	Required.
Oregon	Not required if destination within state reached within 24 hours and death is not by virulent disease.
Pennsylvania	Not required if destination reached within 24 hours and death is not by virulent disease.
Rhode Island	Not required if destination reached within 24 hours and death is not by virulent disease.
South Carolina	Required if shipped by common carrier unless condition prohibits; then sealed outer case required.
South Dakota	Not specified in regulations.
Tennessee	Required if shipped by common carrier unless condition prohibits; then in hermetically sealed container.
Texas	Required if shipped by common carrier unless condition prohibits; then in hermetically sealed container.

Utah	Required if shipped by common carrier unless condition prohibits; then in hermetically sealed container.
Vermont	Regulations of common carriers prevail.
Virginia	Required if shipped by common carrier unless condition prohibits; then sealed outer case required.
Washington	Not required if final disposition is within 24 hours.
Wisconsin	Required if shipped by common carrier unless condition prohibits; then sealed outer case required. Exception: if destination is medical college and is reached within 60 hours.
Wyoming	Not specified in regulations.

Public Celebrations for Deceased Christians

[The following is a reprint of the Decree regarding public celebrations of Mass in the Catholic Church for other deceased Christians. The Decree was prepared by the Congregation for the Doctrine of the Faith, dated June 11, 1976, and promulgated on September 16, 1976.]

In various places Catholic ministers are asked to celebrate Mass for *deceased* persons baptized in other Churches or ecclesial communities, particularly when the departed showed special devotion and honor for the Catholic religion or held public office at the service of the whole civil community.

There is, of course, no difficulty about the celebration of private Masses for these deceased persons; indeed there can be many reasons in favor, such as piety, friendship, gratitude and the like, provided that no prohibition stands in the way.

With regard to public celebration of Masses, however, the present discipline lays down that they shall not be celebrated for those who have died outside of full communion with the Catholic Church (1).

In view of the present change in the religious and social situation that gave rise to the above-mentioned discipline, the Sacred Congregation for the Doctrine of the Faith has received inquiries from various quarters to ask

Reprinted from Bishops' Committee on the Liturgy *Newsletter* 12 (1976).

if in certain cases even public Masses can be said for these deceased persons.

The Fathers of the Sacred Congregation for the Doctrine of Faith duly examined the whole question and in the ordinary congregation of 9 June 1976 made the following decree on the matter:

I. The present discipline regarding the celebration of public Masses for other Christians who have died shall continue to be the general rule. One reason for this is the consideration due to to the conscience of these deceased persons, who did not profess the Catholic faith to the full.

II. Exceptions can be allowed to this general rule; until the new code is promulgated, whenever both the following conditions are verified:
1. The public celebration of the Masses must be explicitly requested by the relatives, friends or subjects of the deceased person for a genuine religious motive.
2. In the Ordinary's judgment, there must be no scandal for the faithful.
These two conditions can be verified more easily in the case of our brethren of the Eastern Churches: we have a closer fellowship with them in matters of faith, even if it is not complete.

III. In these cases public Mass may be celebrated, provided, however, that the name of the deceased is not mentioned in the eucharistic prayer, since that mention presupposes full communion with the Catholic Church.

If there are other Christians present as well as the Catholics who are participating in the celebration of the Masses, the rules made by the Second Vatican Council (2) and the Holy See (3) with regard to *communicatio in sacris* must be observed faithfully.

In the audience granted to the undersigned Cardinal Prefect of the Sacred Congregation for the Doctrine of the Faith on 11 June 1976, The Supreme Pontiff Pope Paul VI, repealing to whatever extent is necessary canon 809 (along with canon 2262, paragraph 2, 2°) and canon 1241, all things to the contrary notwithstanding, ratified, approved and commanded to be promulgated the above-mentioned decision of the Fathers.

Rome, at the Sacred Congregation for the Doctrine of Faith, 11 June 1976.

Franjo Cardinal Seper
Prefect

✠ Jerome Hamer, O.P.
Secretary

1. See Canon 1241, taken with Canon 1240, paragraph 1, 1°.

2. Decree on the Catholic Eastern Churches *Orientalium Ecclesiarum*, 26-29, *AAS* 57 (1965), 84-85. Decree on Ecumenism *Unitatis Redintegratio*, 8, *AAS* 57 (1965), 98.

3. See *Directorium de Re Oecumenica*, 40-42 and 55-56, in *AAS* 59 (1967), 587, 590-591. *Instructio de Peculiaribus Casibus Admittendi Alios Christianos ad Communionem Eucharisticam in Ecclesia Catholica*, 5-6, *AAS* 64 (1972), 523-525.

Bibliography

This bibliography is compiled with the understanding that the reader will consult bibliographical source works such as Harrah, *Funeral Service*, and Miller, *Death*, for specialized areas of concern beyond the scope of this present volume.

Ariès, Philippe. "Death Inside Out." In *Death Inside Out: The Hastings Center Report*, ed. Peter Steinfels and Robert M. Veatch. New York: Harper and Row, 1975.

―――. *Western Attitudes Toward Death: From the Middle Ages to the Present*, trans. Patricia M. Ranum. Baltimore: The Johns Hopkins University Press, 1974.

Ashworth, Henry. "The Prayers for the Dead in the Missal of Pope Paul VI." *Ephemerides Liturgicae*, 85 (1971), 3-15.

Atchley, C. *A History of the Use of Incense in Divine Worship*, Alcuin Collection 13. London: 1909.

Becker, Ernest. *The Denial of Death*. New York: The Free Press, 1973.

Bendann, E. *Death Customs. An Analytical Study of Burial Rites*. New York: Knopf, 1930.

Berger, Placidus. *Religiöses Brauchtum im Umkreis der Sterbliturgie in Deutschland*, Forschungen zur Volkskunde 41. Münster: Regensberg, 1966.

Bishops' Committee on the Liturgy. *Environment and Art in Catholic Worship*. Washington, D.C.: NCCB, 1978.

Bishops of West Germany. "A Death That Is Worthy and Christian." *Origins,* 9 (1979).

Bleeker, C.J. *Egyptian Festivals*. Leiden: Brill, 1967.

Boase, T.S.R. *Death in the Middle Ages*. New York: McGraw-Hill, 1972.

Bürki, Bruno. *Im Herrn entschlafen*. Heidelberg: Quelle & Meyer, 1969.

Centre Nationale de Pastorale Liturgique. *La Célébration des Obsèques* I. Paris: Desclée-Mame, 1972.

Champlin, Joseph M., and James E. Flynn. *The Lord is My Shepherd: A Book of Wake Services*. Notre Dame, Ind.: Ave Maria Press, 1971.

————. *Toward a New Life*. Notre Dame, Ind.: Ave Maria Press, 1971.

Choran, Jacques. *Death and Western Thought*. New York: Macmillan, 1963.

Clark, James M. *The Dance of Death in the Middle Ages and Renaissance*. Glasgow: 1950.

de Clercq, Carlo. *La Législation Religieuse Franque de Clovis à Charlemagne*. Louvain–Paris: Bibl. de L'Université-Sirey, 1936.

Collopy, B.J. "Theology and the Darkness of Death." *Theological Studies*, 39 (1978), 22-54.

Commission on the Sacred Liturgy. *The Rite of Christian Burial*. Chicago: Archdiocese of Chicago, 1968.

Congregation for the Sacraments and Divine Worship. "De celebratione exsequiarum pro iis, qui proprii cadaveris cremationem elegerit." *Notitae*, 126 (1977), 45.

Consumer Union. *Funerals: Consumers' Last Rights*. New York: Norton, 1977.

Cumont, Franz. *Recherches sur le Symbolisme Funéraire des Romains*. Paris: Paul Geuthner, 1942.

————. *Lux Perpetua*. Paris: Paul Geuthner, 1949.

Curl, James Stevens. *The Victorian Celebration of Death*. Detroit: Partridge Press, 1972.

Deferrari, Roy J., trans. *Saint Cyprian: Treatises*, The Fathers of the Church, Vol. 36. New York: Fathers of the Church, 1958.

Deiss, Lucien. *It's the Lord's Supper: Eucharist of Christians*. New York: Paulist, 1976.

Dreves, Clemens, and Guido Blume. *Analecta Hymnica Medii Aevi* 49 (Leipsig, 1906; repr. Johnson Reprint Corporation, New York–London, 1961.

Emery, Pierre-Yves. *The Communion of Saints*. London: The Faith Press, 1966.

Evans, Joan, ed. *The Flowering of the Middle Ages*. New York: McGraw-Hill, 1966.

Feifel, Herman, ed. *The Meaning of Death*. New York: McGraw-Hill, 1959.

Fischer, Balthasar. *"Das Rituale Romanum* (1614-1964): Die Schicksale eines liturgischen Buches." *Trierer Theologische Zeitschrift*, 73 (1964), 257-271.

Flannery, Austin, ed. *Vatican Council II. The Conciliar and Post-Conciliar Documents*. Northport, N.Y.: Costello Publishing Co., 1975.

Geisey, Ralph E. "The Royal Funeral Ceremony in Renaissance France." Dissertation, University of California at Berkeley, 1954.

Gorer, Geoffrey. *Death, Grief and Mourning*. New York: Doubleday, 1965.

Guardini, Romano. Letter to the Mainz Liturgical Congress, April 1, 1964. In *Herder Correspondence*, August 1964, pp. 237-239.

Gy, Pierre-Marie. "Le Nouveau Rituel Romain des Funérailles." *La Maison-Dieu*, 101 (1970), 20-21. An English translation of this is available in *The Way* Supplement 11, Fall 1970, "The Liturgy of Death. The Funeral Rite of the New Roman Ritual," pp. 59-75.

Habenstein, Robert W., and William M. Lamers. *Funeral Customs the World Over*. Milwaukee: Bulfin, 1960.

————. *The History of American Funeral Directing*. Milwaukee: Radke Bros. et Kertsch Co., 1955.

Halligan, Nicholas. *Sacraments of Initiation and Union*, I. New York: Alba House, 1972.

Harrah, Barbara K., and David F. Harrah. *Funeral Service: A Bibliography of Literature on Its Past, Present and Future, the Various Means of Disposition and Memorialization*. Metuchen, N.J.: Scarecrow, 1976.

Holck, Frederick H., ed. *Death and Eastern Thought*. New York: Abingdon Press, 1974.

Holy Cross Funeral Liturgy. Notre Dame, Ind.: Congregation of Holy Cross, 1976.

Huizinga, Johan. *The Waning of the Middle Ages*. New York: Doubleday, 1954. (Dutch original, 1924.)

Hunt, Noreen, ed. *Cluniac Monasticism in the Central Middle Ages*. Hamden, Conn.: Archon, 1971.

Huntington, Richard, and Peter Metcalf. *Celebrations of Death: The Anthropology of Mortuary Ritual*. New York: Cambridge University Press, 1979.

Irion, Paul. *The Funeral: Vestige or Value?* New York: Abingdon, 1966.

Isbell, Harold, trans. *The Last Poets of Imperial Rome*. Baltimore: Penguin, 1971.

Jungmann, Josef. *The Mass*. Collegeville, Minn.: Liturgical Press, 1976.

Kaczynski, Reiner. *Enchiridion Documentorum Instaurationis Liturgicae I*. Rome: Marietti, 1976.

Kelly, Thomas A., ed. and trans. *Sancti Ambrosii Liber de Consolatione Valentiniani*, Catholic University of America Patristic Studies, 58. Washington, D.C.: Catholic University of America Press, 1940.

King, John Phillip. "Death, Burial and Baptism in Romans 6:1-14." Dissertation, Emory University, Atlanta, 1977. Ann Arbor, Mich.: University Microfilms International, 1978.

Die Kirchliche Begräbnisfeier in den katholischen Bistümern des deutschen Sprachgebietes, hrsg. im Auftrag der Bischofskonferenzen Deutschlands, Österreichs und der Schweiz und des Bischofs von Luxemburg. Einsiedeln–Köln–Freiburg–Basel–Regensburg–Wien–Salzburg–Linz, 1973.

Kurtz, Donna D., and John Boardman. *Greek Burial Customs*. Ithaca, N.Y.: Cornell University Press, 1971.

Lewis, C.S. *A Grief Observed*. New York: The Seabury Press, 1971.

Liturgical Commission. *Christian Death and Burial.* New York: Archdiocese of New York, 1978.

Liturgical Secretariat, Irish Episcopal Conference. *Christian Burial.* Portarlington: Mount St. Anne's Liturgy Centre, 1976.

Liturgy for Christian Funerals. Green Bay, Wis.: Commission on the Liturgy, 1968.

Löwenberg, Bruno. *Das Rituale des Kardinals Julius Antonius Sanctorius.* Ein Beitrag zur Entstehungsgeschichte des Rituale Romanum. Dissertation, Teildruk, 1937. München: Druk der Salesianischen Offizin., 1937.

Mannix, Mary D., ed. and trans. *Sancti Ambrosii Oratio de Obitu Theodosii,* Catholic University of America Patristic Studies, 9. Washington, D.C.: Catholic University of America Press, 1925.

McManus, Frederick. "Liturgy of Final Commendation." *American Ecclesiastical Review,* 162 (1970), 405-408.

————. "The Reformed Funeral Rite." *American Ecclesiastical Review,* 116 (1972), 45-59; 124-139.

Mead, Margaret. "Ritual and Social Crisis." In *Roots of Ritual,* ed. James Shaughnessy. Grand Rapids: Eerdmans, 1973.

Meier, John P. "Catholic Funerals in the Light of Scripture." *Worship,* 48 (1974), 206-216.

Miller, Albert J., and Michael James Acri. *Death: A Bibliographical Guide.* Metuchen, N.J./London: Scarecrow, 1977.

Moody, Raymond A. *Life After Life.* Covington, Ga.: Mockingbird Books, 1975.

————. *Reflections on Life After Life.* Covington, Ga.: Mockingbird Books, 1977.

National Office for Liturgy. *Catholic Funeral Rite.* Ottawa: Canadian Catholic Conference, 1973.

Nichols, Roy, and Jane Nichols. "Funerals: A Time for Grief and Growth." In *Death: The Final Stages of Growth,* ed. Elisabeth Kubler-Ross. Englewood Cliffs, N.J.: Prentice-Hall, 1975.

Ntedika, J. "L'Evocation de l'au-delà dans la prière pour les morts, Etudes de patristique et de liturgie latines (IVe-VIIIe S.). *Recherches Africaines de Théologie* 2. Louvain–Paris, 1971.

Order of Funerals for Adults. Experimental Rite for use by permission of the Holy See. Washington, D.C.: National Council of Catholic Bishops, 1967.

Ottosen, K., N.K. Rasmussen, and C. Thodberg, eds. *The Manual from Notmark.* Bibliotheca Liturgica Danica, Series Latina, I. Copenhaven: G.E.C. Gad, 1970.

Paul VI. *Indulgentiarum doctrina. The Pope Speaks,* 12 (1967), 135.

————. *Mysterium Fidei. The Pope Speaks,* 10 (1965), 309-328.

————. *Sacrum diaconatus ordinem. The Pope Speaks,* 12 (1967), 237-243.

Pieper, Josef. *Death and Immortality,* trans. Richard and Clara Winston. London: Northumberland Press Ltd., 1969.

Raby, F.J.E. *A History of Christian-Latin Poetry from the beginnings to the close of the Middle Ages.* Oxford: Clarendon, 1973.

Raether, Howard C. "The Place of the Funeral: the Role of the Funeral Director in Contemporary America." *Omega,* 2 (1971), 131-149.

Rahner, Karl. *On the Theology of Death.* New York: Herder and Herder, 1961.

Rahner, Karl, and Angelus Häussling. *The Celebration of the Eucharist.* New York: Herder, 1968.

Reynolds, Frank E., and Waugh, Erle H., eds. *Religious Encounters with Death.* Pennsylvania State University Press, 1977.

Riemer, Jack, ed. *Jewish Reflections on Death.* New York: Schocken, 1974.

Rite for a Catholic Wake. Ottawa, Canada: Canadian Catholic Conference, 1973.

Rite of Anointing and Pastoral Care of the Sick. New Yo.k: Pueblo, 1974.

Rite of Christian Burial. Adapted for use in the Archdiocese of Chicago by the Commission on the Sacred Liturgy. Chicago: Archdiocese of Chicago, 1968.

Rite of Christian Burial in the Diocese of Albany. Albany: The Liturgy Center, 1976.

Rite of Funerals. Celebrant's Manual for the Church Service. With Pastoral Directives for use in the Archdiocese of Chicago. Chicago: Liturgy Training Program, 1971.

Rite of Funerals: Study Edition. Washington, D.C.: United States Catholic Conference, 1971.

Rite of Penance. Washington, D.C.: United States Catholic Conference, 1975.

The Rites of the Catholic Church as Revised by the Second Vatican Ecumenical Council. New York: Pueblo Publishing Co., 1976.

Rituale Romanum ex decreto sacrosancti oecumenici Concilii Vaticani II instauratum auctoritate Pauli PP VI promulgatum, *Ordo Exsequiarum.* Typis Polyglottis Vaticanis, 1969.

Rituale Romanum Pauli V Pont. Max. iussu editum. Rome, 1916.

Rituale Sacramentorum Romanum Gregorii Papae XIII Pont. Max. iussu editum. Rome, 1584.

Robinson, J. Armitage, ed. *The Apology of Aristides*, Texts and Studies 1. Cambridge: The University Press, 1893; rpt. Nendeln, Liechtenstein: Kraus, 1967.

Roguet, A.-M. "La prédication de la mort." *La Maison-Dieu* 44 (1955), 104-110.

Rowell, Geoffrey. *The Liturgy of Christian Burial,* Alcuin Club Collections, No. 59. London: SPCK, 1977.

Rush, Alfred C. *Death and Burial in Christian Antiquity,* The Catholic University of America Studies in Christian Antiquity, 1. Washington, D.C.: The Catholic University of America Press, 1941.

———. "The Eucharist: The Sacrament of the Dying in Christian Antiquity." *The Jurist,* 34 (1974), 10-35.

―――. "The Rosary and the Christian Wake." *American Ecclesiastical Review*, 152 (1965), 289-297.

Sacred Congregation of Rites. *Eucharisticum Mysterium.* Washington, D.C.: United States Catholic Conference, 1967.

Saint Andrew Bible Missal. Bruges: Biblica, 1962.

Schmaus, Michael. *Dogma VI: Justification and the Last Things.* Kansas City/London: Sheed and Ward, 1977.

Schmitz, Walter, and Terence Tierney. *Liturgikon: Pastoral Ministrations.* Huntington, Ind.: Our Sunday Visitor, 1977.

Schnitker, Thaddäus A. *Publica Oratio: Laudes matutinae und Vesper als Gemeindegottesdienste in diesem Jahrhundert,* Dissertation, Münster, 1977. Privately printed.

Schreiber, G., ed. *Das Weltkonzil von Trient,* 2 vols. Freiburg: Herder, 1951.

Shaughnessy, James, ed. *Roots of Ritual.* Grand Rapids: Eerdmans, 1973.

Sicard, Damien. "The Funeral Mass." *Reforming the Rites of Death,* ed. Johannes Wagner, Concilium 32, 45-52. New York: Paulist, 1968.

―――, "La liturgie de la mort dans l'église latine des origines à la réforme carolingienne," Liturgiewissenschaftliche Quelle und Forschung, no. 63. Münster: Aschendorff, 1978.

Siegler, G.J. *The Roman Ritual. The history of a canonical sourcebook.* Dissertation Gregoriana. Rome, 1963.

Simpson, Michael. *Death and Eternal Life.* Hales Corners, Wis.: Clergy Book Service, 1971.

Staniforth, Maxwell. *Early Christian Writings. The Apostolic Fathers.* Baltimore: Penguin, 1972.

Stannard, David E., ed. *Death in America.* University of Pennsylvania Press, 1974.

Storey, F. *et al.*, eds. *Morning Praise and Evensong.* Notre Dame, Ind.: Fides, 1973.

Szöverffy, Josef. *Die Annalen der Lateinischen Hymnendichtung: Ein Handbuch* II. Berlin: E. Schmidt Verlag, 1975.

————. "Folk Beliefs and Mediaeval Hymns." *Folklore*, 66 (1955), 219-231.

"The Demise of Christian Burial." *Liturgy*. Archdiocese of Seattle, May 1978.

Tissier, Marcel. "L'Homélie aux Funérailles." *La Maison-Dieu* 101 (1970), 117-126.

Toynbee, Jocelyn. *Death and Burial in the Roman World*. Ithaca, N.Y.: Cornell University Press, 1971.

van der Meer, Frits, and Christine Mohrmann. *Atlas of the Early Christian World*. London: Nelson, 1966. (Dutch original, 1958.)

van Dijk, Stephen J.P. *Sources of the Modern Roman Liturgy. The Ordinals of Haymo of Faversham and related documents (1243-1307)*, II. Leiden: Brill, 1963.

Veit, Ludwig Andreas, and Ludwig Lenhart. *Kirche und Volksfrömmigkeit im Zeitalter des Barock*. Freiburg im Breisgau: Verlag Herder, 1956.

Wagner, Johannes, ed. *Reforming the Rites of Death*, Concilium 32. New York: Paulist Press, 1968.

Walpole, A.S. *Early Latin Hymns*. Hildesheim: George Olms, 1966; Reprografischer Nachruck der Ausgabe Cambridge, 1922.

Walsh, Gerald G., and Daniel J. Honan, trans. *Saint Augustine: The City of God*, The Fathers of the Church, Vol. 24. New York: Fathers of the Church, 1954.

Waugh, Evelyn. "Death in Hollywood." *Life*, 23 (1947), 73-83.

————. *The Loved One*. Boston: Little, Brown and Co., 1948.

Weisner, William T., ed. and trans. *S. Ambrosii De Bono Mortis*, The Catholic University of America Patristic Studies, 100. Washington, D.C.: Catholic University of America Press, 1970.

Weller, Philip T. *The Roman Ritual*, II. Milwaukee: Bruce, 1952.

Williamson, G.A. *The History of the Church*. Baltimore: Penguin, 1965.

Winstone, Harold, ed. *Pastoral Liturgy. A Symposium.* Glasgow: Wm. Collins Sons & Co., Ltd., 1975.

Wordsworth, John, trans. *Bishop Serapion's Prayer-Book.* Hamden, Conn.: Archon, 1964; rpt. 1923 revised.

Zandee, J. *Death as an Enemy according to ancient Egyptian Conceptions.* Leiden: Brill, 1960.

Zimmerman, Odo J., trans. *Saint Gregory the Great: Dialogues,* The Fathers of the Church, Vol. 39. New York: Fathers of the Church, 1959.

Index

C

304

310